Charles Cleveland Nutting

Narrative and Preliminary Report of Bahama Expedition

Charles Cleveland Nutting

Narrative and Preliminary Report of Bahama Expedition

ISBN/EAN: 9783337329747

Printed in Europe, USA, Canada, Australia, Japan

Cover: Foto ©Andreas Hilbeck / pixelio.de

More available books at **www.hansebooks.com**

BULLETIN

FROM THE

LABORATORIES OF NATURAL HISTORY

OF THE

STATE UNIVERSITY OF IOWA.

PUBLISHED

BY AUTHORITY OF THE REGENTS.

IOWA CITY, IOWA:
JANUARY, 1895.

NARRATIVE AND PRELIMINARY REPORT OF BAHAMA EXPEDITION.

BY

C. C. NUTTING.

Secretary WM. J. HADDOCK:

We take pleasure in submitting herewith Bulletins Nos. 1, 2, Volume III, from the Laboratories of Natural History, State University of Iowa.

THE EDITORS.

PREFACE.

The following pages contain the history of an educational and scientific experiment. That this history is deemed worthy of publication is in itself a proof that the experiment is considered a success, and the various letters of inquiry which have been received by the author have been taken as an indication of the interest which has attended the cruise of the "Emily E. Johnson." The narrative is intended to give all the information drawn from our experience that would be of benefit to any one who in future might desire to undertake a similar cruise at the minimum of expense. To the zoölogists who may read this account the writer desires to say that he has endeavored to treat the faunæ of the various regions visited from the standpoint of the general zoölogist only, with a view to giving an idea of the facies of the collections from the several localities. The limitations imposed by the somewhat meagre literature at the disposal of the writer, as well as those necessitated by the routine of his official work in connection with the University, must be a partial excuse for the errors which the specialist will undoubtly find in the identifications of the species noted. A fair degree of accuracy in this respect is claimed only in the following general groups, namely,—the birds; the insects, which have been worked up by the various parties named on the last page of the narrative; that part of the Crustacea which is being reported on by Mr. James E. Benedict and Miss Mary J. Rathbun, of the National Museum, who have kindly sent the author the names of the species which he desired to mention; and the Hydroida, a group for which the author is responsible. The Echini and reef corals are probably identified correctly. It is hoped that there is an approximately correct naming of the greater part of the Mollusca. Concerning the remaining groups the identification of species can not be relied upon to any great extent. Practically no attempt has been made to discuss the worms, actinians and sponges.

Species known to be new have not, with the exception of a few hydroids, been described or figured.

The author is greatly indebted to Mr. H. F. Wickham for constant assistance during the preparation of this narrative, and in the necessary drudgery involved in proof reading, a task which has also been shared with Professor T. H. McBride.

To my father, Dr. Rufus Nutting, I am indebted for the unusually complete index at the end of this volume. The illustrations are from the excellent series of photographs taken by Mr. Gilbert L. Houser, and the pen-drawings by Miss Mary F. Linder speak for themselves.

C. C. NUTTING.

STATE UNIVERSITY OF IOWA.
January 17th, 1895.

CONTENTS.

		PAGE
CHAPTER I.	PLANS AND EQUIPMENT,	1
CHAPTER II.	FROM BALTIMORE TO EGG ISLAND, BAHAMAS,	20
CHAPTER III.	EGG ISLAND AND THE BAHAMA BANKS,	37
CHAPTER IV.	HAVANA,	59
CHAPTER V.	THE DRY TORTUGAS,	103
CHAPTER VI.	KEY WEST AND THE POURTALÈS PLATEAU,	136
CHAPTER VII.	HARBOR ISLAND AND SPANISH WELLS,	182
CHAPTER VIII.	LITTLE CAT ISLAND AND HOMEWARD BOUND,	217
APPENDIX A.	LIST OF COMMISSARY STORES ACTUALLY USED,	231
APPENDIX B.	DREDGING AND SHORE STATIONS,	232
INDEX,		235

CHAPTER I.

PLANS AND EQUIPMENT.

KNOWING, as we now do, the immense wealth of biological material awaiting investigation in the depths of the sea, it is hard to realize that this new world to science has been practically discovered and occupied during the last forty years. It seems strange that the significant discoveries of Torell in the waters of the far north, proving the existence at considerable depths of animals belonging to every group of invertebrates ordinarily found in shallow salt water, did not attract more attention at the time of their announcement. Nearly ten years later the two Sars, father and son, became interested in deep sea forms of life, and accumulated a number of specimens which were destined in time to fire the zeal of Sir Wyville Thomson. The science which has since become known as "Thalassography" may have had its birth in the mind of that grand zoologist when he went to Norway and examined the Sars' collection, in which he found much food for reflection. As is usual with such men, reflection bore fruit, and we next find him, in conjunction with his associate, Dr. Carpenter, applying to the Admiralty, through the Council of the Royal Society, "to place the means at our disposal to go into the whole question of the physical and biological conditions of the sea bottom in the neighborhood of the British Islands." The "Lightning," a "somewhat precarious little gun-boat," was placed at their disposal for two months. They found that there was "abundance of animal life at the bottom of the sea, to a depth of six hundred fathoms at least, and that the life there was not confined to the more simply organized animals, but "extended very irrespectively through all the invertebrate classes, and even included some true bony fishes." Next a more suitable vessel was furnished by the Admiralty, and the "Porcupine" in 1869 and 1870 carried the investigation of the sea bottom down to a depth of 2,435 fathoms, at which depth a fair representation of animal life was found.

Having been so largely instrumental in opening up this new field of scientific activity, Sir Wyville Thomson and his colleagues were determined that "Great Britain should be 'Mistress of the Seas' in this as in other matters," and proceeded to organize the most remarkable and successful undertaking for the acquisition of knowledge concerning marine physics and biology that the world has ever seen.

Through the influence of the Royal Society the Admiralty was induced to send the "Challenger" a spar-decked corvette of 2,306 tons, on a four years' cruise for the purpose of examining the physical and biological conditions in the great oceanic basins of the globe. Sir Wyville Thomson was placed in charge as director of the civilian scientific staff, consisting of five eminent naturalists, besides the director himself.

The "Challenger" Expedition marked a new era in marine investigation. Notable as were the discoveries made during the four years' absence of the "Challenger," the splendid series of Reports, by which the results were laid before the scientific world, will ever be the most imposing monument to perpetuate the fame of the director and his associates, and also an exhibit of the manner in which Her Majesty's Government completes work once undertaken.

Alexander Agassiz is to America what Sir Wyville Thomson was to England, in the domain of "Thalassography."[1] In 1849, although but a boy, he accompanied his father, Professor Louis Agassiz, in the "Bibb," and in 1851 we find him aiding his father in the survey of the Florida Reefs.

In 1867-8 Count Pourtalès made memorable discoveries

[1] "The need of some single word to express the science which treats of oceanic basins has led to the construction of this term." — *Agassiz*.

while dredging off the Florida Keys, and Agassiz reported on a portion of the collection secured at that time. "And," says he, "since that time I have been engaged, with little interruption, more or less directly in deep sea work." Under his direction the "Blake," a United States Coast Survey steamer of 350 tons, made three cruises in 1877 to 1880, which have been the means of demonstrating that we have in the neighborhood of our own southern coast a field for marine investigation which offers more attractions to the zoölogist than any other in the world, with the possible exception of the Japan Sea. The amount of material collected, and the number of new species obtained, was in many groups greater than was secured by the "Challenger," a much larger vessel, equipped at greater expense. The Reports from these cruises are contained in the Bulletins and Memoirs from the Museum of Comparative Zoölogy at Cambridge.

Not the least important work done by Agassiz and his associates has been in the line of improvements in instruments for deep-water sounding and dredging. Piano wire has been introduced for sounding, and the expense and labor of dredging in deep water have been amazingly reduced by Agassiz' introduction of iron instead of hemp rope, constituting, perhaps, the most important advance in method since the birth of the science of thalassography.

The "Blake" was followed by the United States Fish Commission steamer, the "Albatross," which is probably the best equipped dredging vessel in existence. She has made three cruises in the West Indies with Mr. James E. Benedict as naturalist in charge, and is now at work in the Pacific. The results of these cruises have not yet been worked up, but an immense amount of material was secured.

These expeditions, with many others, only less notable, have resulted in discoveries of immense importance to zoölogical science. The classification of many groups of marine invertebrates has been profoundly modified in order to accommodate the host of new species, genera, and even families, which are now known to inhabit the deep waters of the globe

Teachers of zoölogy have found themselves almost bewildered by the demolition of old classifications and the erecting of new ones, often as incomprehensible to them as primeval chaos. The original material collected by these expeditions was placed, very properly, in the hands of the most noted specialists in the various groups, and the scientific laity was forced to be content with an exceedingly misty idea of these multitudinous forms which have so thoroughly disturbed old-fashioned classifications. The splendid monographs constituting the "Challenger" Reports are too expensive to be attainable save by the favored few, and so the average teacher of zoölogy has been forced to content himself with placing before his unfortunate pupils a succession of rearrangements of zoölogical classifications, of which he himself can secure no rational basis for comprehension.

Aside from the insects, by far the greater part of the animal life of the globe is marine. Several of the great sub-kingdoms are almost exclusively inhabitants of salt water. The investigations carried on of late years in the deep sea have probably more than doubled the number of known marine species. It will thus be evident that all but a very few naturalists and teachers of zoölogy have been deprived of the opportunity of studying perhaps half of the forms a knowledge of which is necessary to any broad understanding of the subject of marine invertebrates.

When we come to consider the case of students in our colleges and universities, the possibilities of their understanding the relationships of marine animals seems remote indeed, as under no circumstances, except at Harvard, Johns Hopkins and a few other eastern institutions, have they access to any considerable number of deep-water forms of life, and only in isolated cases are they permitted to study these animals when fresh from their native depths.

It was such considerations as the above that gave the original impulse to the plan which culminated in the Bahama Biological Expedition from the State University of Iowa. Western institutions are particularly hampered in their attempts to impart zoölogical knowledge by the remoteness of salt water, with its myriads of animal forms. No adequate conception of zoology can be obtained without a study of marine organisms, and the western teacher is sadly handicapped by the misfortune of geographical position.

Even where a tolerably fair representation of marine types is included in museums, they are as a rule either dried and distorted objects, or repulsive and shriveled specters of their true selves, immersed in alcohol. Few forms are found in any western museum in sufficient abundance to admit of dissection in the class-room.

In the spring of 1888, the writer made a zoological reconnaissance in the Bahama Islands, and obtained a vivid impression of the exceptional value of that region as a field for study. Even with the most limited facilities, two months spent around the coral reefs and shores is bound to result in an enthusiastic appreciation of the great advantage of studying in such a region, and a longing to place such advantages within the reach of students who will use them aright.

In the fall of 1891, the idea of the Bahama Expedition began to take a more definite shape, and an organization of those most interested in the project was effected. It was decided that a vessel be chartered and fitted up for the use of a party of twenty biological students and instructors during a three months' cruise in the West Indies. It was further decided that this enterprise should differ materially from those previously attempted, in the fact that provision would be made, not only for the study of pelagic and shoal water forms, but also for obtaining a fair idea of characteristic deep sea types. It was a peculiarly unfortunate time to apply to the University for financial aid, as all departments were almost crippled on account of a recent cutting down of legislative appropriations. In spite of the scarcity of funds, however, there was much that the University could do to help along the enterprise. It could give leave of absence to the necessary instructors, furnish from its laboratories the microscopes and other appliances requisite to good work in marine biology, and provide a working library of reference from the general

University library. President Schaeffer could, and did, interest himself most efficiently in the enterprise, and secured letters from our Department of State which proved of great service in foreign ports. In addition to all this, a sufficient amount of cash was squeezed out of meagre appropriations to pay for the necessary appliances for dredging at a considerable depth, and for the preservation and transportation of the collections.

As soon as the plan of this expedition was announced, applications for membership began coming in, and there arose a question of considerable importance. Several young ladies of excellent standing as students applied for membership. After mature consideration, it was agreed that it would be doing violence to the co-educational principles of the University to deny privileges to competent ladies which were accorded to young men.

This matter being settled, the organization of the expedition was soon effected, there being more applicants than could be accommodated. The management was left to an executive committee consisting of three professors of the University. Professor Samuel Calvin was to undertake all preparations for the biological work in the field, including laboratory supplies and material. To Professor L. G. Weld was entrusted the planning of appliances for effective work down to at least one hundred fathoms, the matter of economy being regarded as of prime importance. The selecting of a suitable vessel, and the direction of all matters pertaining to the collecting and preservation of specimens, was placed in charge of the writer.

Owing to his appointment as State Geologist in the early summer of 1892, Professor Calvin was obliged to relinquish all hopes of accompanying the expedition, much to his and our disappointment. He very kindly consented, however, to act on the executive committee until the departure of the party, and planned the very effective laboratory equipment which added so much to the success and profit of the enterprise. Professor Weld, also, found himself unable to accompany the expedition, and for a time it looked as if the scheme was going to pieces. Mr. William Powell ultimately filled Professor Weld's place, so far as seeing to the dredging equipment was concerned. A commissary committee was appointed, with instructor G. L. Houser as chairman, whose duty it was to attend to the provisioning of the expedition, and later he had charge of the equipment for laboratory work. This equipment consisted essentially of twelve dissecting microscopes and ten compound microscopes, provided with three-quarter and one-fifth objectives, and a high grade Zeiss instrument with immersion objectives, for any special investigation in which a good instrument was necessary. A quantity of reagents, glass ware, chemicals, dissecting tools, etc., was also provided. In addition to these microscopes and their accessories, a good photographic outfit was secured, with an abundant supply of films and dry plates for hand and tripod cameras. Experience proved that a much smaller number of microscopes would have been sufficient. It rarely happened that any considerable number of the party made use of the instruments at the same time. While we were dredging almost every one had his or her specified duties to attend to, in the way of watching the dredge, assorting or caring for the quantities of material coming up with almost every haul, and making rough and hasty notes of the specimens which seemed to be of the most interest. Again, when we were in port, all hands were eager to go on shore and see the characteristic sights of foreign lands. A half dozen compound microscopes would doubtless have answered all requirements, and at the same time left more room for other things.

Professor Weld had a difficult task before him in the planning of equipment which should come within the exceedingly limited means at our disposal, and at the same time do effective work of a kind hitherto attempted only by government vessels with equipment costing thousands of dollars.

Correspondence was entered into with various gentlemen whose experience could help our cause. It is worthy of grateful record that in every case the response was prompt, and the desired information given with great care and courtesy. Among those who kindly rendered aid in this direction were Hon. Marshall McDonald, United States Commissioner of Fish and Fisheries; Mr. James E. Benedict, who was naturalist in charge of the "Albatross" during her first cruise in the West Indies; Captain J. W. Collins, Commander of the United States Sailing Dredger "Grampus;" and especially Doctor Alexander Agassiz, whose long experience as a naturalist in charge of the various "Blake" expeditions in the West Indies and Florida Keys made his advice of the utmost value. The amount of trouble this gentleman took to help entire strangers with detailed plans of equipment best suited to their wants, was almost as astonishing as it was gratifying. He alone, of all our kind advisers, thought Professor Weld's plan of using iron instead of hemp rope practicable. The others advised the use of Italian hemp rope. The final adopting of the iron instead of the hemp proved a most valuable and practical idea. After once having used it, we felt that the success of our deep water work was assured. Of course iron rope had already superseded hemp in deep-sea work with steamers; but our vessel must necessarily be a sailing craft, and scientific dredging had never before, so far as we could learn, been attempted with iron ropes on a sail vessel. The many points of superiority of iron over hemp will be noted further on.

It soon became evident that even the simplest sort of donkey engine for working the dredge was beyond our means, and a device that could be worked by hand was substituted. This consisted in a hoisting machine, technically known as a "crab," constructed after plans by Professor Weld. It consisted essentially of a horizontal drum, fifteen inches in diameter and thirty inches long, resting on a heavy iron frame bolted to the deck. This drum was provided with a single and double purchase for cranks, by which a sufficient degree of power could be applied to meet any demands likely to be made upon the machine. The lowering of the dredge was regulated by a powerful friction brake, which kept the speed of the descending dredge under complete control. This simple machine was found to be entirely adequate to meet all demands which were made upon it during the cruise, and was constructed by the Yale & Towne Manufacturing Company of Stamford, Connecticut, at a very reasonable price. One thousand nine hundred and twenty feet of $\frac{5}{16} \times 7$ cast steel rope was purchased of John A. Roebling's Sons & Company, of Newark, New Jersey, the drum of the hoisting machine being designed to comfortably accommodate that length of cable. The single purchase only was used in hoisting, unless the dredge hung on the bottom, when the double purchase furnished enough power to bend the strongest dredge frames used, or even the heavy iron bar of the tangles. After leaving the bottom, the dredge or tangles came up easily, the single purchase being used. We found that a single haul, including lowering the dredge until all the rope was out, dragging on the bottom for twenty-five minutes, and reeling in again, usually took about an hour and a half. Experience proved that four or five hauls of this kind was about all that we cared to attend to in a day, and even that amount was at first no child's play, in tropical heat.

In order to have something to fall back upon, should the iron rope prove a failure or be lost, 225 fathoms of $2\frac{1}{4}$ inch Italian hemp rope was purchased of the Sewell & Day Cordage Company of Boston, Massachusetts. Although this rope was never used for dredging, we found it useful,—indeed indispensable,—in making tangles, our most effective instrument, and actually used about half of this rope for that and other incidental purposes, such as hanging the trawls, painters for boats, etc.

The trawls and dredges were all made in the University machine shop, by Mr. William Powell, an engineering student who accompanied the expedition, and proved an exceedingly useful member of the party. The trawl frames were made after the "Blake"[1] model, so far as shape is concerned, but gas pipe was used as the easiest material to manage and join securely. Agassiz says, "The trawl is by far the most

[1] Agassiz, "Three Cruises of the Blake," page 26.

useful instrument in deeper water, where the bottom generally consists of ooze or fine mud." In our work we found the bottom down to our deepest dredging, about two hundred and sixty fathoms, almost invariably rock, and the trawl nets were quickly demolished by the severe usage. It is evident that the trawl can safely be omitted from the equipment of a vessel, unless really deep dredgings (say five hundred fathoms) are to be made.

The dredges were of two patterns. The "naturalist's" dredge, for use in shallow water with row-boats or small sailboats, was made in three sizes, with the frames 15 by 6 inches, 18 by 8 inches, and 21 by 10 inches. The largest of these sizes is small enough for any sail-boat work, and still larger sizes would be better for any but the smallest boats. The "Blake"[1] dredge has the advantage of a frame to protect the dredge net or bag. In both kinds of dredges it is necessary to punch a series of small holes around the lower edge of the frame, by means of which the dredge nets can be seized to the frames.

Nets for dredges and trawls can be ordered in any dimensions or size of mesh, or in any quantity, of the Gloucester Net and Twine Company, of Boston, Massachusetts, whose long experience enables them to understand the requirements better than any other firm in this country, perhaps.[2]

In order to protect the dredge nets, it is necessary to make a canvas bag for each, using good new canvas. (We used second hand canvas, to our sorrow.) The mouth of the bag should be as large as the outside of the dredge frame, to which it is securely seized with marline. The bag should be bottomless, so that the water can pass freely through the dredge. It is surprising how soon this dredge covering will be worn out and require renewal.

At the suggestion of Captain Flowers, we also took along a

---

[1] Agassiz. "Three Cruises of the Blake," page 21, Fig. 22.

[2] So much difficulty was encountered in finding just where the various items of equipment for marine dredging could be bought, that the author has decided to be explicit in such matters for the benefit of others who may desire to secure similar equipment.

small oyster dredge, such as is used in the Chesapeake. This we found of excellent service on shallow, sandy bottom, such as the Bahama Banks, but it will not do to use it on rocky bottom, as the teeth get such a firm grip on the rocks that there is danger of disastrous breakage of some part of the dredging equipment. Such a dredge with the teeth broken out would probably do good service if lined with netting, to prevent the loss of the smaller and more delicate objects. No matter what kind of dredge is used, it should be strongly built, and hung so that it will "trip" before breaking the dredge rope. This is effected by fastening only one of the iron arms of the dredge frame directly to the dredge rope, the other arm being lashed to the first by marline, which, when the dredge fouls on the bottom, will usually break, allowing the dredge to be extricated without breaking the dredge rope, involving a loss both of dredge and rope. We found in practice that the tendency is to underestimate the strength of the marline, making the lashing so strong that the dredge frame itself bends in order to slip by the obstruction, instead of the tension being relieved by the breaking of the marline.

The necessity of heavily weighting the trawls and dredges is obviated by use of the iron rope, which tends by its own weight to take the dredge to the bottom. We found, however, that a forty or fifty pound weight attached a short distance in front of the dredge facilitated matters considerably, and usually insured successful hauls at the depth at which we worked. When the "Blake" dredge is used, a couple of twenty pound weights attached to the lower end of the frame will tend to keep the front edge from digging into the bottom. Lead weights at eight cents per pound are rather expensive material for sinking dredges or tangles. If any considerable amount of work is to be undertaken, it would be cheaper in the end to have a number of castings made in the shape of iron balls, with rings for lashings. These could be provided in various sizes, and thus save considerable expense. In spite of every precaution, a number of weights will be lost. In using lead sinkers we were surprised to see the rapidity with which they were worn away by scouring over the sandy bottom.

In dredging, there is a tendency on the part of beginners to use too little rope. It is best in the long run to be generous in paying out the line, twice the amount needed to go straight to the bottom being none too much as a general thing. The oyster men have a saying to the effect that "the man with a long line has the biggest pile by night."

Perhaps three-fourths of our specimens from deep water were brought up with the tangles. We found the bottom rocky almost everywhere at depths of from sixty to two hundred and sixty fathoms. Large patches of smooth bottom would be encountered, but the peculiar jerking of the line, which is soon recognized as the danger signal, indicating rocks and trouble with trawl or dredge, was a frequent occurrence, so that we were always uneasy until the dredge left the bottom. The tangles are by far the most efficient instrument for such moderate depths, and we finally came to rely almost entirely upon them. These tangles were made after a pattern suggested by Mr. James E. Benedict, of the Smithsonian Institution. A four foot length of one by two inch iron bar is bent in the middle at nearly a right angle. Five iron rings are bolted at regular intervals to the inner side of this bar. The ends of five two foot lengths of chain are fastened to these rings, and through each link is passed a six foot strand of two and three-fourths inch Italian hemp rope. Each strand is tied to the link at the middle, and then carefully unravelled throughout its entire length on each side of the knot. There are six such strands to each six foot length of the rope. The dredging cable is attached by a hook to a ring bolted to the outer side of angle bar. "Mousing" should be placed over the hook to keep it from slipping out of the ring when in use. This tangle differs from that previously used, in the fact that the bar is bent and not straight, and in the use of the chains instead of fastening the ropes directly to the bar. This latter feature we found to be an excellent one, as the chain weighted the swabs sufficiently to insure their dragging closely to the bottom. The angle in the bar, however, is rather a disadvantage than otherwise, as it seems prone to cause the affair to become securely wedged in between rocks, in which case a tangle will foul quite as badly as a dredge. It is advisable to provide a considerable number of extra tangle bars and a quantity of suitable rope for the tangles, as the bars will often be lost, in spite of every precaution, and the tangles will wear out every two or three days, and have to be renewed. We were advised to use *old* Italian hemp rope, and were told that it made much more effective tangles than new rope. In practice, however, we did not find any very perceptible difference, a fortunate thing for us, as the supply of old rope taken was not sufficient for us to do our actual work.

Our sounding line was two hundred fathoms in length, twelve thread, furnished by the Gloucester Net and Twine Company, of Boston, Massachusetts. Not expecting to dredge below one hundred fathoms, we thought this sufficient. In fact, however, much of our work was done in water nearer two hundred than one hundred fathoms, and we found our line of little use. Soundings made by hand at such depths are at best unreliable, owing to the currents and drift of the vessel. Hence we were forced to depend largely on the charts to estimate the depth before putting over the dredge, which itself proved more reliable in indicating the depth than did our sounding line. Our experience indicates that sounding at any considerable depth cannot be managed with accuracy with an old-fashioned line and lead. Piano wire and detachable sinkers are now used in all deep-sea work. Another device which is used on many steamers records the depth by barometric pressure, and can be used when the vessel is under full headway. I do not know whether or not this method has been used for very deep soundings

For dredging it is necessary to provide some device for carrying the iron rope over the bulwarks without friction, and hoisting the dredge high enough to clear the side of the vessel. This was effected by stepping a dredging spar to the foremast above the galley, so that it would swing aft of the mast. The hoisting machine was placed about six feet in front of the mainmast. The iron rope led from the reeling drum to a twelve-inch iron block fastened to the centre of the deck just aft of the galley, thence to a similar block hooked to the ends of the dredging spar, and then overboard. When in use the spar is guyed fore and aft so as to be practically immovable. These guys should be sufficiently strong to bear the entire strain of the dredge line. Indeed, great strength is necessary in all parts of the equipment when a sail-vessel is used, as it is impossible to back, and the strain is something terrible when the dredge suddenly fouls. This strain could doubtless be materially lessened by the use of some sort of accumulator, such as was used on the "Blake."[1] This does not seem to be an actual necessity, however, for, as Alexander Agassiz says, "the curve made by the wire rope, as it leads from the vessel to the trawl, is of itself the best accumulator, as a comparatively slight strain will constantly tend to change the form of the catenary." With the primitive dredging equipment used by us, it is necessary for some one to guide the line so that it will coil properly in reeling in under tension. Our means of doing this was crude, but effective, consisting of a strip of inch plank about four feet long, provided with a slot through which the rope ran, by which it was kept from slipping horizontally. The end of the board was placed on the deck, and leverage exerted to the right or left, as the reeling demanded.

Each day, when the dredge, trawl, or tangles were let down for the first haul, the entire length of the iron rope was oiled by hand. In addition to this, the whole coil was thoroughly sopped with oil whenever it was dry.

In addition to the trawls, dredges, and tangles a number of simple appliances were provided for surface and shoal water collecting. Convenient and cheap dip nets can be secured by purchasing crab nets at any sea-port, and replacing the net by silk bolting cloth, cheese cloth, or mosquito netting, thus securing a series of netting from the finest to a sufficiently

---

[1] Agassiz, "Three Cruises of the 'Blake,'" page 31.

Winding in the Dredge.   G. L. H.

coarse mesh. Some of the crab nets should be left in the rings as they are, for use in dipping up sea-weed, or large objects of any kind. Surface nets should also be provided for towing astern. They are essentially the same shape as the dip nets, but the net itself is much longer, and the ring is hung to a line instead of being attached to a long handle. When a sail vessel is used, the surface work must be done almost exclusively in small boats, as pelagic animals as a rule come to the surface only during calms and at such times there is, of course, no headway on a sailing vessel. The remaining portions of the equipment can best be discussed in connection with the description of the actual work of the expedition.

A matter of the most vital importance was the selection of a suitable sailing master. It was essential that he should not only be trustworthy in all matters pertaining to the navigation and safety of the vessel, but acquainted with the general features of the region to be visited, and perfectly familiar with practical dredging with a sail vessel. Such a man was found in the person of Captain Charles B. Flowers, with whom the writer had sailed on his previous visit to the Bahamas, during which time there was ample opportunity to form an estimate of his abilities as a sailor and character as a man. That this estimate was entirely satisfactory is proved by the fact that one of the first things attended to after the "Bahama Expedition" was decided upon, was to write to secure the services of Captain Flowers. His experience as a practical oyster dredger in the Chesapeake during the winters, and as skipper for Bahama fruiters during the summers for many years, was exactly such as best to fit him for sailing master on such a cruise as ours. The result proved that a better selection could not have been made. He seemed to meet every requirement with excellent judgment, and his consummate skill in handling the vessel while dredging in deep water was a constant source of remark to all on board. It is simple justice to acknowledge that the success of our enterprise, so far as deep water work is concerned, was due very largely to his ability as a practical dredger.

The vessel selected for our cruise was a two masted, double top-sail, centre-board schooner, the "Emily E. Johnson," of Baltimore, owned by Captain C. C. Paul. We were no less fortunate in our selection of a vessel than in our choice of sailing master. The "Emily E. Johnson" had a net tonnage of 116 tons, was 95 feet long, with 26 feet beam, and with 7 feet depth of hold. The extra beam made her unusually staunch and "dry" in rough weather. She had a small cabin aft, into which four state-rooms and a toilet room opened. This furnished excellent accommodations for the seven ladies of our party. The vessel was solidly ballasted with pebbles, most of which was placed well aft. Over the ballast a tongue and groove flooring was put in. The hold was painted on the sides, bulk-heads and sides of well, and white-washed overhead. The after hatch was covered with a glass skylight made of four sashes, all of which could be raised to admit air when desired. Movable steps secured to hooks on either side of the hatch led from the skylight into the hold. Although the glass in these skylights was protected by iron grating, and when necessary by stout reefing boards, every pane but one was broken long before the cruise ended. The hatch leaked badly, and, like most of the joiner work done by a Baltimore firm in refitting the vessel, was botched, in spite of the exorbitant prices demanded.

A series of shelves placed against the after bulk-head on the starboard side accommodated the microscopes and other laboratory instruments and supplies. A book-case was extemporized by fitting shelves on the port side of the same bulk-head, a door leading from the cabin to the hold being between the "library" and "laboratory."

A small, dark-room for photographic work was built on the starboard side next the laboratory shelving. Eight bunks were fitted along each side of the vessel, there being two tiers of four each. These bunks were extra wide, and furnished with good matresses. Cheese cloth curtains were hung in front of the bunks, so that they could be concealed when necessary. Two tables, each twenty feet long and four feet broad, were placed under the after hatch, one on each side. These tables were covered with white oil-cloth, and were used for dining tables, and between meals for laboratory work with the microscopes, or for writing or drawing. A large lamp with a reflector was hung over each.

The stores were stowed forward. As boxes and barrels were emptied by the consumption of their contents, they were refilled with specimens of natural history, which seemed to accumulate just about as rapidly as the provisions were eaten.

The hold was thus made as comfortable as circumstances would admit. As a matter of fact, however, very little time was spent below after we reached a tropical climate. The top of the cabin made a commodious work table during the day, and was usually occupied at night by a double row of sleeping men. When the vessel was at anchor, awnings were stretched from the foremast to the stern, making a grateful shade under which to study or to work.

The wisdom of commencing our preparations eighteen months before the party sailed, became apparent as the time drew near for the departure of the expedition. The number of items which required consideration, and questions which demanded decision, was astonishing. Meetings of the members of the expedition were held from time to time, at which reports from the various committees were presented and questions asked and discussed. Each member of the party heartily attended to any duty assigned by the executive committee, and willing hands made comparatively light work.

At the beginning of the collegiate year 1892-3, the members of the party were organized as a regular University class, to pursue studies preliminary to the work of the expedition. Previous to that time the personnel of the party had been practically determined. It was made a prerequisite to admission that the applicant should have demonstrated special aptitude for biological work.[1]

By this plan it became practicable to divide the party for

[1] This rule was departed from in two cases only, when individuals were especially adapted to be useful to the expedition, in one case as an engineer, and in another as a special correspondent.

more effective work, giving each one a special group of marine animals to study, it being understood that each person should be prepared to care for and keep track of his or her special group, when dredging or collecting was in progress. This method worked excellently, and resulted in larger and better cared for collections, as well as more effective concentration in the work of each member of the party.

The "commissary committee," in charge of Mr. G. L. Houser, had by no means a light task before it in determining the amount and variety of stores which would be needed. It was decided to take a sufficient supply from Baltimore to last through the entire cruise, as it would not do to take chances in the matter of securing stores in out of the way ports. It was estimated that twelve dollars per month for every person on board would furnish good wholesome food in adequate abundance and variety. The result proved this estimate to be very nearly correct. Mr. Houser has kindly furnished a list of these supplies, amended so as to include changes which our experience would suggest as desirable.[1]

An important item was the matter of transportation from Iowa City to Baltimore and return. We found that the Chicago, Rock Island & Pacific, and the Baltimore & Ohio Railroads were inclined to be generous in the matter of rates, and when the party went over their roads, it was treated with great courtesy, and everything within reason was cheerfully and voluntarily done to make the trip pleasant and comfortable.

Early in April, 1893, the writer went east to complete the arrangements and have everything in readiness for the reception of the party on May 1st. Persistent rainy weather delayed the painting of the vessel, and, as usual, various unforseen complications arose at the last. In spite of these drawbacks, however, the vessel was in readiness for occupancy in four days after she was turned over to us. The party arrived on the evening of May 4th. The next day water was taken aboard and stowed in the hold, twenty-seven barrels being the original supply, and they were refilled three times during the

[1] See Appendix A.

cruise. After a delay of several hours in getting our clearance from the Custom House, on the account of the wariness of the Spanish Consul in view of a reported revolution in Cuba, the long looked for hour of departure arrived, and the "Bahama Expedition" set sail for Havana, its first port of entry. The members of the party, as it was finally organized, were as follows:

Executive committee: Professor C. C. Nutting, instructors G. L. Houser and H. F. Wickham. Members: Professor M. F. Arey, State Normal, at Cedar Falls; Professor Steven Stookey, of Coe College, Cedar Rapids; Professor Gilman Drew, Oskaloosa; Mrs. H. F Wickham, Mrs. Gilman Drew, Doctor Leora Johnson, Miss Margaret Williams, Miss Bertha Wilson, Miss Minnie Howe, Miss Edith Prouty, Messrs. A. G. Barrett, E. G. Decker, Henry Ditzen, W. P. Powell, William Larrabee, Jr., A. M. Rogers, Edwin Sabin, Webb Ballord.

The crew consisted of Captain Charles B. Flowers, mate George Murrill, a cook, steward, and three ordinary seamen.

CHAPTER II.

FROM BALTIMORE TO EGG ISLAND, BAHAMAS.

It is doubtful if any skipper ever started on a three months' cruise with a more inexperienced lot of "land-lubbers" than Captain Charles Flowers had on board the "Emily E. Johnson," as she was towed out into the stream on the evening of May 5th, 1893. Only a small percentage of those on board, aside from the crew, had ever so much as seen salt water before. Everything pertaining to the sea, the vessel, and marine life, was novel, and the more experienced members of the party awaited developments with no little anxiety.

It would be hard to suggest a more severe test of character than was involved in the necessary close quarters and mutual forbearance and concessions of a three months' cruise. From the very nature of the case, the true character of each person was bound to be manifest, and each viewed his companions as they really were, and not as they simply seemed. The educational and disciplinary value of such a test, especially when, as in this case, the results are creditable, can hardly be overestimated.

The sail down the Chesapeake was a delight to every one on board, and it would have been pleasant to indolently enjoy the beauties and novelties of the first few days; but there was much that it was necessary to accomplish before getting to sea, and work was commenced at once.

According to agreement, the assignment of work was left to the executive committee, and it is a pleasure to state at the commencement that the entire party promptly and efficiently attended to the work assigned, and that the amount of grumbling over obnoxious tasks was surprisingly small.

Some were put to work at unpacking and arranging the

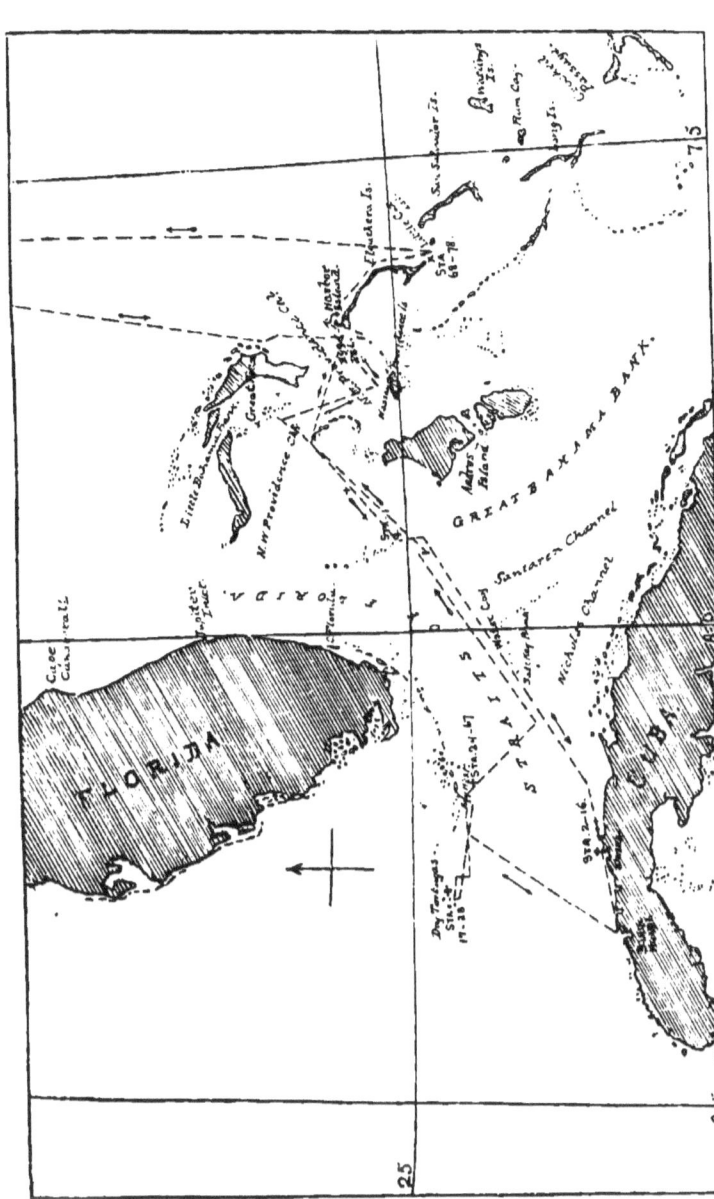

CHART OF THE BAHAMAS, CUBA AND THE FLORIDA KEYS, SHOWING COURSE AND DREDGING STATIONS OF BAHAMA EXPEDITION.

microscopes and other laboratory material; others unpacked the books and placed them on the shelves of the "Library," fitting a movable wooden bar in front of each row, so that no movement of the vessel could displace the books. Before leaving home, all of the larger and more expensive volumes, such as the "Challenger" Reports and monographic works, had been carefully covered with oil-cloth, lettered on the back with white paint.

A convenient place was found under the cabin floor, for the twenty-four ten gallon alcohol tanks, where they helped trim the vessel and were safe from accident. Then the three hundred fathoms of iron rope had to be reeled upon the drum of the dredging machine under tension, and at the same time thoroughly oiled to prevent corroding in the sea air. All of the stores had to be carefully re-stowed before we got out into the Atlantic, a work accomplished under the superintendence of the mate, who directed the young men in disposing of the various packages so as to properly distribute the weight, and at the same time be accessible when wanted.

Many of the party, although warned against it, had brought along an excessive amount of baggage, which caused considerable annoyance before it was finally disposed of. In spite of this, however, it was astonishing to see how satisfactorily the baggage and stores were accomodated in the hold of the "Emily E. Johnson," room being found for everything, leaving sufficient space for comfortable sleeping, eating and working quarters.

Another matter of great importance was the appointment of two committees. One of these, known as the "steward's committee," had in charge the matter of issuing supplies to the cook, and looking out for any waste or loss of water or provisions. It was the duty of this committee to know where everything in the line of eatables was stowed, how much had been consumed, and what quantity remained, at any given time. It can readily be seen that, with such a long cruise before us, it would not do to guess at the condition of the stores, neither could any waste be tolerated.

Another committee was the "bill of fare committee," whose province it was to make out the daily bill of fare, using the various articles of food so as to give as great a variety as possible, and at the same time to make them "come out even," so far as practicable. It may be of interest to note that throughout the cruise it was an actual fact that more provisions were consumed each week than had been the preceding week. The appetites of the party seemed to increase in a compound ratio from first to last, so that a shortage seemed imminent during the last few days.

These duties being successfully disposed of, considerable time was left to enjoy the really delightful passage down the Bay. The weather was bright and fairly warm for the season, and every passing sail or steamer was of interest to these young men and women from the prairies. Indeed, a long familiarity with the sea does not diminish the interest of a thoughtful person in all that pertains to ships and shipping, although the sea has lost a considerable proportion of its romance with the advent of the ponderous machines, working with the regularity of clock work, and almost regardless of wind and waves, that have replaced the sailing craft of the past. The modern traveler fails to catch the spirit of Old Ocean, unless he has the hardihood to "go shipmates" with some rough but congenial skipper on board a sailing vessel.

On Sunday morning, May 7th, the "Emily E. Johnson" passed between the capes, and was at last fairly at sea. The wind was brisk and the white caps on, and, as might have been anticipated, it was not long before the terrible and familiar "mal de mer" made itself apparent.

Although generally regarded with little concern except by its victims, there is no doubt that this distressing complaint is a fatal bar to any comfort in sea travel for perhaps a majority of persons. There seem to be no criteria by which one can judge as to the likelihood of its attacking any particular individual. The semi-invalid seems as apt to escape as the man in the most robust health. The idea entertained by many persons that, like the measles, a single attack of seasickness exempts from further visitation, is without any foundation in fact. The writer knows a sea captain who has followed the sea for over fifty years, and suffers more or less from seasickness every time he commences a voyage.

It seems evident that the cause of this complaint is not understood, and equally evident that no cure is known, although innumerable "sure preventives" are given with the most entire confidence. These means of avoiding seasickness are often taken with such absolute assurance of their success, that the downfall of the victim is all the more trying when it does come. After considerable opportunity to observe the workings of the various remedies proposed, I am of the opinion that they are all equally useless. One thing is fairly evident, however, and that is, that the man or woman who keeps on deck and in the open air, and makes a brave fight in spite of his or her distress, will recover sooner than the one who gives up to the malady and takes to his berth.

Of the twenty-one passengers on board the "Emily E. Johnson," three escaped entirely; one had so slight an attack as to be considered practically exempt; eleven were temporarily sick, — that is, they recovered within a week and were not afterward incapacitated by seasickness; and six were more or less affected all of the time when the vessel was at sea. Two of the latter class were so distressingly afflicted by this malady that they were forced to leave the vessel at Key West.

Of the four who practically escaped, three were men of good constitution and robust health, and one was a lady who had been in rather poor health before starting.

Of the eleven who were temporarily sick, there were eight gentlemen, all but one in robust health, and three ladies in good health.

Of the six who were persistently sick, there were three gentlemen in good health, and three ladies, one of whom was in poor health.

In comparing the sexes, it would appear that the ladies as a whole suffered somewhat more than the men, and that they were more apt to be persistently affected.

One of the best proofs of Darwin's moral greatness is the fact that, during the voyage of the "Beagle," he was always seasick when the weather was at all rough, and yet had the sublime force of character to keep constantly at work, accomplishing more in the way of collecting and observing than any other naturalist has done in the same length of time.

On Monday, May 8th, the Gulf Stream was entered. The wind having been high during the night, the water was decidedly "lumpy" in the morning, much to the distress of the miserable seasick victims.

Sir Wyville Thomson[1] calls the Gulf Stream "one of the most marvelous things in the ocean" and "probably the most glorious natural phenomenon on the face of the earth."[2] It forms the subject of some of the most interesting chapters in the modern science of thalassography.[3]

To quote from Sir Wyville Thomson's "Depths of the Sea." "Mr. Croll calculates the Gulf Stream as equal to a stream of water fifty miles broad and a thousand feet deep, flowing at a rate of four miles an hour; consequently conveying 5,575,680,000,000 cubic feet of water per hour, or 133,-816,320,000,000 cubic feet per day. This mass of water has a mean temperature of 18° C. as it passes out of the Gulf, and on its northern journey it is cooled down to 4°.5 C. The total quantity of heat therefore transferred from the equatorial regions per day amounts to something like 154,-959,300,000,000,000,000 foot pounds." This, he says, is enough heat to equal the entire amount received from the sun by the arctic regions.

It has been my fortune to cross the Gulf Stream ten times between longitude 70° and 76° W. On at least six of these occasions, the weather was decidedly squally, and on three severe storms were encountered. Sailors always feel a decided relief when they get across "the Gulf," as it is called. This great volume of warm water coming into cooler latitudes thus

[1] "Depths of the Sea," page 306.
[2] *Loc. cit.* Chapter VIII.
[3] "Three Cruises of the Blake," Chapter XI; "Voyage of the Challenger," Atlantic, Vol. I, Chapter 5. The condensed statements which follow are based on facts taken from these sources, unless otherwise indicated.

creates atmospheric disturbances which are a constant source of anxiety, and often of peril, to the sailor. The vast area of warm water being covered by a thick stratum of warm air constantly tending to rise and be replaced by the inrushing cooler air from the edges, presents all the conditions favorable to squalls of rain accompanied by wind, and frequent storms of great severity, which, however, are not usually of long duration.

The edge of the Gulf Stream can always be distinguished, especially the northwestern edge, by the long bands of sargasso weed that are stretched out along the "rip," and mark the exact edge of the stream. In calm weather this great oceanic river is as clearly defined as if it flowed over the land, the deep blue of the stream showing distinctly in contrast with the dull green of the Atlantic. In a dead calm the stream is clearly discernible at a considerable distance, on account of the difference in reflection on its surface from that of the surrounding water, the surface being always more or less broken on the Gulf Stream, even though perfectly smooth outside.

The surface temperature rarely rises above $89°$, the general temperature of the stream being about $81°$. On one occasion a large steamer was stopped so that her bows were outside, while her stern was inside the edge of the Gulf Stream. Temperatures taken in the water at each end showed a variation of over twenty degrees within the length of the vessel.

This great oceanic river profoundly affects the distribution of life and warmth over both shores of the Atlantic. England, although on about the same latitude as Labrador, is blessed with a mild climate and abundant moisture, while Labrador is almost uninhabitable, one of the bleakest and most desolate spots on earth. The Gulf Stream is the main, if not the only, cause of this striking difference in climate between countries approximately in the same latitude.

Corals of the reef building species grow luxuriantly around the Bermuda Islands, which lie about six hundred miles east of Charleston, South Carolina, this being the northernmost spot on the globe where these species grow. The cold winds and water from the north are here intercepted by the warm current from the tropics, acting as an effectual barrier for the protection of the sensitive coral polyps. Doctor J. Walter Fewkes speaks of a Physalia which he found carried as far north as the Bay of Fundy, where it was doubtless surprised by the cold reception given it by the icy arctic current.

Numerous attempts at an explanation of the Gulf Stream have been made. Some have sought to explain it by the different density of the water in polar and tropical regions; others find its cause in the convexity of the earth's surface, and still others regard the trade winds as the prime agent in causing the flow of the stream. However that may be, it is evident that the great equatorial current splits itself on Cape St. Roque, on the South American coast, one portion going south along the Brazilian shores, and another flowing northward to the Carribean Sea. Here it again breaks, part going to the east of the Windward Islands, and the remainder, which is ordinarily regarded as the source of the Gulf Stream proper, banking up in the Gulf of Mexico by way of the Yucatan Channel, the old Bahama Channel, and the Bemini Channel. After swirling around in the Gulf of Mexico and becoming greatly heated in the process, this great volume of warm water finds an outlet, and scours along between Cuba and the Florida Reefs, and then between the Bahamas and the peninsula of Florida, where it is concentrated into a stream about forty-five miles wide, with a current of at least four knots per hour. Pouring out of this channel it widens as it proceeds northward and eastward, finally reaching the shores of Great Britain and Northern Europe, rendering habitable vast areas of land which would otherwise be as bleak as Labrador. Sir Wyville Thomson says, "I have seen no reason to modify the opinion . . . . that the remarkable conditions of climate on the coasts of Northern Europe are due in a broad sense solely to the Gulf Stream."[1]

The beneficent work of this great hydrographic feature is not confined to warming the northern shores of Europe. At the very beginning of its course *as* the Gulf Stream, it has pre-

[1] "Depths of the Sea," page 196.

pared for the marine biologist a field for work perhaps not excelled on the globe. Sweeping along the coast of Cuba on the south, and over the Pourtalès Plateau off the Florida Keys, it furnishes the conditions best suited to a profusion of marine life, a slope leading off from a land mass and swept by a strong steady current.

It does not seem to be necessary that such a current be of warm water, however. The writer has seen as great profusion of marine life[1] in the Bay of Fundy, swept by an inrush of the arctic current, as has been found anywhere beneath the flow of the Gulf Stream.

It was while crossing this marine river that our first collecting was done. The crab nets, with their long handles, proved effective instruments for dipping up quantities of the sargasso weed. A number of tubs were filled with sea water, and glass jars were placed on the top of the cabin. The sea weed was first immersed in the tubs, and the larger inhabitants picked out. Then portions were placed in the glass jars for more careful study.

Agassiz, in his interesting chapter on "Pelagic Animals,"[2] gives a very complete account of the sargasso weed, and mentions many of the animal frequenting it. Considerable quantities of this interesting alga were encountered as we crossed the Gulf Stream. Some of the specimens were in fruit. The receptacles are on specially modified leaves, which they cover in wart-shaped protuberances. The globular "floats" are so hard, and apparently solid, that one is surprised to find them possessed of extraordinary buoyancy. After an immersion of eight months in strong alcohol, these little globes still float on the surface of the fluid with almost unimpaired buoyancy, when an opportunity is given them. The writer once saw great patches of this sea-weed, seemingly acres in extent, about three hundred miles to the southeast of our present course. This was more like the accounts of old writers than is often seen, but even there the weed offered little impedi-

---

[1] By this I mean the quantity of marine organisms, not number of species, which is far greater on the Pourtalès Plateau, over which warm water sweeps.

[2] "Three Cruises of the Blake." Volume 1, page 290.

ment to a sailing vessel. The "Sargasso Sea" itself is said to equal the continent of Europe in extent, and lies between 20⁰ and 35⁰ north latitude, and 30⁰ and 60⁰ west longitude.

The inhabitants of this gulf weed form an exceedingly interesting subject for study, the following being especially worthy of mention: The most characteristic fish is a little *Antennarius*, which has become wonderfully adapted to life among the sea-weed, and is one of the very best examples of protective form and coloration that could be found. The fleshy tags streaming from the rostral spine, dorsal fins and abdomen, resemble very closely the ends of the young leaves of the sea-weed, while the maculations of brown, white and olive assimilate perfectly with the brown stems blotched with white bryozoa, and the olive of the leaves. It would be a sharp-eyed bird indeed that could see the fish surrounded by a mass of the sargasso weed. A still more wonderful adaptation to its environment is found in the geniculated pectorals, which look grotesquely like arms and hands, the terminal spines with the membrane between them curiously resembling a hand with widely spread fingers. These strangely modified fins are capable of being used as grasping organs, wherewith the fish can firmly cling to the stems of the plant.

A small *Balistes*, or "file fish," was secured, characterized by having one abdominal and three dorsal spines. A *Monocanthus* of grotesque shape, with its enormous head and minute mouth, was especially interesting on account of its greatly developed rigid dorsal spine, which is strongly serrated. This spine can be erected with a snap, or laid back almost out of sight in a groove on the dorsal surface of the animal. A little *Diodon*, or "porcupine fish," was also taken with the gulf weed, but seemed quite disinclined to give an exhibition of its peculiar powers of inflating itself, and showing off its bristling armature for our instruction.

All of the fish, it will be observed, were especially protected to meet the demands of their exceedingly exposed position, the *Antennarius* being passively protected by its form and coloration, and the others aggressively protected by formidable spines, which would surely make themselves felt, upon any attempt to swallow their possessors.

The crustaceans were no less interesting as examples of protective coloration than were the fishes. Sir Wyville Thomson says, " I know of no more perfect example of protective resemblance than is shown in the gulf weed fauna. Animals drifting about on the surface of the sea with such scanty cover as the single broken layer of the sea weed, must be exposed to exceptional danger from the sharp-eyed sea birds hovering above them, and from the hungry fishes searching for prey beneath; but one and all of these creatures imitate in such an extraordinary way, both in form and coloring, their floating habitat, and consequently one another, that we can well imagine their deceiving both the birds and the fishes."

These crustacea, several of them, are characterized by pure white, not simply livid, markings, in sharp contrast to brown blotches, thus resembling the *Antennarius*, and the sea-weed, with its growth of silvery white bryozoa.

The following species of crustacea were noted at this time: *Latreutes ensiferus*, *Palaemon natator*, *Nautilograpsus minutus*, and *Neptunus sayi*. A small barnacle of the genus *Lepas* was found in great quantities on the sea weed. From the fact that this species is quite conspicuous, it would seem that its shell affords a sufficient protection against attack.

A minute gasteropod mollusk was secured, but has not yet been identified. The most abundant mollusk, however, was a nudibranchiate (*Dendronotus*), which furnished still another excellent example of protective coloration, resembling as it did the sea weed, the *Antennarius*, and the brachyuran *Nautilograpsus*.

At that time and place but few birds were feeding on the inhabitants of the sea weed, the only one at all abundant being Wilson's petrel, a species of " mother Carey's chicken." But the sargasso weed, in the course of its extensive travels, passes through localities swarming with sea birds, which render the special protective coloration exhibited by its inhabitants of vital importance.

Among the worms found on the sea weed, the most abundant was a *Spirorbis*, which thickly dotted the olive surface with its minute spiral shells.

But the hydroids furnished the most interesting, or at least most beautiful, animal forms found inhabiting the gulf weed. Campanularians predominated, four very distinct species being found, several of which seemed to be new. Fortunately the reproductive buds, or gonophores, were present in each case. Perhaps the most interesting campanularian was one characterized by its green color. This was the first green hydroid which had been seen by any one on board; of course we except the fresh water *Hydra viridis*. A microscopic examination showed that this color was apparently due to the presence of chlorophyl, which seemed to be a part of the animal itself, as in *Hydra viridis*, and not an alga which is parasitic, such as is described by Cienkowsky, Hertwig, Brandt and Geddes.[1] The distribution of these chlorophyl bodies seemed to be uniform throughout the bodies and tentacles of the hydranths, as well as in the pedicels. Of course no physiological test was available to positively prove the nature of the green cells, but there was no ocular difference discernible between them and true chlorophyl bodies. The reproductive organs were enclosed in flask-shaped gonangia, having a collar and lid. The hydranth of this remarkable campanularian has a disk-shaped proboscis borne on a short, rather slender pedicel, and surrounded by twenty or more tentacles.

Of the remaining species, two are apparently new *Campanularia*. One has a gonangium which is shaped like a Chinese lantern and contains a single planoblast borne on a blastostyle, and filling the entire gonangium. *Obelia hyalina* is another very beautiful hydroid found at this time attached to the gulf weed, its graceful branching form and triangular calicles making it particularly elegant in appearance. Two species of plumularian hydroids were also found attached to the sea weed, one being *Aglaophenia minuta* Fewkes, growing in the shape of delicate plumes, fairly covering the

[1] "Three Cruises of the Blake," page 211.

branches, leaves and spherical floats of the gulf weed. We were greatly interested in watching the branching streams of protoplasm issuing from the nematophores, which are so characteristic of the Plumularidae. A small sertularian completed the list of hydroids found on the gulf weed at this time.

To sum up, the total list of animals which we collected, which were leading a wandering life as they followed the fortunes of the sargasso weed, was as follows: Fishes four, crustaceans five, mollusks three, worms two, bryozoa one, hydroids eight, making twenty-three in all, and affording a study of great value to those whom the merciless seasickness would allow to work.

On Tuesday, May 9th, the wind was northeast and worked around later to the east, the barometer sinking toward evening. The weather being squally, the vessel was kept under reefed mainsail and foresail. The study of sea weed was continued by those well enough to care for it. The occupation of dipping up the weed took the attention of some from their distress, and doubtless hastened their recovery. The east wind forced us to sail in the trough of the sea, and greatly aggravated the rolling of the vessel, although the " Emily " proved remarkably dry, more so than many much larger vessels would have been under similar circumstances.

From this time until we reached Egg Island, the schooner passed through large areas thickly dotted with *Linerges mercurius*, a small thimble-shaped jelly-fish, which, with others, has formed the basis of an interesting study by Dr. J. Walter Fewkes. This afforded an excellent opportunity for our students to become acquainted with the general structure of the medusae, and a class was formed, microscopes being brought up and used on the cabin top. With Dr. Fewkes' excellent account before them, and an abundance of material for dissection, a very satisfactory hour was spent with *Linerges*.

At night the brilliancy of the phosphorescence of the sea claimed our attention. The dip nets were again brought into requisition, when it was found that by far the greater part of the phosphorescence was due to this same *Linerges*.

It was manifestly impracticable to do much studying at night, as the motion was too great to admit of basins or dishes of water being used on the tables in the hold, and there was no available light on deck. Collecting of pelagic forms is carried on at a serious disadvantage on a sailing vessel, as most of these animals come to the surface only during calm weather, and at such times the vessel has no headway, so that the tow nets cannot be used, and skippers dislike to have the boats leave the vessel during a calm, not knowing when a favorable breeze may spring up. Thus it happened that the amount of pelagic material secured by us was not nearly so great in proportion to other forms, as is usually secured when steam vessels are employed.

Wednesday, May 10th, latitude 29° 50′, longitude 76° 5′. The weather was still inclined to be squally, and the vessel was kept under reefed fore and mainsail. About four o'clock P. M. an ominous bank of black clouds appeared in the north, its upper margin being regularly convex and clear cut, with a fringe of white scud rolling on before. It came upon us with appalling rapidity. Some of the young men proved of real use in helping take in sail, the mainsail being too heavy and bulky to be quickly managed by the crew. Their college athletic training stood the young men in good stead, and they gave effectual aid on this, as on many subsequent occasions when prompt action was necessary. A torrent of rain came with the squall, and a furious wind, sending the rain with stinging force into the faces of those who remained on deck. The execrable joining in the sky-light over the main hatch caused the water to pour in streams into the hold, although our effects were so stowed that no damage was done beyond making the hold exceedingly damp. It was, however, somewhat uncomfortable to have a stream of water trickling down the back of one's neck while at the table, as was the fate of some whose places were unfortunately directly under the hatch combing.

The squall gave rise to a heavy sea, and destroyed all comfort for the rest of the day. The seasick ones were made

utterly wretched by the wallowing to which the " Emily " now
abandoned herself. In justice to the unfortunates, however,
it must be said that they bore their trials stoically, and made
as little trouble as possible, although they doubtless thought
the romance of a life on the ocean wave a delusion. A trial
of the pumps showed that the vessel was remarkably tight,
not much more water coming up than had gone down the
hatches.

Thursday, May 11th, latitude 28° 25,' longitude 76° 5'.
A very "lumpy" sea was running all day, so that little could
be done on board in the way of study or work. Some of the
stores had become shifted in the hold, and a barrel of water
upset during the storm. It was no easy matter for the men,
most of them at least semi-seasick, to go into the hold and put
things to rights while the vessel was rolling so outrageously.

Attempts were made to secure specimens of the stormy
petrels flying about near the vessel. I have never seen one
caught with a pin-hook and thread, as is so often attempted;
neither can a net be handled so skilfully as to catch these expert
flyers. The origin of the name "mother Carey's chicken,"
or "Carey chicken" as the sailors call it, is unknown to the
writer, but they have a "peep" almost exactly like that of a
young chicken. Their manner of treading water with outstretched
wings and feet is highly amusing. On one occasion
I saw a large flock of these birds sound asleep on the water
in the daytime during a calm in the "horse latitudes."

Many flying-fish were seen during our outward passage,
and the students were interested in trying to solve the question
as to whether theirs' is a true flight or not. There seems,
however, little room for doubt, as a careful observer can soon
convince himself, that these fish are capable of genuine, although
very limited, flight. The flutter of the large pectoral
fins which serve these animals as wings, is so rapid that it
takes close watching to detect it, but it is nevertheless evident.
It takes longer watching to satisfy the observer that the animal
can rise in the air by this fin motion, independent of the
impetus with which it leaves the water, but this, also, seems to

be a fact. In the undulating flight of the fish the water is not always touched on the "dip." Sometimes the vigorous flutter of the fins lifts the animal when it does not touch the water at all. The direction of flight can be suddenly changed without contact with the water. These fish often fly aboard large vessels, especially at night, when they seem to be attracted by the lights. In one instance a man is said to have been knocked down by being struck on the chest by a large specimen of this species, and at another time enough flew aboard during a single night to make a mess for the passengers of a Pacific Mail steamer next morning.

A small squid was picked up on deck by the captain, having probably been thrown on board by one of the high seas running during the night.

Most of the seasick people seemed nearly over their troubles when the weather moderated somewhat about noon, and a number set to work putting canvas covers over the dredges. When they came to be used, however, it was found that the canvas provided for the purpose was so rotten that it was usually demolished during the first haul, exposing the nets to wreck and ruin on the rocky bottom.

A tow-net was also put on a frame, such as was used on the "Blake;" but the motion of the vessel was too great to admit of its being used to any purpose at that time. In general we found the dip-net more serviceable than the drag-net.

About four o'clock in the afternoon a strong gale blew from the eastward, and we were forced to lay to, not wishing to unnecessarily risk our canvas, some of which was not so strong as could have been desired. Of course this thing of lying to in a gale and "wallowing it out" is far from a comfortable experience, especially to those not yet accustomed to the sea.

It seemed as if old Neptune was determined to show how disagreeable he could make himself. It was not by any means a bad thing, however, to have the sea do its worst in the way of discomfort solely, as there was no danger, and thus get the party in a proper frame of mind for enjoying its gentler moods, which came afterward, and in abundance.

Friday, May 12th, latitude 26° 3', longitude 76° 49'. At about seven A. M. the reefs were shaken out of the mainsail for the first time since leaving the Chesapeake, and the light sails were set. At ten A. M. the cry of "Land ahoy!" proved a most welcome one to those whose first experience at sea had been, after all, a somewhat unreasonably rough one. The land sighted was the northeast end of the island of Abaco, the northernmost of the Bahama group. The accuracy of Captain Flowers' navigation, as well as that of his instruments, was attested by this excellent "land fall." Early that morning he had announced that we would see land at about ten o'clock, and his prophecy was verified to the letter. We had two quadrants on board, one for the captain's use and another for the use of those students who desired a little practice in the science of navigation. The latter instrument, however, was faulty, although it served very well for purposes of instruction. The sea had calmed down until there was comparatively little motion, and every one was in excellent spirits and developed astonishing appetites, as might have been expected. During the day we made the first set of tangles of Italian hemp rope, as described on page 12, and hung our largest trawl net on its gas-pipe frame. The mate proved of great service in giving practical aid and suggestions in hanging our various instruments for dredging. The novice finds himself pitifully ignorant regarding the various peculiarities of rope, marline and twine, as well as of the innumerable mysteries connected with the "clove hitch," "half hitch," and scores of other hitches and knots, each of which has its proper function in the eyes of the "sailor man," who may have little book learning, but will make university professors feel exceedingly insignificant when it comes to tying knots and hanging dredges, trawls and tangles.

In the afternoon the wind died down to an almost imperceptible breeze, and the barometer fell to thirty degrees, the lowest point reached during the outward voyage. On account of this fact, as well as a general desire to land, we decided to make Egg Island anchorage before night if possible. About noon the higher prominences of the island of Eleuthera appeared in the south, and we were drifted toward them by an almost imperceptible breeze. Egg Island light was made about four P. M., and the white speck of a pilot's sail was the center of attraction, as it grew larger and larger, until the little craft came alongside, and most of the party got their first sight of the natives of the British West Indies. The pilots, as usual, asked about three times the price which they were willing to accept, but Captain Flowers had dealt with these worthies for many years, and soon brought them to reasonable terms, when one of their number clambered aboard, bringing with him a supply of the famous Bahama straw hats, which are the best possible head-gear for that climate, and cost only a shilling (twelve cents) each.

The light breeze held until we rounded the west end of Egg Island, and dropped anchor in the beautiful little harbor. The worst of the voyage was over at last.

CHAPTER III.

EGG ISLAND AND THE BAHAMA BANKS.

Egg Island is the last outlier of Eleuthera to the northwest, and is situated, latitude 25° 30′, longitude 76° 55′. Although it was not measured, its area is probably not far from a square mile. In its center is a large pond, or lagoon, which was nearly dry at the time of our visit, but in 1888 I found it filled with water, rendering a boat necessary to cross it. This island is of importance to the world at large from the fact that between it and Abaco is the passage from our eastern coast and Europe to Havana and the Florida Keys, the rapid current of the Florida Straits between Great Bahama Island and Little Bahama Bank on the one hand, and the Peninsula of Florida on the other, rendering that passage impracticable for sailing vessels.

For many years a single white house on the highest point of the island was a noted "land fall" by day, and a light in the window of the same house was all that warned the mariner by night. Recently, however, the British government has placed a small light-house by the side of the old house, and now a light-keeper is regularly employed, and this important point is shorn of most of its dangers.

After dropping anchor off Egg Island on the evening of the 12th, one of the boats was lowered and a number of the men went ashore for their first swim in tropical waters. Landing in a little cove hemmed in by a coral sand beach, they were soon luxuriating in a delicious bath, with rustling palms almost over their heads, and the soft swell of the rollers around them. The seasickness and other discomforts of the past week were forgotten as soon as land was sighted. One of the few redeeming features, by the way, of this dreadful malady is the ease and completeness with which its terrors are lost sight of as soon as relief comes.

That night there was a general overhauling of fire-arms and other equipment for land work. Guns which had been put away dry and new, covered thickly with oil, were found to be rusted a bright red all over the metal work. Our experience proved that eternal vigilance is the price of even a measurably clean gun, and that in spite of the most scrupulous attention they are bound to rust more or less in the sea air. When a weapon is laid away for several days, it is advisable to plug up both ends of the barrels with a wad of cotton oiled with porpoise or some equally good animal oil.

The ornithologists overhauled their kits of tools, the botanists got out their collecting cans, note books and presses, and the entomologists unpacked their nets and collecting bottles, in eager anticipation of their first field day in the Bahamas.

The morning of May 13th dawned clear and beautiful. The scene from the anchorage was gratefully quiet and restful after the continuous tossing of the past eight days. The rising sun was flecking the ripples with fire, while the delicious morning breeze gently waved the fronds of the cocoanut palms which lined the adjacent beach. The water around the vessel was clear as only Bahama waters can be, and the crabs could be distinctly seen crawling among the algae at the bottom, eighteen feet below the surface.

After an early breakfast, the members of the party were assigned work for the day. One boat-load was dispatched to Little Egg Island, a rocky reef near the entrance to the harbor, where the numerous sea birds were seen circling around, indicating a promising rookery. Another party was detailed to work up the larger Egg Island, where they beached the boat in the little cove right under the cocoanut palms.

A path led to an empty sugar house, in which was a tank of fresh water, rather better than is usually found in the Bahamas. There being no streams in these islands, the inhabitants have to depend entirely upon the rain-fall for their water supply, unless they are content with the exceedingly brackish water found in the so-called " wells." The principal products of the island seemed to be cocoanuts and manilla plants. The immensely tall, flowering stalks of the latter we had taken in the distance for trees, the stems being fifteen or twenty feet high, crowned with graceful fronds of leaves somewhat resembling oak leaves, under which were clustered the clumps of fruit, resembling miniature cocoanuts. The bayonet-like leaves, radiating in every direction from the surface of the ground, proved hard to penetrate, as they easily pierced any clothing and seemed capable of penetrating side leather.

A large palm grove near the shore had lately been sadly damaged by fire, the beauty of these picturesque trees being marred by blackened trunks and charred leaves.

The view from the foot of the light-house is one of the most superb bits of marine coloring imaginable. At one's feet stretches a reach of dazzling white coral beach, relieved by a fringe of glistening palm leaves. Beyond, the water exhibits a wealth of color absolutely amazing in its weird and bizarre contrasts, the purest of nile green alternating with intense purple, and mottled with a bewildering jumble of browns, pinks and terra cottas, flecked here and there with snowy white-caps; still further out is the intense blue of the deep sea, a blue never seen in northern waters, the blue of stained glass, pure, deep, translucent. The clouds over these waters present colors seldom or never seen in northern regions, a decided purple being the dominant hue.

Mr. Pindar, the light-keeper, proved a hospitable host, and gave us a good deal of interesting information concerning the island and its products. The ends were deftly sliced off a number of green cocoanuts, and several of the party had their first taste of cocoanut water as used by the natives of the tropics the world over. The water is taken from green nuts, each yielding from half a pint to a pint of perfectly clear, sparkling, slightly sweetish liquid. Many persons do not relish it at first, but a taste for it is readily acquired. Being perfectly pure and healthful, it can be used as freely as spring water, and without fear of bad results.

The ladies of our party were greatly interested in the household arrangements of this "Robinson Crusoe," who lives alone with his old father on Egg Island. This house, like all others in the Bahamas, was scrupulously neat and clean. Indeed, where there is neither dust nor mud, on account of the island being composed of coral rock and pure white coral sand, it is much easier to be cleanly than otherwise.

The ornithologists found it hot work penetrating the thickets of wiry bushes which cover the greater part of the island. One of the greatest obstacles to collecting in such regions is the difficulty of finding a bird after it is shot. A majority of the land birds are small, of course, and falling into the dense thickets perhaps half of them are lost, unless the collector is possessed of both experience and patience. A very good aid in this kind of work is the auxiliary barrel, such as was formerly made by the American Arms Company, of Boston. This barrel fits into the bore of a breech-loader, having an extractor which is worked by the extractor of the gun, and carrying a thirty-eight calibre blank cartridge, which is shoved in after a pledget of cotton and a small charge of dust shot. Equipped with this ingenious device, the writer has collected with gratifying results in the thickest jungles of tropical America, where small birds could be shot at a distance of four or five yards without material damage, and almost invariably found after being dropped.

Messrs. E. G. Decker and Webb Ballord, who undertook the ornithological collecting for the expedition, put in a good day's work, securing a fair representation of the avifauna of the island, their collection embracing the following species:

Sterna anæsthetus Scop., bridled tern; *Sterna dougalli* Montag., roseate tern; *Anous stolidus* Linn., noddy tern; *Tringa minutilla* Vieill., least sandpiper; *Ægialitis wilsonia rufinucha* Ridg., rufous-naped plover; *Ægialitis semipalmata* Bonap., semipalmate plover; *Columbigallina passerina* Linn., ground dove; *Myiarchus lucaysiensis* Bryant, Bahama flycatcher; *Euetheia bicolor* Linn., grass finch; *Loxigilla violacea* Linn., grosbeak; *Vireo altiloquus barbatulus* Cab., black-whiskered vireo; *Certhiola bahamensis* Reich., Bahama honey creeper; *Mimus gundlachii* Cab., Bahama mockingbird.

Out of seven species of land birds collected, it will be noticed that only one, the ground dove, is a North American form.

"The most striking feature of the insect fauna of Egg Island appears to be the great prevalence of spiders (which are of course carnivorous in habit), combined with the apparent absence of any adephagous Coleoptera. Nearly all of the few beetles taken were species that afterwards proved to be of quite extended distribution in the Bahama Islands, and almost without exception either phytophagous or lignivorous. Among the weevils the most common species is an *Artipus* near *floridanus* Horn; several specimens of *Pachnaeus opalus* Oliv., a very fine green species about half an inch in length, were taken. Search on the beach under seaweed revealed a few specimens of species usually found in such places and belonging to the genera *Cafius* and *Phaleria*. The bulk of the captures consisted, however, of inconspicuous Hemiptera and Coleoptera, which were beaten from leaves in the dense brush."[1]

Toward the middle of the day, the heat became somewhat oppressive, although the thermometer registered only 78° in the hold of the schooner. The whiteness of the coral sand was so glaring as to be painful to the eyes. A rocky point juts into the cove from one side, the rock being worn into various fantastic shapes with numerous pot-holes containing small tide-pools, and forming excellent collecting grounds. Quantities of gasteropods were found in these pools, the most abundant species being:[2]

Littorina lineata, Littorina lineata var. *angulifera, Tectarius nodulosus, Nerita tessellata, Purpura hæmastoma, Strophia glans, Fissurella sp.,* and a large *Chiton*, which was par-

[1] For this, as for all other entomological notes, the author is indebted to Mr. H. F. Wickham, of the State University of Iowa.
[2] For the identification of most of the Mollusca here mentioned, the author is indebted to the kindness of Mr. B. Shimek, of the State University of Iowa.

ticularly abundant, most of the individuals apparently spawning. It was no easy matter to detach these Chitons from the rocks, if they were given time to use their wonderful powers of adhesion. If taken unawares, however, they could be easily and quickly removed. The shells of nearly, if not quite, all of the species of gasteropods furnished homes for minute hermit crabs. *Strophia glans* and *Cerithium* being favorite abodes for these most persistent of homesteaders. Some of these hermits seem to be in a fair way to become as terrestrial in their habits as the land crabs of the Bahamas. The writer has found them considerable distances from the water on the highest parts of some of the rocky islets near Spanish Wells, Bahamas.

The modification of the chelæ to serve as an operculum for the individual shell chosen as a domicile, is a good instance of what might be called the plasticity of the organism. It would be interesting to make a study of this matter with a view to ascertaining whether there is any tendency to inherit this peculiar class of acquired characters, and thus adduce an argument for the Neo-Darwinian or Neo-Lamarckian school, as the case may be. Another striking fact concerning these crustaceans is the brilliant color of the chelæ, which are about as conspicuous as they could be made, as if the economy in color on the rest of the body was compensated for by a concentration of pigment on the only exposed parts of the animal.

The botanists noted the following land plants on Egg Island.

[1] "In a first view of Egg Island, the two most striking representatives of its flora are the cocoa palms and the agave, or American aloe plant. The characteristics of the former are well known. Their trunks are often very crooked, bent in the most fantastic shapes, and in color are striped alternately pale ashen grey and dark, almost black. They are endogenous and bear at the summit of the stem the great cluster of mammoth feather-like fronds. A leaf is unfolded from its coarsely

[1] Miss Bertha Wilson has kindly furnished the following list of plants. It must be remembered that this narrative does not enter the province of a Report, and only notes a few of the characteristic forms of each locality visited.

reticulated fiber-like envelope about once a month, and a large spadix of small cream colored flowers disclosed. On the same tree one may see every gradation of development, from the budded blooms at the top to the ripened nut lower down. The nuts hang in clusters by stems about as thick as a lead pencil.

"The agaves or 'pita plants,' as they are called by the natives, are much like century plants in appearance. The great sword-like fleshy leaves grow from four to seven feet in length, and are tipped with a sharp thorn. The flower stalk is from sixteen to eighteen feet high, and is called a 'pole.' We did not see it in bloom here. The fiber of the leaves is used in the manufacture of cordage, a very paying industry to the Bahamans. At Egg Island these striking plants were everywhere,—along the shore, under the cocoa palms, in the sandy, open places inland, and even springing among great jagged masses of the coral formed rock. They are supposed to be indigenous to the Bahamas, and occasionally are as pestilerous as weeds.

"Along the shores are the mangroves, with their glossy leaves, and the sea grape, a shrub-like tree, with rigid spreading branches, round cordate leaves, and long racemes of small greenish flowers. It has a succulent violet calyx in which the nuts are developed; hence the name, 'sea-side grapes.' The berries are acid and pleasant to the taste. The wood dyes a red color.

"As we proceed inland we find thick hedges of shrub lantana four to seven feet high. It is sprinkled with its small dense heads of white flowers, and makes the air redolent with its sagey odor. Lantanas have run wild and have become as uncontrollable as the rankest weeds.

"The *Lippia*, a small creeping relative of the *Lantana*, grows near by in the sandy places. There are other coarse and woody shrubs not yet identified,— one with a small white star-shaped flower, nestling right in the axils of its small leaves, glossy as holly, and its stems are bristling with long sharp thorns. Still another has tiny bright green fleshy leaves, scarcely one fourth of an inch long, springing in whorls along the coarse woody stems, and spotted with the brightest of small orange flowers. These and some others formed high, almost impassable thickets, and over them trailed the moon-flower, with its delicate, evanescent white blooms, and several varieties of leguminose climbers, and a beautiful reddish passion-flower.

"In the sandy, open places, bristled the prickly-pear cactus, with its yellow flowers and globose fruits, and near these was found one of the most beautiful of the *Leguminosæ*, a trailing pea-vine with showy lavender blossoms almost two inches long. We also recognized many of our northern 'weeds.'— the vervain, with its purple spikes, and the purslane, with its fleshy leaves and quickly perishing yellow flowers; the *Capsella*, or common shepherd's purse; the *Solanum*, or night-shade, with its starry flowers of white or lilac or pinkish, and round, poisonous berries; a milk-weed, with pale greenish white blossoms, and its near relative the *Apocynum*, or Indian hemp; the showy *Argemone mexicana*, with prickly leaves like a thistle and a flaring yellow flower; the spider-worts, with their purple three parted flowers and grass-like leaves, and even the pestiferous sand-burr. The composites are also represented.

"Among cultivated fruit trees were the lemon, lime, orange, sapodilla, mango, papaw and guava."

The party detailed to visit Little Egg Island returned with abundant collections. Noddy and bridled terns were numerous and tame. The former is known throughout the British West Indies as the "egg bird," and is far more abundant in most regions than any other bird. Its rookeries are often visited by the natives for the purpose of collecting the eggs, which are fully as large as the diminutive excuse for a hen's egg usually found on these islands.

The coral rock of which this and all the other Bahama Islands is composed, is worn and weathered into a bristling array of sharp points, rendering walking a dangerous operation, and destroying the stoutest shoes in a remarkably short time. The rocks generally overhang the water with jagged points, making a troublesome landing for boats except in very still water. These overarching rocks are fairly alive on their under surfaces with peculiarly hideous crabs, *Grapsus maculatus Catesby*,[1] called "rock crabs" by the natives, but not the rock crabs of our northern shores. These are remarkably flattened forms with conspicuous stripes in regular patterns over the carapace and appendages. The facility with which they run along, clinging to the *under* surfaces of rocks, is amazing. It is exceedingly difficult to catch them even with a dip-net, so long as they are out of the water, but we found that by forcing them to drop from the rocks they could be scooped up with comparative ease.

The handsome gasteropod *Livonia pica* is found in abundance, clinging to the under side of these overarching rocks, and most of the species found on the rocks in the cove at Egg Island were also encountered on Little Egg Island.

Six or eight species of serpent stars were collected here, among which was a remarkably pretty blue *Ophiothrix*, an exquisite object under the lens, with its glassy serrated spines and beautifully colored disk. The genera *Amphiura* and *Amphiuma* were also represented. Here, too, our students first collected that striking but only too common sea-urchin *Diadema setosum*, with its exceedingly long and sharp spines, from which many a painful wound was received by our collectors during the cruise.

Quite a number of Gorgonidæ were secured, the most conspicuous being the common sea-fan, *Rhipidigorgia flabellum*. It is hard to see what has prevented authors from separating the red and yellow "varieties" of this gorgonian into two species. The difference in color seems absolutely constant, and there is also a marked difference in size, the purple form being decidedly the larger on the average. A constant difference both in size and color would seem to be sufficient for specific distinction. It is also a fact worth noting that the two varieties do not usually grow together, but in communities in which one or the other is exclusively found or greatly predominates.

[1] Miss Mary E. Rathbun, of the Smithsonian Institution, has very kindly identified most of the brachyuran crabs mentioned or figured in this narrative.

Plexaura dichotoma, *Eunicea* and *Pterogorgia* were also secured. Good specimens of these with expanded polyps were preserved by plunging the entire zoanthodeme, expanded, into water as warm as could be borne by the hand. *Plexaura dichotoma* is an excellent species for use in class work, especially when fresh, the various characters of the family Gorgonidæ being well shown.

In the evening all who were able to handle a scalpel helped to extricate the ornithologists from the difficulties which they had brought upon themselves by their activity in collecting during the day. The top of the cabin made an excellent table for dissecting and skinning the birds.

Specimens collected in the tropics must be promptly attended to, and never left over night, unless an ice-box is available. We soon found that it would not do to attempt any dissecting below, as many specimens became tainted before they could be disposed of.

Sunday, May 14th. Captain Flowers got the schooner under way, bound for Havana via Stirrup Key, which bears west northwest from Egg Island, and marks the entrance to the "N. W. Providence Channel" of the charts. During the entire cruise Sunday work was discouraged. When the weather permitted, service was held at the usual hour in the morning, and the remainder of the day was spent in reading, writing and resting.

This Sabbath was a typical West Indian day, with a fair wind, affording a "free sheet," which was a delight after sailing close-hauled for so long. "Hole in the Wall," at the southern extremity of Abaco, was sighted about noon, and at six P. M. Stirrup Key was made, and the "Emily" dropped anchor for the night, Captain Flowers preferring daylight for entering upon the "Banks."

The "Great Bahama Bank" is a submerged plateau or sand flat, extending westward from Andros Island and the numerous islets of the Berry group, the greatest length being over two hundred nautical miles, and the width south of Andros over one hundred miles. The average width is about sixty miles, giving a total area of something like twelve hundred square miles. The depth of water over this area varies from one to ten fathoms. All of our soundings on the "Banks" indicated a greater depth than was given by the chart, but our soundings were not extensive enough to be of much permanent value. On account of the shallow water, there is rarely a very high sea running, and as good anchorage can be found anywhere on the Banks, captains consider them the safest place in case of severe storms, although the numerous rocks and shoals in some parts are anything but reassuring to the navigator. The bottom is sandy, the sand being composed largely of triturated shells and corals, covered in patches with algæ of various kinds, and a "grass" which grows in tufts and has long lanceolate leaves very much like certain swamp grasses in the north.

The color of the water on the Banks is usually a clear light green, varied by dark purplish blotches, marking the presence of algæ or gorgonians. I have often noticed that wherever this green water prevails in the Bahamas, the clouds take on a rich purple hue. What causes this curious coloration of the clouds is not known to me, but the fact is striking enough to attract the attention of even the least observant persons.

It was while anchored on the Banks that we first saw the Southern Cross, which we had not expected to be visible at this latitude. Truth compels the remark that this celebrated constellation is not so striking an object as many suppose. In fact, a number of northern star groups far surpass it in splendor.

During the next three days the prevailing wind was so nearly dead ahead that our progress was necessarily slow, and we decided to take advantage of the opportunity afforded by the shallow water of the Banks to secure some practice in the use of our dredging equipment, so that the deep water should not find us actual novices at the business. The dredging spar was therefore stepped to the foremast above the galley, and the men assigned to the positions which they were to occupy during the trip while dredging. A certain one always attended to the friction brake when the dredge or tangles was being lowered; others were assigned the duty of putting over and taking in the dredge, and seeing that it was started properly on its downward passage; others always oiled the iron rope as it was unreeled for the first time each day; others attended to the assorting and labeling of the material as it came on deck and still others saw to it that everything was properly cared for and set aside for study or permanent preservation, either dry or in alcohol.

It will thus be seen that there was little chance for idleness while active dredging was being prosecuted. Each one soon became accustomed to his or her special duties, and the work was carried on without confusion or friction.

Three instruments for collecting were employed while on the "banks," the "Blake" dredge, the tangles, and an oyster dredge, which Captain Flowers had brought along for trial in this new capacity. This latter proved the best instrument for work on the "Banks," where the bottom was sandy and free from rocks. Its teeth tore up the largest gorgonians with ease, and everything in its path seemed to find a sure destiny in the net. In the beautifully clear water of these seas we could see just how our instruments acted as they passed over the bottom, and could correct any defect in the way they were hung or in the speed of the vessel.

The "Blake" dredges were covered with such poor canvas that the nets became exposed after a short time, and we did not find them so serviceable as they otherwise would have been. The tangles at once proved their usefulness, sweeping up everything from minute corals and gasteropods to the solid round *Echinanthus*, and even small coral heads. Strangely enough, fish were not infrequently brought up on the tangles and landed in good order on deck. No class of animals encountered seemed able to evade the sweep of the long swabs, and were it not for the difficulty of getting the specimens clear of the hempen strands, nothing better in the way of a collecting instrument could be desired. As a usual thing we kept two tangles at work, using them alternately and clearing the specimens from one while the other was over the side. In this way an astonishing amount of material was sometimes collected during a favorable day.

That part of our equipment about which there seemed to be the most doubt was the iron rope. It was claimed that it was necessary to keep it constantly under tension, and that this could not be done except by the use of a steam vessel and hoisting apparatus. As a matter of fact, it was bound to be under tension all the time the dredge was overboard, the weight of the dredge with its sinkers, and of the rope itself, being adequate to give a sufficient amount of strain to secure it against kinking, the thing most to be feared. The only danger, apparently, is in allowing the rope to pay out too fast, thus forming a coil on the bottom, and an eventual kink. This danger, however, is just as great where steam is used, the dredge in either case being lowered by its own weight, controlled by a friction brake.

The practical trial of our equipment worked entirely to our satisfaction, and gave us good grounds for confidence in its adequacy for dredging in deeper water. We soon saw that there was little danger of kinking the rope if care was used in not allowing the dredge to go down too rapidly, and that Captain Flowers was master of his vessel when it came to dredging.

We were greatly surprised at the number of specimens collected on the "Banks." Indeed, this region would amply repay a careful investigation, as it supports an interesting assemblage of animal forms. The most striking fish was one clearly allied to *Ceratias uranoscopus* (*Murray*), which was brought up by the trawl of the "Challenger" from a depth of twenty-four hundred fathoms. Our specimen, although closely allied to the one secured by the "Challenger," differs in many matters of detail. It is a more robust species, capable of still more increasing its girth by distention of the abdomen, after the manner of the *Diodon*. It is considerably larger than *C. uranoscopus*, the length being five inches. The anterior spine of the first dorsal is implanted right back of the margin of the upper jaw, and is much shorter than in *uranoscopus*. It is hinged so that the pear-shaped flesh-colored bulb can be hung right above the large vertically cleft mouth, and thus serve as a bait in securing prey, which seems to me a much more reasonable explanation of this peculiar structure than to discover in it a "sense-organ intended to give notice of the approach of the prey."[1] The animal has good eyes, situated so as to be effective much further than this hypothetical sense-organ. The two short fleshy tubercles forming the second part of the first dorsal of *uranoscopus* are represented in our species by two round, rather club-shaped spines, covered with spiny skin, and lying flat upon the dorsal surface of the head and body. The ventral fins are small and thoracic in position, while the pectorals are geniculate and ten rayed. It agrees with *uranoscopus* in being laterally compressed, of a uniform black color, gill openings at lower axils of pectorals, the skin being covered with minute imbedded conical spines, in the vertically cleft mouth, "fishing rod and bait," dorsally placed eyes, geniculation of pectorals and number of pectoral rays. The animal was capable of great distention, assuming an almost globular outline. It emitted a distinct grunt when handled.

Among the other fishes secured at that time might be mentioned a *Malthus*, or "bat-fish," an exceedingly grotesque creature with long geniculate pectorals, flat body, and a forehead produced into a lumpy prominence reaching in front of the mouth. The animal doubtless lives buried in the sand, with nothing but its staring eyes to be seen. Its color would assimilate well with the sandy bottom, and the warty dorsal protuberances would still further deceive by a simulation of small pebbles or worm castings.

A small flounder belonging to the genus *Etropus* was secured, having the eyes sinistral, the scales cycloid on the blind side and ctenoid on the left. A species of *Monocanthus*, or "file-fish," was also secured.

Here, as elsewhere during our dredging operations, the crustacea were constantly a source of wonder and interest.

[1] "Challenger" Narrative, the Atlantic, Volume 2, page 68.

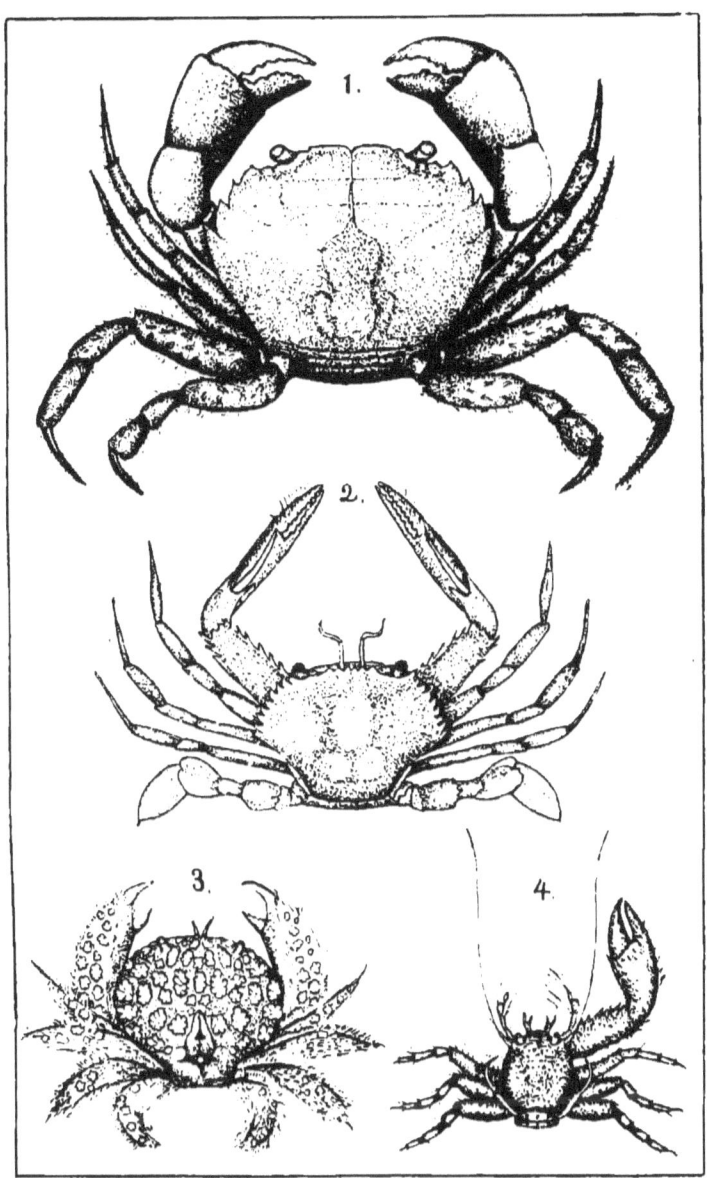

Crabs from Egg Island and Bahama Banks.

Fig. 1. PANOPEUS HERBSTII, M. Edw.
Fig. 2. NEPTUNUS DEPRESSIFRONS, Stm.
Fig. 3. ACTAEA PALMERI, Rathbun.
Fig. 4. PETROLISTHES SEXSPINOSUS, Gibbes.

The grotesque forms which these animals assume can only be
appreciated when seen. Here is Nature's art of protective
form and coloration carried to perfection. Scuttling among
the "grass" might be seen a very strikingly marked species
of *Neptunus*, which was conspicuous only after being brought
on board, its alternate olivaceous and light markings assimi-
lating perfectly with the grass and sand over which it crawls.
A very peculiarly ornamented species of *Ictæa* (*A. palmeri*
Rathbun) was secured, with the carapace and upper surface
of chelæ ornamented with regularly disposed round groups of
nodules, looking like sparsely distributed cobble-stones, between which a dense furry hair appears. The legs are greatly
flattened, the chelæ sharp and dentated, while each ambulatory leg is provided with a horny claw at its distal extremity.

The genus *Pilumnus* was represented by an extremely
hairy species, *P. caribæus* Desbonne and Schramm, with jet
black fingers to the chelæ, which were coarsely granulated.
Among the spider-like crabs, two species of *Macrocœloma*
came up on the tangles, one of them being very closely allied
to *C. camptocera*, with a triangular body, parallel rostral spines,
tubular eye sockets, and prominent spines on dorsal surface of
the carapace.

Massive sponges came aboard, fairly alive with crustacea of
various species. As might have been expected, specimens of
Dromidia antillensis Stimpson, were included, each covered with
its mass of sponge, and further protected by a coloration
exactly matching that of the sponge under which it lived. The
carapace, moreover, is covered with short, dense hair, giving a
splendid means of attachment to the sponge, which is still
further prevented from being lost by the pseudo-chelæ with
which the fourth and fifth pairs of legs are provided, these
latter being habitually carried over the back of the animal so
as to be available in holding on to the sponge.

But the strangest of all the strange crabs collected here was
a little fellow made to resemble a bit of shell so perfectly
that any one but the sharp-eyed young man who attended to
the crustacea would have been likely to overlook it altogether.

This is *Cryptopodia concava* Stimpson, having a triangular carapace so concave on the dorsal surface as to resemble a bit of shell, but with three prominent ridges meeting at a point near the anterior margin of the carapace. The chela is long and trigonal. When its various appendages are retracted, only the closest inspection discloses the fact that this animal is a crab at all, the real dorsal surface resembling the concave surface of a piece of shell, a deception still further enhanced by its color, which is whitish.

Among the macroura the only one which we will notice was an *Alpheus*, which occurred in great numbers in the various water channels of the massive sponges. They were pale brown in color, and like others of the genus were characterized by the enormous chela, which is longer and heavier than all the rest of the animal. A number of specimens of this species were placed together in a glass jar, and every once in a while a noise was heard resembling more than anything else the cracking of thin glass under the pressure of freezing water. The animals were taken out and placed in a tin dish, but the noise still continued. Careful observation disclosed the fact that this peculiar noise was made by the snapping together of the two fingers of the great chela. How this particular sound could be produced by a substance so comparatively soft as these organs, is a mystery. This species seems to be on the road to losing its eyes, these organs being completely overgrown by the rostrum, which seems to actually press upon the upper surface of the eyes.

The above are only a few of the interesting crustacea secured on the Great Bahama Banks, but they serve to show what a delightful experience our naturalists enjoyed at this time. About twenty-eight species of mollusca were collected, while we were at work on the Banks, among which were interesting species of *Avicula*, *Astralium*, *Cerithium* and *Trivia*. The most conspicuous Echinoderm was *Pentaceros reticulatus*, of which enormous specimens were secured, some being too large to go into the collecting tubs. The dried specimens of this star-fish usually seen in museums do not con-

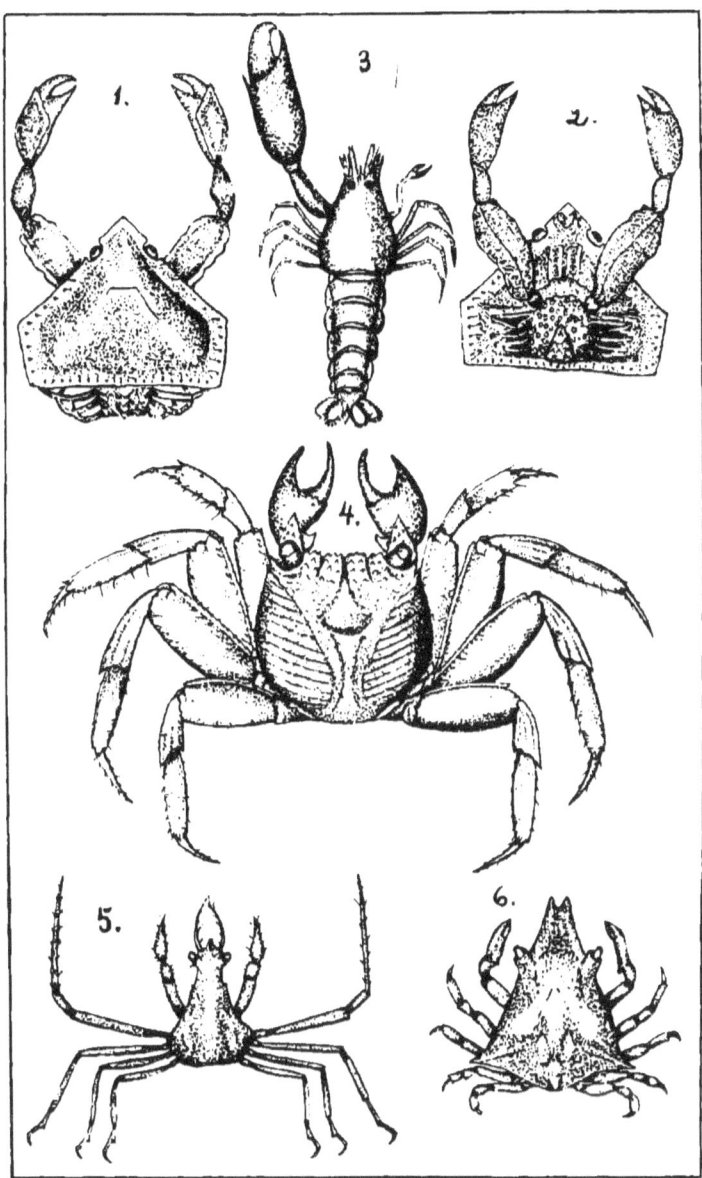

Crustacea from Egg Island and Bahama Banks.

Fig. 1. CRYPTOPODIA CONCAVA, Stimp. Dorsal view. x 3.
Fig. 2. Ventral view of same.
Fig. 3. ALPHEUS sp. x 3.
Fig. 4. GRAPSUS MACULATUS, Catesby. x 1½.
Fig. 5. PODOCHELA MACRODERA, Stimp. x 1½.
Fig. 6. MACROCOELOMA TRISPINOSA, Latreille.

vey any adequate idea of their real beauty when fresh from the water, the most conspicuous having a deep red body-color, relieved by the bright yellow blunt spines arranged in symmetrical patterns over the surface. Others present various shades of red, deepening into a rich maroon, alternating with orange and yellow. The natives of the Bahamas have a way of preserving these specimens dried, and sell them so cheaply that, for ordinary cabinet specimens, it hardly pays the scientific collector to take the time to dry them, even if he knows how to do so successfully.

A species of *Archaster* and one of *Echinanthus* were abundant echinoderms. Of course quite an assemblage of serpent-stars were secured. A haul is almost never made without bringing up some of these animals, which appear to be practically omnipresent in West Indian waters. A very prettily marked little species of *Ophiocantha* was noticeable from the fact that it uniformly possessed six rays, a not very common feature in this group. Two species of *Ophiothrix* were secured, one of which had very large, jagged spines, thickly matted over the entire dorsal surface of the disk. All of the ophiurans secured here were of small size, and not so abundant as in other regions where we dredged.

Sea-urchins, curiously enough, were scarce on these flats, although one would think the region particularly favorable to this form of life. *Echinanthus rosaceus* was secured in abundance. Like most of its relatives, it seems to flourish best on a sandy bottom.

Gorgonians of various kinds were common. Hydroids of several species were found clinging to all sorts of objects brought up by the dredge. A species of *Halecium* exhibited a new style of gonangium for this family, the reproductive calicles being oval and surmounted by a very conspicuous acrocyst. The gonangia contain ova, and each acrocyst contains a single developing medusa.

Another, a beautiful little campanularian, with tubular hydrothecæ, has a gonangium with regular corrugations, and a well marked collar and lid. Three sertularians belonging to the genus *Desmoscyphus* were found growing on the sea weed. An interesting species of *Thuiaria* was secured in abundance. Its gonangia are bottle-shaped with small necks and everted margins. These were among the largest reproductive calicles which we encountered. *Aglaophenia minuta* Fewkes was found with the corbula which very much resembles those of *Aglaophenia perforata* Allman.

It was at this time also that our whole party enjoyed the exceedingly rare privilege of seeing the zooids of *Millepora* fully expanded. A fragment of this hydrocoralline, having been brought up by the dredge, was placed in a jar of sea-water, without any particular care being taken to avoid exposure to the air or other shock. Knowing the difficulty with which the zooids are said to be induced to expand, we were not expecting to be thus highly favored, when a cursory examination of the specimen showed a considerable portion of its surface to be covered with what appeared to be fine white down. An examination with the lens disclosed the fact that both the gastrozoids and dactylozoids were fully and beautifully expanded, and they remained so for nearly an hour. We did not dare to disturb the specimen by transferring it to another vessel for the purpose of placing it where it could be viewed with the compound microscope. The characteristic features, however, of the two kinds of zooids could be very well seen with a Coddington lens, and they appeared to correspond closely with the figures in Agassiz' "Contributions to the Natural History of the United States," Volume III, Plate XV.

On another occasion, while at the Dry Tortugas, we were favored with a good view of expanded *Millepora*, although the expansion was not so complete as at the time under consideration. These *Millepora* are known throughout the English-speaking regions of the West Indies and Florida Keys as "*pepper coral*," a name exceedingly appropriate in view of the great stinging powers possessed by the animals.

At night, while crossing the Banks, we enjoyed the most brilliant exhibition of phosphorescence that occurred during the cruise. Every wave was flashing with light, and every ripple luminous. The vessel seemed to be bathed in ghostly flame, as the millions of light-emitting animals gave each its quota to the display. Nothing is better calculated to impress one with the infinite number of living things to which Old Ocean yields home and livelihood. We found that here, as in the Gulf Stream, the little thimble-shaped *Linerges mercurius* was the cause of the greater part of the luminosity, although ctenophores, pelagic crustacea and *Noctiluca* added greatly to the general effect, while more than once we saw the ghostly trail of what we took to be *Pyrosoma*, although the animal was not secured.

The most brilliant phosphorescence seen during the voyage of the "Challenger" was encountered in the Guinea current, not far from the Cape Verde Islands. Sir Wyville Thomson says,[1] "The wake of the ship was an avenue of intense brightness. It was easy to read the smallest print, sitting at the after port in the cabin." We saw no such brilliant effects as this, but the writer has seen in the Gulf of Nicoya, on the Pacific coast of Costa Rica, an equally intense display, distinctly lighting up the decks of a large steamer, and enabling one to read at intervals the print of an ordinary newspaper.

The purpose of this phosphorescence is somewhat difficult to explain on the supposition that it must be of use to its possessors. Verrill regards it as protective, at least among the gorgonians where, he suggests, the light may act as a warning to predatory fishes. Doubtless it may be explained in many instances as an aid to the sexes in finding each other at night or in deep water. Again, it probably assists carnivorous fishes and crustacea in discovering and capturing their prey in deep water.

Until the physiology of the light-emitting organs in various animals is better understood, it will perhaps be impossible to do more than conjecture regarding their true significance.

On Tuesday, May 16th, no dredging was done, the wind allowing us to make some headway on our course. Most of

[1] Voyage of the "Challenger," Atlantic, Volume 2, Page 71.

the day was occupied in taking care of the material already obtained.

Mr. James E. Benedict, of the Smithsonian, had suggested a means by which alcoholic specimens could be saved in good condition without using anything like the ordinary amount of alcohol. His plan was to use large tin pans in pairs, the rim of one being slightly wider than that of the other. The wide-rimmed pan is filled with specimens which have been in alcohol for two or three days. The specimens are heaped up as high as they can conveniently be placed, and then the pan with the narrow rim is inverted over pan number one. The rims are then carefully soldered together all around, so as to be air-tight, and the specimens are safe for transportation, the pans being much lighter, of course, than vessels of equal capacity filled with alcohol in the old way.

We found this plan to work admirably to the great saving of alcohol and weight. Large crinoids, especially, came through in much better shape than if they had been allowed to swash around in tanks. One important point, however, should be remembered. The pans must be of good heavy tin or they will rust through. Our collection suffered slightly from the fact that part of our pans were of cheap tin, and were rusted through before the end of the voyage. The damage was not from the specimens drying or decomposing so much as from the rust making unsightly spots upon the specimens with which it came in contact.

We tried both square and round pans, but preferred the latter when of good quality, because they are easier to solder together than square pans, and are not so apt to leak from careless workmanship. The pans, when filled, were crated for transportation, in sets of five, but we found it necessary to examine them occasionally, so that any leakage could be stopped with solder.

On Wednesday, the 17th, a head wind again gave us an excuse for dredging, with the result that many good specimens were added to our collection. On the 18th and 19th the vessel was delayed by squally weather, although some head-

Near View of the Rookery, Water Key. G. L. H.

way was made, and the western edge of the Banks reached. On the morning of Saturday, May 20th, we found the Double Headed Shot Cays in sight. Water Cay, the westernmost and largest of these, is in latitude 24°, and longitude 80°, 15. Reading in the book of instructions that this island contained a "natural well of excellent water," we determined to cast anchor and send a boat ashore, in hopes of refilling some of our empty barrels. The captain, with praiseworthy caution, anchored several miles out, thus necessitating a long and heavy pull in a rough sea before we reached the Cay. There is no landing place for boats on the north side, but a little agility will enable one to make a flying leap onto the jagged overhanging rocks with which the coast on this side is fringed. We found the "well of excellent water" to be a delusion as it was almost unbearably brackish, although used by the native spongers, who consider anything good that will sustain life. The island is about two miles long and half a mile broad, and is the home of countless sea-birds, particularly man o' war-birds, bridled and noddy terns. Both the latter species were remarkably tame, the noddies in particular, being apparently oblivious of our presence, and allowing themselves to be taken from their nests by hand. A large number of the eggs of both species were secured. Considerable quantities of gorgonians and sponges were found dried upon the rocks, having probably been cast up by the waves, and then blown inward by the wind. The rocks seem to be extensively excavated beneath the centre of the island, and in several places were openings through which the roar of the underlying sea could be heard. Near the north shore was a picturesque amphitheatre carved in the coral rock, at the bottom of which was a round pool of deep blue sea-water, in which many gorgeous fish could be seen. The highest point of the rocks is about fifty feet above the sea level. On the south side is a very pretty stretch of sand beach around the margins of a semi-circular cove, affording a good landing for boats.

Mr. Wickham furnishes the following note: "The three hours' work on Water Cay served to give an idea of the somewhat limited insect fauna supported by this barren rock. The space under loose stones which in more northern climates would be occupied by numerous beetles of various species, was here given over to hermit crabs, a number of which would scurry away when the protecting cover was disturbed. A single scorpion was seen, but escaped, and a species of *Phrynus* was captured. No butterflies were seen, and only a few inconspicuous moths, none of which were taken. Ants were rather numerous, and some of the species appear not to have been met with elsewhere during the trip. A Tabanid fly was seen, and a few flesh flies were attracted by the carcasses of birds shot for skinning.

"The coleoptera were not numerous eitherin specimens or species, the most remarkable capture being a Cetoniid, which I take to be *Euphoria sepulchralis* Fabr., though it is not exactly like those found in the United States. It was at rest under a spreading yellow-flowered plant, which grew quite commonly wherever a little soil was to be found in hollows of the rock. A Mordellid was beaten from another species of plant (not then in flower, I think), and with it several specimens of a minute black weevil, totally unlike anything with which I am acquainted, and a few *Artipus* near *floridanus*. The sea-weed along the beach covered a number of *Phileria*, of course. They seem to occur on sandy sea-shores everywhere."

CHAPTER IV.

HAVANA.

Early on the morning of Sunday, May 21st, we found ourselves in view of the Cuban coast, off the city of Matanzas, back of which loomed high mountains, one raising its majestic top, flat and massive, above the clouds which hung over the island. All day long the "Emily E. Johnson" sailed along this picturesque coast with a light but fair wind, just a little more than holding her own against the strong current of the Gulf Stream, which sweeps the coast at the rate of three, and in places perhaps four, knots per hour. An occasional village was seen nestling at the foot of the hills, each hamlet with its inevitable church on the one hand and barracks on the other.

One who travels far from home is constantly reminded of how little we realize the magnitude of countries, rivers, etc., of which we seldom hear. Few persons, for example, are aware of the fact that the island of Cuba is over seven hundred miles long, and that one could travel in a straight line, theoretically at least, a distance equal to that from New York City to eastern Illinois, or from New Orleans to Quincy, Illinois, in going from one end of Cuba to the other.

As we neared Havana, the towns along the coast became larger and more pretentious. Then came charming country villas, where the aristocracy of Havana retreat from business cares. Telegraph lines, and perhaps telephones, connected the metropolis with these suburban retreats. Finally the lighthouse tower on Morro Castle loomed up in the misty atmosphere, and the long line of fortifications came into view.

As we neared the harbor entrance a little steam launch with officials in uniform made its appearance off the point. A fierce and sudden rain squall drove them back, and sent the "Emily" several miles to the eastward and southward. The squall over, we again made the harbor entrance, and this time secured our pilot and passed a brief examination on the part of the health-officer of the port, a courteous and affable gentleman, whose object in life seemed to be not to make himself disagreeable in the course of official duty.

The setting sun gilded "El Morro" as we passed its frowning battlements and glided beneath the muzzles of its big guns. This fortification is one of the most historic, as well as picturesque, on the American Continent. It was built about three hundred years ago, and has seen many a bloody drama in its day. Report has it that within its walls the massacre of the ill-fated men of the "Virginius" took place. The massive walls and turrets, the old bastions and lofty tower perched on the top of the precipitous rocks, combine to make a scene strangely like those of mediaeval times.

Our captain was evidently loth to trust his vessel to a pilot who didn't know a word of English with which to direct a crew that knew nothing else, but "el practico" brought us safely inside the harbor, assigning us an anchorage opposite the government wharves.

We had been told that the customs regulations were so severe that it would be difficult to avoid infringement of their intricate requirements. We found, however, that there was nothing unreasonable about them, so far as our business was concerned. A distinctly polite official looked over our passenger list and manifest, said a few pleasant words regarding our trip, and left the vessel with the assurance that all was right and we could go ashore whenever we liked. The pilot left us a copy of the harbor regulations printed in several languages. Some of these rules seemed a little severe, but all were evidently for the common good, with a sufficient number of fines attached to trivial offences to enable the Cuban Government to secure some revenue thereby, provided the fines were collected, which seems doubtful.

No one went ashore that night, but all enjoyed the loveliness of the moon-light on deck. The electric lights of the city, the music from the parks, the ghostly forms of the white cruisers, were all welcome signs of civilization to those who had been cooped up on the "Emily" for a week since their run on Egg Island. In the morning a chance was given us to view this matchless harbor by daylight. To the north was the distant entrance, guarded by "El Morro;" on the east the fortifications extended for miles, most of them, however, showing considerable dilapidation; to the south were large warehouses and freight wharves, while to the west lay the city of Havana, "Queen of the West Indies," with its moss-covered cathedral towers rising here and there over the level stretch of buildings, which are low in comparison to those in northern cities, few being over two or three stories high. Immediately in front of us was a government wharf with a huge iron derrick, capable of lifting the mainmast out of a cruiser, and a solid stone water-front, with steps for the use of naval officers when they went ashore.

We had heard so much about the filth of Havana Harbor that we naturally expected to be disgusted. On the contrary, however, we saw less that was offensive than would have been encountered in any harbor in the United States whose shores accomodate so large a city. The whole water-front was scrupulously clean, and devoted to public purposes instead of being given over to the lowest and most wretched inhabitants of the city, as is so often the case.

Three Spanish cruisers lay at anchor between us and the city. They resembled miniature editions of our own "white squadron." Modern in every detail, even to machine and dynamite guns, they looked to be no larger than a good many private yachts, although doubtless admirably designed for the purpose of cruising along the Cuban coast and suppressing incipient rebellions, one of which was said to be under way at the time of our visit.

It was somewhat of a disappointment to find that the "Emily E. Johnson" floated the only American flag in this great harbor, with its forests of masts on hundreds of vessels. We afterward made out some American schooners, but for some reason they neglected to show their colors We were not allowed to enjoy this enchanting view for long, however, for no sooner were we on deck than the vessel was besieged by the "bungo" men. The bungo is a little boat with an awning over the after part, like that which marked the prairie schooner of early days at home. There seem to be hundreds of these little harbor craft, each with its vociferous boatman, who evidently has the insistent methods of the cabman the world over. He is allowed by law to charge twenty-five cents in American money for conveying a passenger anywhere within the harbor. If he is dealing with a stranger, however, the chances are that he will charge as much as he thinks his patron can be bullied into paying. Having our own boats and men, it was not necessary to patronize the bungo man very extensively, much to his evident disgust.

The law required that our vessel be consigned to some resident firm or business man, and the representative of the firm of Gonzales & Co. came off in a pretty steam launch to take the captain and manager ashore. We had letters from the United States Secretary of State to the Hon. Ramon Williams, Consul General to Cuba, instructing him to aid our cause and assist us in securing permission from the Cuban Government to carry on our work without official molestation. Mr. Williams proved affable, and promised to use his influence in our behalf, which he promptly did, securing permission for us to carry on our dredging operations on the coast off Morro Castle, and also at Bahia Honda, a place some fifty miles to the west of Havana. Wishing to be released from the legal requirement of taking a pilot whenever we desired to go in or out of Havana Harbor, the captain and myself went to the Captain of the Port, who was acting Admiral at the time. As is almost universally the case with Spanish officials, this gentleman was courtesy itself, and immediately promised to do what he could for us, and sent us to confer with the "Captain of the Pilots," who had jurisdiction in such matters. Both Captain Flowers and myself were deeply impressed with the courtesy which seemed to be habitual and natural to these officials, a courtesy so strangely in contrast with that which we had both repeatedly encountered in dealing with similar officials in our own country, that we could but exclaim, as did Mark Twain in regard to the French officials. " We are measurably their superiors in some things, but they are immeasurably our superiors in others."

Havana was founded about 1519, and is thus among the very oldest cities of the new world, and was twice visited by Columbus. Some of its fortifications were built by De Soto. It was twice captured by the English, once by the pirate Jacob Sores, and once by Admiral Drake, since which time it has been continuously in the power of Spain, although several insurrections and so-called "revolutions" have given the mother country considerable trouble.

The architecture is Moorish, as might be expected from the fact that for centuries the Moors dominated Spain. The old city, or that originally enclosed within the walls, bears the appearance of being cramped for room, so characteristic of walled cities. The streets are excessively narrow, barely allowing room for two wagons to pass, and are paved with rough cobble-stones, affording anything but a comfortable road-bed over which to ride. In many places the signs are hung across the street, giving a decidedly oriental appearance, but sadly obstructing the view. The sidewalks are ridiculously narrow, not permitting two persons to pass. The rule is " keep to the right," and if one is walking on the left side of the street he must take to the gutter, unless he happens to meet a pedestrian opposite a door, when it is customary for one person to step into the doorway and let the other pass on the walk. Most of the windows above the first story project over the sidewalk, and are enclosed by stout iron bars. Nine-tenths of the notices posted in the windows and on street corners are devoted either to announcements of bull-fights or of lottery drawings. Street peddlers are constantly soliciting the stranger to buy lottery tickets, and this evil is evidently firmly entrenched in Havana, as in most Spanish cities. To a stranger the lottery appears utterly demoralizing in its tendencies, and more harmful in Havana than the drink habit.

although a vast amount of liquor is consumed in the various cafés.

The Cubans are not living at such a killing rate as their brethren of the North, and it is a surprise to the latter to see large rooms filled during business hours with men playing dominos with the greatest assiduity. Very little drunkenness was seen on the streets, in spite of the great amount of drinking indulged in, and aside from the lotteries, which of course are legalized, there is little external evidence of vice.

The men are small and rather slender on the average, many of them with strikingly handsome faces, particularly the eyes. They are well dressed as a rule, and are much more graceful and easy in their movements and attitudes than Americans. Their negligee costume of trousers and light shirt, with a bit of color in the woven sash gathered around the waist, is cool, sensible and picturesque. Many of the store-keepers and clerks appear rather indifferent as to whether they sell you anything or not, as if they regarded the saving of trouble, incident upon your refusal to buy, as an offset to the gain they would realize on the sale.

Cuban ladies are seldom seen on the streets during the day-time, and never without an escort, which is usually in the shape of a grey-haired and solemn-looking duenna. When riding in the city they are often seen puffing cigarettes, and in some cases even cigars. It is doubtful, however, whether we saw many ladies of the higher rank in walking about the city, especially in the daytime.

Havana boasts a number of well kept and attractive parks. The one nearest the harbor is the "Plaza de Armas," fronting on the Governor's residence. A statue of Ferdinand adorns the centre of this beautiful little park, which is tastefully laid out and contains many attractive flowers. Probably the most beautiful tree in the world for park ornamentation, *Pionciana regia* is abundant in Havana, and its rich masses of scarlet blossoms add greatly to the charm of the public grounds.

The municipal palace itself is a not very pretentious structure of two stories, colored yellow with white trimmings. Below, a corridor runs along the whole front under a series of arches, which form in themselves a very characteristic and artistic feature of Cuban architecture.

In all of the parks we recognized that familiar bohemian and unmitigated nuisance, the English sparrow. He is now evidently in possession of the beautiful Cuban parks, and doubtless finds himself in even better quarters than in the United States. If this enterprising bird can overrun a continent with such appalling facility as he has North America, he doubtless finds little to prevent his ascendency in an island so well adapted to his wants as is Cuba. A better example of man's folly in attempting to readjust the infinitely fine balance of nature by importing a foreign element, could hardly be found than his performance with the English sparrow, particularly in the United States.

Some of the names of the streets are curious with their foreign sound, but we were positively shocked to find that the street running by the side of the Plaza de Armas was "O'Reilly Street!"

Another attractive park, some distance west of the water front, is "Parka Centrale," larger and more frequented by people than the Plaza de Armas. In front of this park there stood, at the time of our visit, a handsome triumphal arch, erected in honor of the Princess Eulalia, who had just visited Havana. This arch, although a temporary structure, was so imposing and massive in appearance that, like the "White City," it seemed a pity to tear it down. On one side of this is the principal theatre, and on the other the building devoted to bull-fights, the two main competitors for popular favor.

Parka Centrale is seen at its best in the evening, when the military concerts are given, and all Havana turns out to enjoy the refreshing promenade among the trees and flowers, illuminated by electric lights. The music at such times is excellent. Hundreds, and probably thousands, of chairs are placed near the band stand, and for a "medio," or five cents, a courteous official sells you a ticket which secures the right to occupy any otherwise vacant chair, and to change your seat as often as you may desire during the evening.

Here we had a chance to see the better classes of Havana, and found them very much like other ladies and gentlemen the world over. Many of the men and some of the women were strikingly handsome, and seemed to abandon themselves entirely to the enjoyment of the hour.

The handsomest drive in Havana is along the "Prado," or "Paseo Isabel," which is probably one of the most pretentious boulevards in Cuba, having a long line of park-like strips in the centre and well paved carriage-ways on either side. Cabs there are everywhere, victorias and "volantes" being always within call. The latter accommodate two or three persons each, and will take two, and perhaps three, passengers anywhere within the city limits for twenty cents. Besides these, there are street-cars and numerous omnibuses which run toward the suburbs. The drivers seem utterly reckless as they dash along the narrow streets and whirl around the corners. The citizens must be educated to keep out of the way of these vehicles, as they are evidently expected to look out for themselves, the cabmen being apparently indifferent as to whether people are run over or not.

Out west of the city are the Botanical Gardens, the most beautiful grounds near Havana. Here tropical vegetation may be seen in its luxuriance, and the trees, especially the date-palms, are well kept and induced to attain their complete development. A small stream and miniature lake, bordered by a profusion of aquatic plants, suggested to the biological mind that here was an excellent place for a well equipped biological laboratory in which splendid work could be done, with both salt and fresh water within easy reach. We found little evidence, however, that modern biology occupied any considerable share of the attention of the Cuban authorities. The Gardens, being beautiful, will always receive the support of this beauty-loving people; but pure science has not as yet obtruded itself upon the official mind.

Mr. Wickham visited the museum in the "Iglesias de

Belen," a cathedral founded in 1704. The museum is in a large room opening from the library, and contains collections illustrating the products of the West Indies, particularly the island of Cuba. There is a limited number of specimens of birds, mammals and reptiles. One of the most conspicuous objects is a centre piece of two large sharks, one of which is a "hammer-head." There is also a large collection of labeled mollusks, and a small collection of insects, most of which are without labels and in a poor state of preservation, having suffered greatly from the ravages of moths. The library connected with the museum is quite extensive, containing many rare old works, among them Ramon de la Sagra's "History of Cuba," containing descriptions by specialists of the time, of all the known animals of the island.

The cathedral which has been supposed to contain the bones of Columbus was erected by the Jesuits in 1724. It is sombre and massive, built in the conventional style of all Spanish cathedrals, with two towers at the front containing numerous bells. Here we were accorded scant courtesy by a rotund and surly Padre who seemed to be in charge of this building.

Opposite the municipal palace is a white marble chapel of plain but classic design, built to commemorate the celebration of the first mass held at Havana by Christopher Columbus.

The most striking feature of the city to an American is the omnipresence of soldiery. The militia are the policemen, and besides there are thousands of regular troops quartered in the city. Men in uniform are everywhere conspicuous, in companies, squads, and singly, and the impression conveyed is that of a city in the grasp of a military despotism. Many of the police wear sensible straw hats, and the almost universal uniform is made of a neatly fitting suit of blue cotton cloth, cool and adapted to the climate. At the time of our visit there were rumors of a rebellion, and it may be that a greater number of soldiers were on duty than is usually the case.

In the poorer quarters of the city the garbage is thrown into the gutters, and the smells are horrible. Half, indeed almost entirely, naked children pick over these foul heaps in search for edible scraps. Flies swarm everywhere, and the dirty faces of the children are covered with them. Yellow fever is endemic here, and it is a wonder that its ravages are not more terrible in the squalid districts. The flies must be active agents in spreading contagious diseases, where garbage from all sources is left to rot in the street, and the children and the flies carry on a struggle for existence, although living in apparent amity.

The manufacture of tobacco into cigars and cigarettes is of course one of the most important industries, and every vessel that comes into the harbor is besieged by tobacco dealers, who come out in bungos and use the most approved arts of the peddler in disposing of their goods.

The sudden incursion of so many young men and women from the hitherto unheard of country called "Iowa" was a matter of considerable interest to the good people of Havana, and they doubtless had many a hearty laugh over the attempts of the "Americanos" to make themselves understood. One of the most noticeable traits about Spaniards is the impossibility of inducing them to laugh, or even to smile, at any mistake a stranger makes in attempting to speak Spanish. With perfect courtesy they keep their countenances until they are safe from observation. They would be other than human did they not laugh then. But we had our turn when our laundry bill was handed in, with a printed price list, from which I make a few extracts:

```
"Casimire pans.              80 cents.
 Hand Ferchiefs. .            05 cents.
 Witte linen coats.           40 cents.
 Varioss happes. .            30 cents.
 Nap Kins. .        .    .    05 cents.
```

Washing will be done in feus hour."

Although on shore the heat seemed great during the middle of the day, the thermometer in the hold of our vessel usually stood at about 86°, not going more than two or three degrees above that point. The morning from ten to twelve seemed

the hottest part of the day, as there was usually little breeze
at that time. Just after sunrise the horizon was encircled by
solitary cumulus clouds, which had the turreted appearance so
common in the tropics. Sometimes they assumed the shape of
towering columnar masses with a spreading top. When the
wind was east or south of that quarter the clouds would gather
in the afternoon, and violent rain-squalls would pass westward
over the island. The amount of water which sometimes fell
in the course of half an hour was almost incredible. On
one occasion I saw the water reaching to the horses' bellies in
one of the main streets. Although the drainage seemed good,
the water came so fast that it was actually unable to run off
with sufficient rapidity to prevent this accumulation. It is
said to be unsafe to use the water in the harbor for any purpose after a heavy rain has washed the streets of the city, and
carried the garbage into the bay.

We remained in Havana Harbor for two days and three
nights at this time. The evenings were delightful, and most
of our party preferred to stay on board. One evening the
Spanish cruiser nearest us was going through the search-light
drill, and threw the dazzling beam on the quarter-deck of the
"Emily E. Johnson," keeping it there for some time, and
throwing every object into the sharpest relief. Whether this
was a bold scheme to scrutinize the American "*Senoritas*," or
an indication of some suspicion on the part of the authorities,
we never learned.

About all of the naturalizing done at Havana was accomplished by our indefatigable entomologists. Mr. Wickham
has handed me the following notes:

"The first insects to attract attention on going ashore were
specimens of *Cybister Iherminieri*, and a species of *Hydrophilus*, looking very much like our *H. triangularis*. These were
found on the ground under the electric lights which line the
harbor front, and later we found a very large *Benacus* under
the lamps in various parts of the city. A week later an opportunity presented itself to go across on the other side of the bay
for an hour's work beating, by which it was hoped to add

something to the stock of insects. Vigorous thrashing of the brush over a large net brought to light two species of large weevils, one a *Pachnaeus*, allied to *P. opalus*, the other not now referable to its place in our lists. Both of these were very active, taking wing almost immediately on being disturbed. In the same places a few *Cryptocephalus marginicollis* Latr. were found, and a peculiar longhorn, *Euthuorus filum*, which is also known from the Floridian Islands, looking very much like a small dry twig, the deception being heightened by the insect keeping perfectly still when beaten from its resting place. Locusts were quite abundant in the dusty roads, but time was all too precious to admit of chasing them. Butterflies were fairly common, and a small series of them was secured.

"About this time a yellowish beetle with dark tips to the elytra, *Nacerdes melanura* L., was very common in the hold of the vessel, often running over the tables or crawling in the bunks. It is probable that they bred aboard the schooner, however, as it seems hardly likely that they would come in such numbers from the city. The insect has a very wide distribution. An example of *Callichroma columbina*, a beautiful velvety green longhorn, was found one morning at rest on the hull, and as it is a West Indian species, it is probable that it flew out from the shores of the bay. A scarabaeid beetle, *Scatophilus sarpedon* (Burm.), was also found near Havana."

An excellent series of photographs of Havana and vicinity was taken by Mr. G. L. Houser, besides a great number of more or less successful snap-shots with the Kodak and other hand cameras, with which several of the party had provided themselves. Films seemed to work better than glass plates in the hand cameras, and were apparently less damaged by fungi on account of being tightly rolled while in the camera, leaving the surface exposed for only a very brief time. We found our dark-room for developing so unbearably hot and stifling after the lamp had been burning for a few minutes, that most of us avoided developing our negatives while on the vessel.

On the morning of Wednesday, May 24th, we had an exciting adventure which might have ended disastrously. The mate had brought along a small dog for a ship's pet, and "Paul," as he was called, soon became a general favorite, being of an affectionate and playful disposition. He had been moping and under the weather for a day or two, and on this morning, while all hands were on deck after breakfast, Paul, who was being fondled by one of the young men, suddenly sprang from his arms, and gave apparently unmistakable evidence of rabies, barking and growling at imaginary enemies, trembling violently, and circling around the deck as if seeking a hiding place, but not able to remain in one when found. Finally foamy saliva gathered around the mouth, and we were forced to conclude that the animal was mad. Under the circumstances there was no time for debate. Even the possibility of the animal's being rabid, and free in the narrow limits of the deck, with twenty-eight people on board, was enough to send a thrill of horror through all who saw the dog's condition. One of the crew, with genuine heroism, succeeded in getting the animal by the neck and holding him until a blow from a large iron bolt ended his life and his suffering.

If the animal actually had rabies, which of course could not be definitely proven without a more thorough investigation than we could give, it is evident that the malady had been latent ever since leaving Baltimore, or that this was a spontaneous case of madness.

At 9:40 in the morning, the "Emily E. Johnson" was towed out of Havana Harbor, to attempt to secure a series of *Pentacrinus* from the celebrated "Pentacrinus Grounds," discovered by Lieut. Commander Sigsbee, of the "Blake," in 1878, and ever memorable as the first place where the beautiful "sea-lilies" were dredged in quantities. For this purpose our expedition had visited Havana, although we were told by competent authorities on marine dredging that our plan was "too ambitious," and that dredging at such depths with a sail-vessel was impracticable. Moreover we were informed that an iron rope could not be used on any but a steam-vessel, with steam to hoist the dredge. We, on the contrary, believed our plan practicable, and proposed to demonstrate its feasibility, if possible.

This day, then, was to witness the crucial test of the expedition, and of the equipment so carefully devised by Professor Weld, from hints given by Doctor Alexander Agassiz. Mr. Benedict, Assistant Curator of Marine Invertebrates at the Smithsonian Institution, was naturalist in charge of the United States Fish Commission Steamer "Albatross," when she made her successful hauls of *Pentacrinus* off Morro Light. This gentleman very kindly pointed out for our benefit the exact spot on the chart from which these hauls were made, and gave us valuable suggestions as to the best methods of securing the crinoids, strongly advising the use of tangles rather than trawls or the dredge.

At 10:15 A. M., we made our first soundings. Morro Castle bearing S. W. by W., distance one mile. The lead did not reach the bottom. At 10:43 we made a second sounding, with the same bearings from Morro Castle, and distant about one and one-half miles, finding a depth of one hundred and ten fathoms. The tallow at the bottom of the lead was eagerly scrutinized for indications of the nature of the sea-bottom at this point, and we found, among fragments of coral, a fresh arm-plate of a crinoid. This was good evidence that we were over the pentacrinus ground, and the tangles were immediately lowered, rapidly at first, until they were presumably nearing the bottom, and then slowly, until the jerking on the rope proved that the tangles were dragging. The wind was N. E., and just about enough of it for our purpose. The vessel was headed about N. W., the current running east about three knots per hour. We were thus dredging almost directly off shore, or down the submarine declivity which leads somewhat rapidly into deep water off the Cuban coast. Just enough headway was kept to drag the tangles without their jumping and hitching over the bottom.

After allowing the tangles to drag for about twenty minutes, the crank to the crab was manned, and our first haul in deep water was on its way to the surface. The number of willing hands on board made it possible to work short shifts, the men working in pairs in regular rotation, each pair making thirty turns of the crank, the next pair immediately taking their place at the thirtieth turn. It was necessary for one man to stand in front of the machine with a stick as a lever to guide the rope so that it reeled regularly and did not pile on the drum. Others got out buckets, tubs, sieves and jars, in which to assort the proceeds of the haul. As the tangles neared the surface an anxious group of watchers stood along the rail. It must be confessed that this was a time of very great but suppressed excitement. We hardly dared hope that the first haul would be successful, and were indeed prepared to work for a week, if necessary, before giving up our cherished hope of obtaining the much prized "sea-lilies." Although assuring each other that success must not be expected on this first attempt, there was eager expectancy on every face that leaned over the rail to catch the first glance of the returning tangles. At last a dim yellowish blotch appeared way down in the blue depths, then one of the sinkers, and finally the bar broke above the surface amid breathless silence. The next moment a shout of triumph, for there, clinging to the hempen strands, were over a score of the graceful pentacrini. It was well that no phonograph recorded the wild rhapsodies with which we fondly and caressingly disentangled our prizes from the hempen meshes, placing them as soon as possible into sixty per cent. alcohol, as advised by Mr. Benedict.

During the four days spent on the pentacrinus grounds we made fifteen hauls, mostly with the tangles, dredging down the slope from one hundred and twenty-five to two hundred and sixty fathoms, and securing about one hundred and fifty specimens of these handsome crinoids. *Pentacrinus mülleri* and *P. decorus* were the most abundant, but two beautiful specimens of *P. asteria* were secured, besides a very small *Pentacrinus* which may be new.[1] When fresh. *P. mülleri* is

[1] Dr. Charles Wachsmuth, the veteran authority on crinoids, kindly identified these species for us.

darker colored than *P. decorus*. and is a handsomer species on account of the greater number of arms. *P. decorus* when first out of water usually had the head gracefully drooping and the arms not greatly recurved, the outline of the whole being very much like that of a lily. *Pentacrinus mülleri*, on the contrary, came up with the head erect and the numerous arms very greatly recurved, usually meeting below the calyx as do the leaves of some tiger-lilies. *P. decorus* is much more fragile than the other species, both the cirri and arms being more slender and liable to injury.

Lieutenant Commander Sigsbee reported that the colors of these pentacrini were light brown, white and yellow. We saw none that were either white or yellow, all being of some shade of light brown, usually with a purplish or violet tinge, and sometimes approaching a flesh color. Bright yellow Comatulæ were fairly abundant, and white or nearly white Comatulæ were also secured at this place. It occurs to me as possible that Lieutenant Commander Sigsbee may have had these in mind when giving the colors of the pentacrini.

Several specimens lived some little time after coming on deck. The *P. decorus* would gracefully expand its arms until they assumed a reflexed attitude, similar to that of *P. mülleri*. The cirri were also waved about as if seeking support, and there was some motion of the stem. We did not observe any independent motion of the pinnules.

A majority of the specimens came on deck in good condition. Some were broken in the operation of disentangling from the hemp strands, and a few, not very many, were ruined by their noted proclivity to "fly all to pieces" when displeased, a shocking habit, especially in crinoids worth twenty dollars apiece.

The method of preserving in pairs of pans soldered together, as described on page 56, worked admirably, the specimens thus cared for reaching Iowa City, after three months' tossing about on the "Emily E. Johnson," in excellent condition, not having suffered the slightest damage so far as we could see. The remainder were transported in a large square tank of alcohol,

A Bouquet of "Sea Lilies."

and these also came through with remarkably little damage.

The first specimen of modern *Pentacrinus* brought to the attention of the scientific world was secured from the vicinity of the Island of Martinique, and sent to Paris in 1775. During the next century only a few isolated specimens found their way to Europe, and none of these had the soft parts sufficiently well preserved for satisfactory investigation. The "Challenger" secured quite a series, comprising several new species, but nowhere were they found in any considerable quantities during that memorable expedition. It remained for the United States Coast Survey Steamer "Blake" to discover that there are still spots on the earth's surface where these graceful forms grow in almost as great profusion as during past geological times.

So far as the writer can discover, only two vessels dredged over the pentacrinus grounds previous to the visit of the "Emily E. Johnson." These were the "Blake" and the "Albatross," the latter vessel being, as Agassiz says, "the best equipped dredger for deep sea work in existence." Both of these expeditions secured magnificent series of *Pentacrinus*, which enriched the collections at the Smithsonian, Harvard, and a few other Eastern Institutions. No Western museum had anything like a good series of these interesting animals until our expedition secured an abundance of stalked crinoids for the State University of Iowa.

One attempt to use a dredge on the pentacrinus ground came near resulting disastrously. The dredge caught on the rocky bottom and hung so solidly that it seemed that our dredge rope would certainly part. The strain was evidently tremendous, but the rope held, and after great labor and anxiety the dredge was broken from the bottom, and came up bent out of shape and with little in it to pay for our trouble. The tangle bar is the instrument *par excellence* to use on rocky bottom, such as we found at this station.

The labor of continuous dredging was rather severe on the young men, most of whom were still inclined to be seasick. The heat at times seemed oppressive, and our backs ached long before the evening of each day spent on the pentacrinus grounds. We had the great satisfaction, however, of feeling that we were attaining a marked success, and stuck to the work every day, and all day, until our ambition was satisfied in the matter of crinoids. Besides the pentacrini, a number of species of Comatulæ, including several *Actinometra*, served to enlarge our series of crinoids.

At this station we reaped a rich harvest of marine invertebrates of almost every class, and found the ground well worth working over, even had there been no "sea-lilies" secured. Among the crustacea there were fewer individuals than we encountered elsewhere, and yet those secured were almost invariably of peculiar interest. The macrourans were represented by two striking forms, one a species of *Munida*, having greatly elongated chelipeds and long antennæ widely separated at the base. The eyes are greatly enlarged and deeply pigmented, indicating a constant functional use of these organs, which could doubtless discern both prey and enemies as the animal wandered around the patches of phosphorescent gorgonians so abundant in this locality. What a weird and ghostly world it must be down there! A world of fitful phosphorescent gleams amid the eternal night and unbroken silence, a land tenanted by grotesque shapes wandering among the miniature palm-groves of pentacrini, each living but to kill and eat, and in turn to be killed and eaten. The struggle for existence must be as sharp down there as elsewhere in nature, but it seems to our notion more grim, with less of joy because with less of light and sound, and less of pleasure because with less to impress the senses.

Another still more interesting macrouran was a little fellow with his tail flexed tightly beneath the thorax, and enormously lengthened chelipeds and chelæ, these organs being no less than four times the entire apparent length of the body. The chelæ are, moreover, distinguished by having one large tooth on the inferior cutting edge of the forceps, and anterior to this a number of minute nodules. They are provided, moreover, with conspicuous tufts of hair which project like a cam-

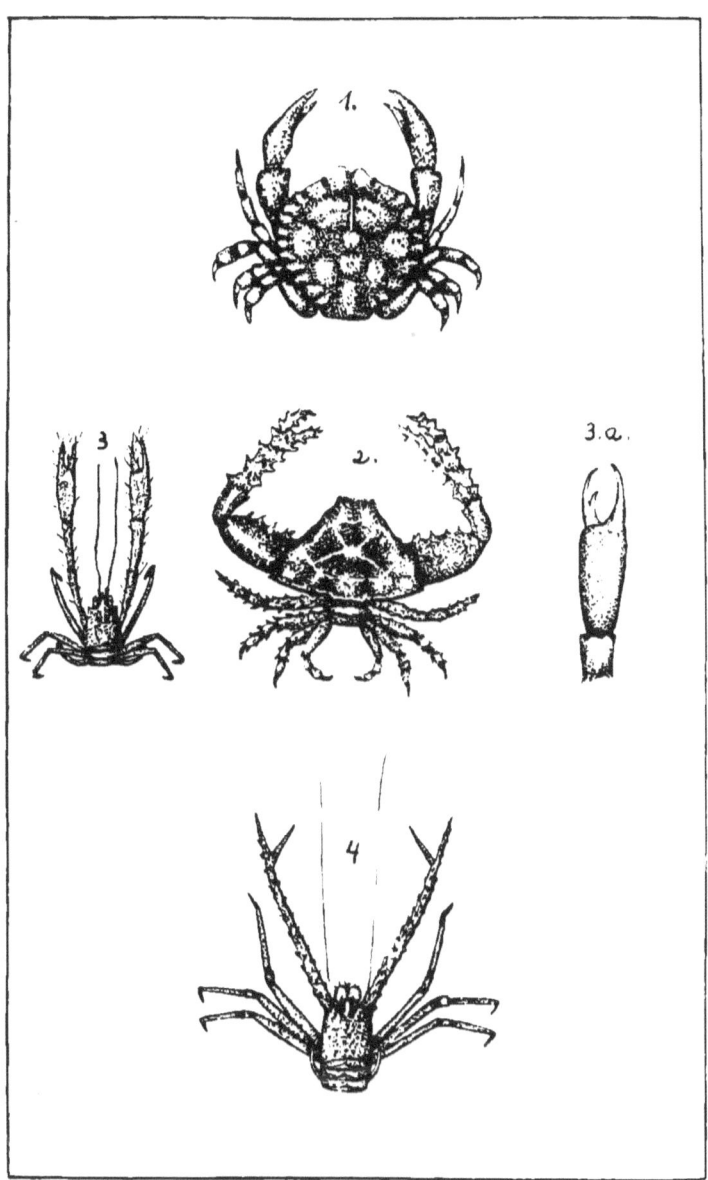

Crustacea from "Pentacrinus Ground."

1. OSACHILA TUBEROSA, Stimp.
2. THYROLAMBRUS ASTROIDES, Rathb.
3. Macrouran with elongated chelipeds.
3a. Chela of same.
4. MUNIDA (?) sp.

el's hair brush in front of these organs. The eyes are small and entirely devoid of pigment, giving the impression that they were not much used. Probably the brushes on the chelae were tactile organs pushed out far in front of the animal on the enormously lengthened chelipeds.

Among the brachyurans the myioids greatly predominated. One species of *Libinia* is characterized by a great horse-shoe-shaped depression on the carapace, as if the animal had been very deeply branded. The concave surface of the depression is glistening and smooth, as if it were in some way artificially produced. This mark is perfectly symmetrical, however, and placed exactly on the median line of the carapace. In other respects this specimen is not remarkable. A species of *Thyrolambrus* was secured, with a transverse and triangular carapace, an exceedingly long cheliped and small chelae with conspicuous spines. All the legs are covered with spines and nodules, and the carapace is marked with curious reticulations of ridges and grooves, as if waterworn. There is no rostrum, and the inconspicuous eyes have the appearance of being functionless. A slender-limbed species probably belonging to the genus *Podochela* is characterized by its long and slender forceps, exserted eyes, and two dark marks on the carapace above the bases of the walking legs.

Among the oxystomata, *Osachila tuberosa* Stimpson was secured. It has the tender mouth-parts well protected by a leaf-like expansion of part of the maxilliped, which forms a triangular plate exactly fitting over the mouth-parts, and, with its fellow, making a sort of operculum which effectually protects all of the appendages engaged in feeding.

One of the interesting things about the macroura is the nicety with which the antennule is folded up like a pocket rule, and tucked away out of sight when not in use. A novice might hunt in vain for this organ in the species in question without discovering it packed out of harm's way in a special pocket hollowed out under the rostrum for its reception.

The most abundant animals at this station were the various classes of Echinodermata. Of these the star-fish were the least numerous, although one striking species was secured, which seems to belong to the family Asterinidæ, but cannot be accommodated in any genus, the description of which is accessible to the writer. The abactinal surface is covered with small rectangular plates arranged in regular rows. These plates bear spines closely resembling paxillæ in their arrangement. The papulæ, or dermal branchiæ, are found on the dorsal surface only. The most striking feature of this species is the peculiar ornamentation effected by conspicuous, irregularly disposed rounded prominences scattered over the dorsal surface, and resembling huge warts. I have seen no similar arrangement of tubercles elsewhere among the Asteroidea.

Among the thirty-odd species of serpent-stars and basket-fish dredged on the pentacrinus grounds, were many forms of unusual interest to the zoologist, a considerable proportion being probably new species. This portion of the collection is particularly worthy of careful study in the hands of a competent specialist. The writer can do nothing more than indicate the general nature of the collection, mentioning a few of the more notable and striking forms, such as catch the attention in a hurried examination of the material.

The Ophuridæ are represented by species of *Ophiura*, *Ophiomusium*, *Ophiozona*, *Ophiolepis*, *Ophiomitra*, *Ophiopæpale*, *Ophiothyreus*, *Ophiocantha*, *Ophioglypha*, and *Ophiocamax*.

A very striking form allied to *Ophiomusium* has the entire dorsal surface covered with rounded, greatly projecting nodules like cobble-stones of several colors in striking contrast. Similar nodules cover the dorsal surface of the arms, from which they pass on to the disk, forming five large bulging ridges which meet at the centre of the back. Alternating with these ridges are the broad, granulated and widely separated radial shields. Below are seen the roughly pentagonal mouth-shields, with conspicuous side mouth-shields, both being set back a considerable distance from the angles of the jaws. Each upper arm-plate alternates with a series of three prominent "cobble-stones," and a still more prominent accessory piece is placed in front of each side arm-plate, the latter being considerably less conspicuous than the accessory piece. There are two short, stubby arm-spines to each side arm-plate, and a large tentacle-scale apparently soldered down to the lower arm-plate, there being no visible tentacle-pores. The mouth-papillæ are six on each side of each jaw, and they too are apparently soldered together, a character of the genus *Ophiomusium*. Another interesting fact is that the arms roll in a vertical plane, a feature heretofore, I believe, observed only in the Astrophytidæ, or basket-fish. This resemblance is further helped out by the prominent ridges on the top and sides of the arms, these ridges *not* being formed by the upper and side arm-plates. Indeed it is doubtful that this strange ophiurian is an *Ophiomusium* at all, and it may be regarded as the first of a series of no less than eight species secured at this station, which lead from the true serpent-stars on the one hand to the true branched Astrophytidæ on the other.

The species above described would seem to be on the serpent-star side of the line, still retaining the characteristic mouth-parts, i. e., mouth-shields, side mouth-shields and mouth papillæ, combined with several features characteristic of the Astrophytidæ.

Next in our progress toward the typical basket-fish, we come to a species of *Sigsbeia*, with a highly vaulted disk covered with harsh granules, and exhibiting pronounced radiating ridges, and, in addition, raised ridges which form concentric pentagonal markings, crossing the radiating ridges at right angles. The bases of the arms are swollen, and the arms throughout are ringed as in the next genus. The radiating ridges on the disk are formed not by radial shields, but by series of nodules or small plates. The arms are harsh with rough granules arranged in ridges as in the next genus, and roll naturally in a vertical plane, forming a stiff coil which can hardly be unrolled after the animal is dead without breaking the arm. There are large and prominent accessory plates on the sides of the arms. This species differs from *Sigsbeia murrhina* in having a highly vaulted instead of a flat disk, as represented in Agassiz' "Three Cruises of the Blake," and described in the "Blake" Reports. The arrangement of the dorsal plates is also different.

Next we have the genus *Ophiomyxa*, which is placed on the basket-fish side of the line. Our collection seems to contain at least two species of this genus. Here we have forms with the arm-plates and disk markings of the serpent-star replaced by a tough, leathery membrane. The mouth-papillæ are furnished with serrated edges, an approach to the spines in this region characteristic of the basket-fish. The tentacle-scales are obliterated, and the arm-spines are reduced to inconspicuous stumps. The radial ridges are not prominent. A step farther is reached in the genus *Ophiocreas*, of which we secured at least three species at this station. This genus has the astrophyton-like characters of *Ophiomyxa*, and, in addition the spiniform mouth-papillæ and prominent radial ridges reaching in some cases clear to the middle of the dorsal surface. The arms are immensely lengthened, reaching the maximum of length to diameter to be found among ophiurians. The three species secured may be differentiated as follows, the writer not being willing to risk naming them:

(a) A form in which one radial shield of each pair overlaps its fellow. Length of arms to diameter of body is as twelve to one. The color in alcohol is a decided brown.

(b) An exceedingly slender form, with prominent but narrow radial plates which do not touch each other. Length of arms to diameter of disk as twenty-five to one. This is a small and delicate species, of a light pinkish brown color, highly vaulted disk, and remarkably attenuated arms.

(c) A small but stouter form, with radial shields not reaching to center of disk, but extending not much more than half that distance. Disk flat; segments of arms very distinct, much more so than in any other *Ophiocreas* which I have seen. Length of arms to diameter of disk as eight to one.

Last of all we come to two species of *Astrogomphus*, a genus discovered by the "Blake" near the Florida Keys. This genus seems to exhibit nearly all of the characters of an astrophyton except the branching arms, and is probably nearer that genus than any other specimen secured by us. Neither of our two species can be referred to *Astrogomphus vallatus*. They may be briefly diagnosed as follows:

(a) Radial ridges broader than in *A. vallatus*; spiniform mouth-papillae much smaller. The ventral surface is not smooth, but bears a number of regularly but sparsely distributed granular nodules. There is no "fence of pickets" separating the mouth region from the interbrachial spaces. Color in alcohol almost white.

(b) Radial ridges not continuing to near center of disk, and apparently five instead of ten in number, owing to the fact that each pair of radial plates is soldered together by their apposed faces, forming one broad elevated ridge instead of two, as in other species. The ridges on disk and arm bases resemble those of *Astrocnida isidis*. Spines on radial ridges smaller than in *Astrogomphus vallatus*, and the mouth parts much as in the latter species. The ventral surface is crowded with spiny granules, but there is no "fence of pickets."

It is seldom that such an array of species of simple armed ASTROPHYTIDÆ is found in any one locality. Most of these forms appear to be new, and are certainly well worthy of careful study.

Among the great number of typical serpent-stars our space will admit of but the briefest mention of a few. *Ophiothyreus goësi* is a short-armed species having the disk covered with swollen plates. The first upper arm-plate is split in two and interposed between the radial shields. Each half of the split arm-plate bears on its outer side a row of minute scales resembling genital scales. *Ophiopepale goësiana* is a daintily marked slender-armed species, with divided under arm-plates and prominent radial shields. Disk brown, conspicuously spotted with white.

A very conspicuous species is an *Ophiocantha* (?), with a disk colored light brown, with five broad radiating bands of pure white and long glassy spines. There are few more beautiful objects under a low power of the microscope than these glassy spined ophiurans. For some reason they are particularly apt to be provided with conspicuous radiating bands of color, giving a remarkably elegant pattern against which the pure transparent spines are outlined. Another fact worth noting is that, so far as the writer has been able to discover, these glassy spines are never colored, as are the gorgeous calcareous spicules of the GORGONID.E, for instance. Nature has infinite resources, and the contrast of color is probably just as effective in the one case as in the other. There may be little significance in the fact that a deep violet or purple is perhaps the commonest color in spicules of gorgonians, and is also found in the conspicuous color bands on the disks of many species of glassy spined ophiurans.

Perhaps the most remarkable spines possessed by any species dredged from the pentacrinus grounds, are those of an *Ophiocamax* (?), in which some of the arm-spines are six times the diameter of the arm in length. These beautiful spines are beset with symmetrically arranged spinelets sharp as needles (how poor the comparison!), and set nearly at right angles to the main shaft. The disk of this species is remarkable for being highly vaulted and sharply divided into five swollen lobes. The mouth-papillae are arranged in rosette-shaped tufts, and tooth-papillae are present. Taken as a whole the OPHIURID.E secured at this station are characterized by the paleness of their colors, although bright pigment is by no means wanting.

Among the Echini a number of striking forms were secured. Perhaps the handsomest species was *Porocidaris sharreri*, one specimen being a truly magnificent one, with spines about seven inches in length, and the peculiar serrated radioles resembling some of the ivory spear-heads used in Africa. *Porocidaris bartletti* exhibited remarkable variation in its radioles or primary spines, those in young specimens being conspicuously banded with scarlet and white, and coarsely serrated, while the older and longer spines appear to have lost both their color and their serrations.

It seems to me that such striking coloration in regular pattern as is often found among the deep-sea echinoderms is good presumptive evidence that there is a considerable quantity of light at the sea bottom, whether the illumination comes from the upper world or is furnished entirely by the various phosphorescent animals.

Cœlopleurus floridanus, a beautifully colored species allied to the *Arbacca* of our coasts, made a pleasing display with its brilliant crimson and white spines. The four triangular anal plates of this species is usually given as a family character of the ARBACEIDÆ, but among our specimens of *Cœlopleurus floridanus* was one with three plates, others with four, and one with five. In examining the series it so happened that the writer found the three in the order named, much to his astonishment. *Salenia pattersoni*, another species with spines banded with vermilion and white, is rendered still more attractive by bands of deep violet following the ambulacral furrows, and outlining the plates of the apical system, the ground color being a dove or cream color. The anal opening is quite eccentric in this sea-urchin, and Alexander Agassiz thinks that the suranal plate is the homologue of the centro-dorsal of star-fishes and crinoids. A beautiful specimen of *Aspidodiadema* may represent a new species, the spines being ringed with rich purplish violet and white in striking contrast.

Some small specimens of Echini probably belonging to the genus *Temnechinus* were secured, and also a few small Petal-osticha which have not yet been identified.

The cœlenterates of the pentacrinus ground are little less interesting than the echinoderms. The assemblage of forms belonging to this subkingdom embraced almost nothing that is familiar to the naturalist whose work has been confined to shallow water.

The corals are almost all of the simple old-fashioned type, not one of the familiar West Indian reef-builders being found at this station. Pourtalès, who had the honor of first calling the attention of the scientific world to the deep-sea corals of the Gulf Stream, says, "The total of sixty-four species is nearly as large as the total of the shoal water or reef corals of the same region, if we reduce the number of the latter to its proper proportions by the rejection of merely nominal species.[1] Probably the most beautiful simple coral secured by us was a *Deltocyathus italicus*. This exquisite little disc-shaped coral is noted for being a living fossil, as it were, being found living on the Portales Plateau and other parts of the Gulf Stream, and fossil in the Miocene rocks of Italy. We found excellent specimens of both forms figured by Agassiz in "Three Cruises of the Blake." None of our specimens showed any indication of a base of attachment. Other genera represented were *Rhizotrochus*, *Caryophyllia*, *Paracyathus* and *Thecopsammia*. A small branching form was also secured with slender costate calicles, from the upper walls of which other individual calicles spring. The most conspicuous coral here was a profusely branching form which appears to be *Axohelia mirabilis*, although the original description of this species is not at hand. The specimen secured has a remarkably hispid surface, with calicles having ten to twelve exserted septa, giving it the appearance of an *Oculina*. An unusual character is the prevalence of ten septa to each calicle, the number twelve appearing to be exceptional. The corallum is buffy or creamy white, with brown polyps.

To those accustomed to the shallow-water Hydrocorallinae, the deep-water forms are a revelation. The daintiest "coral" secured was the *Stylaster filogranus*, with its exquisite lace-like tracery of delicate branchlets and its rosy hue. Unfortunately, the beautiful color had altogether disappeared before we reached home. *Pliobathus symmetricus* is, as its name implies, a form characterized by unusual symmetry, being fan-shaped with a number of regularly disposed palmate branches. *Distichopora contorta* has curiously bent branches, along the edges of which are double ridges with deep furrows between. The gastrozoids inhabit large pores arranged in an irregular double row along the bottom of the furrow, while the dactylo-

---

[1] Report on Corals and Antipatharia by L. F. Pourtalès, Bulletin Mus. Comp. Zool., Vol. VI., No. 1.

zoids inhabit smaller slit-like pores placed on either side along the edge of the two ridges. The specimens of this form secured by us attain a height of about two inches.

Two other species of this genus were found which attained a considerable size. Both were profusely branching forms, with the branches in the same plane. One, *D. sulcata* (?), had the edges cut by deep grooves, which were continuous and included large pores, and ill-defined nodules scattered rather freely over the broad surfaces of the branches. Color, light buffy. The other species was characterized by very shallow, discontinuous grooves along the edges, small pores, comparatively smooth surface, and a white color.

So far as we discovered, these deep-water Hydrocorallinæ did not possess stinging powers at all comparable with their shallow-water relatives, which have an urticating effect hardly surpassed by any cœlenterates which we encountered, with the exception of certain Siphonophora.

The Alcyonaria were no less interesting than the hard corals, and were in a better state of preservation, making their approximate identification possible. The classification used is the one adopted in the "Challenger" Report on the *Alcyonaria*.[1]

Two beautiful crimson species of *Gorgonia* were found, with sub-flabellate system of branches and slightly raised calicles. The Chrysogorgidæ were represented by species of the genera *Dasygorgia* and *Chrysogorgia*. The former does not have the branches spirally arranged, and the branches are sparse and do not break up into branchlets, as is usual in this genus. On the other hand, the calicles are long and at an acute angle to the branch, and have the spicules arranged as in the genus mentioned. The specimens of *Chrysogorgia* are branched in an exceedingly profuse dendritic manner, giving an unusually delicate and pleasing appearance to the colony. The calicles are much smaller than in the preceding species,

---

[1] It is surprising how greatly these magnificent Reports differ in the convenience with which they may be used by the general zoologist, the Report on the *Alcyonaria* being particularly satisfactory in the synopsis of classification in the introduction, which greatly enhances the utility of the work to the non-specialist.

and conform to the definition of *Chrysogorgia* in the disposition of the spicules.

A beautiful *Acanthogorgia*, apparently complete, but only two inches high, is symmetrically flabellate and very profusely branching, with lengthened columnar calicles and bristling with thorny spicules, two layers of which protect the included polyp, the inner layer closing over the distal end and forming a complete operculum. Two species of *Paramuricea*, both brown in color, flabellate in form, and very profusely branching, differ in size and in the arrangement of the verruciform calicles, one being characterized by distinctly separated calicles, and the other by having the branches covered with a dense mass of crowded calicles with their bristling spicules. A bright crimson species probably belongs to this genus, and bears a striking superficial resemblance to the beautiful colored plates of *Siphonogorgia* in the "Challenger" Report. Under the lens this species is exquisitely beautiful, with its coating of large crimson spicules.

These extremely hispid species get so involved in the fine hempen strands of the tangles, that a great deal of patience is required to separate them from their unnatural environment, and it is almost impossible to pick off all the threads that wind in and out among the myriad thorny points of the spicules.

The family GORGONELLIDÆ is represented by a slender whip-like *Scirpearella*, with irregular rows of verruciform calicles arranged on two sides of the unbranched colony. The general surface is smooth, and the color orange in some specimens and light yellow in others.

Among the most interesting of all was a representative of the family CORNULARIDÆ, which gives an idea of the stock from which the primitive TUBULARIDÆ, or organ-pipe coral, and also the original GORGONIDÆ, may have sprung These specimens, which are fragmentary, appear to belong to the genus *Telesto*, although I am not aware that representatives of this genus have heretofore been reported from the Atlantic. It is characterized by having a long axial polyp-tube, in our specimens, about four inches long. A cross section of this polyp-tube reveals a central cavity surrounded by the eight mesenterial chambers, which reach from the base of the branch clear up to the terminal polyp. The ridges indicating these mesenteries can be seen externally running along in parallel lines to the extremity of the axial polyp. At rather short intervals lateral polyp-tubes appear, ending distally in calicles with eight longitudinal ridges. The polyps can be partially, and perhaps wholly, protracted from the calicles. Color of entire colony, orange. The specimen closely resembles *Telesto arborea*, as figured and described in the " Challenger " Report.

Two other species of the Alcyonacea belong to the widely distributed genus *Spongodes*. The colony at first glance seems to be nothing but an agglomeration of spicules. The polyps are in dense, short clusters or clumps, and are so compactly surrounded by large jagged spicules that the calicles are almost concealed. One species is brown and about an inch high, and the other is brilliant scarlet and somewhat smaller.

The difference between this assemblage of Alcyonaria from the pentacrinus ground and those from shallow water in the same general region, is probably as great as would be found in specimens from the polar and tropical seas, and forcibly illustrates the revelations that await us when investigations are undertaken in the science of bathymetrical distribution of animals, a science which bids fair to be as productive of suggestive facts as is that of geographical distribution, as first conceived and elaborated by Alfred Russell Wallace.

One or more species of *Antipathes* was collected here, all being of the branching type. They were at first taken for plumularian hydroids, to which they bear considerable superficial resemblance.

In this locality about twenty-one species of hydroids were dredged from depths averaging from one hundred to two hundred and fifty fathoms. Of the eight campanularians, five appear to be new. The heretofore described species are *Obelia marginata*, *Thyroscyphus ramosus*, and *Cryptolaria conferta*. Two parasitic campanularians were secured, one being characterized by a more robust calicle than its nearest ally, *Lafœa venusta*, and also by the fact that the margin is very slightly, if at all, everted. The other species is still more robust, and perfectly smooth, the annulations which make *L. venusta* so attractive being entirely absent.

Two new species of *Cryptolaria* were added to this interesting genus. One was among the most graceful forms of hydroids secured, having exceedingly large and long hydrothecæ gracefully curved with their bases twisted together, a very distinct and striking species. Another form is distinguished by profusely annulated hydrothecæ which are nearly opposite on the polysiphonic stem. Another interesting find was a species which bears a very striking resemblance to *Lafœa convallaria*, but a closer examination shows that each calicle is separated from the stem by a distinct partition or septum, a character which, according to Allman, must throw the Havana species into the genus *Lictorella*. The gonangia are of the peculiar anchor shape described by Clarke, but the top is produced into a tube through which the ova apparently escape, and not through the lateral flukes of the anchor.

Some novel forms were encountered among the sertularians. One species, growing to a height of about six inches, was provided with the largest hydrothecæ the writer ever saw. These were further remarkable in being in the form of a parallelopipedon, with a square aperture and an operculum composed of four flaps. The margin is ornamented with a number of false margins, as if produced by successive periods of growth. *Sertularia integritheca* has very large cylindrical hydrothecæ without opercular flaps. The gonangia of this species are almost unique in springing apparently from the side of the hydrothecæ. An exceedingly delicate *Sertularia* is characterized by having the hydrothecæ in pairs with their backs contingent, and borne on the side, not the front, of the stem as in the genus *Desmoscyphus*. *Sertularia tubitheca* completes the list of sertularians from this region.

A number of interesting PLUMULARIDÆ were dredged on the pentacrinus ground. *Plumularia megalocephala* and *Antennella gracilis* were found. A fragmentary specimen, with

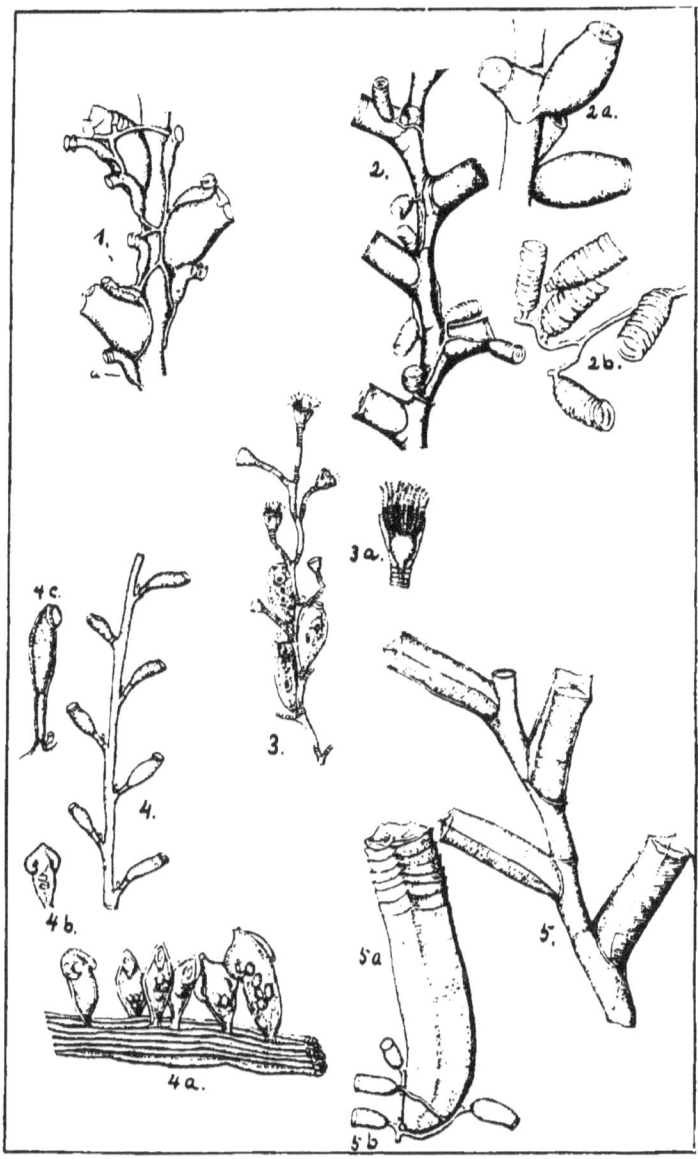

Hydroids from "Pentacrinus Ground."

Fig. 1. SERTULARELLA GAYI VAR. ROBUSTA, Allman.
Fig. 1a. FILELLUM sp., a parasitic Hydroid.
Fig. 2. SERTULARELLA FORMOSA, Fewkes.
Fig. 2a. Gonangium of same.
Fig. 2b. LAFOEA VENUSTA, Allman.
Fig. 3. ORELLA HYALINA, Clarke (found on floating sea-weed)
Fig. 3a. Magnified hydranth of same.
Fig. 4. LICTORELLA CONVALLARIA (?) Allman'.
Fig. 4a, b, c. Details of same.
Fig. 5. SERTULARELLA QUADRATA, Nutting.
Fig. 5a. Magnified hydrotheca of same.
Fig. 5b. Parasitic campanularian.

four supracalicene nematophores, two of which were excessively elongated, is not far from the genus *Diplopteron* of Allman, but may require a new genus for its accommodation. *Aglaophenia rhynchocarpa* and *A. lophocarpa* were accompanied by a probably new species of *Aglaophenia*, characterized by having the mesial nematophores long with the distal portion projected at a large angle from the anterior face of the hydrotheca. Corbulæ with eight perfectly free leaflets, each bearing two rows of nematophores. The distal ends of the leaflets from opposite sides meet each other above, rather than alternating as in other species. A new *Nematophorus* is remarkable for the possession of "double barrelled" mesial nematophores, which are very long and project forward and slightly downward. An apparently new *Cladocarpus* is allied to *C. dolichotheca*, from which it differs in having much shorter and more closely approximated hydrothecæ, in having the gonangia in pairs instead of single, and in less profusely branched phylactogonia.

Too much cannot be said in praise of the manner in which Captain Flowers handled his vessel while dredging. He amply demonstrated the practicability of working at considerable depths with a sail-vessel, and it was evident that with sufficient iron rope we could have done successful work at a depth of five hundred fathoms or over. The captain staid at the wheel during the entire four days of our work on the pentacrinus ground, and also stood his watch at night while the vessel was standing off and on, in order to be on the dredging ground early in the morning. Even his endurance, however, was not sufficient for such a continued strain, and on Friday evening, May 26th, we decided to return to Havana in order to get a rest. But this was easier said than done. The wind held fair but close, until the "Emily E. Johnson" was right in the narrowest part of the channel, when it suddenly drew around, blowing directly out of the harbor and in our teeth. There was room neither to tack nor to bring the vessel about, and the situation was decidedly precarious. Then it was that our captain showed his judgment and seamanship, for he succeeded in *backing* the schooner out of the channel as neatly as though she had steam propulsion. With consummate skill his orders were given and executed, every pull at the halliards and sheets having the exact effect upon which he had calculated. A glance at the sea-wall opposite Morro Castle showed that it was black with people, who realized that a wreck was imminent. Slowly and steadily the "Emily" glided stern first, back past the grim port-holes of "El Morro," until she reached blue water and put about.

It being impracticable to get into harbor that night, it was decided to spend one more day on the pentacrinus grounds, and then we tried the channel with better success, the "Emily" being forced to make almost the entire circuit of the harbor on account of a big steamer blocking the direct way to our anchorage. A stiff breeze sent the schooner cutting through the water like a yacht, as she dodged in and out among the various craft, and at last dropped anchor, as before, among the Spanish cruisers.

Sunday, May 28th, was passed in resting and in visiting the city and Botanical Gardens. This is the day on which one sees the people of a Spanish city to the best advantage. In the evening, especially, the military concert in Parka Centrale seemed to attract a multitude of citizens of the better classes.

The next day was spent in preparation to leave for our next station. The American Consul General had requested us, in case we were successful in securing *Pentacrinus*, to present one to each of three or four prominent officials, in recognition of courtesies extended to us. This we were perfectly willing to do, and five superb specimens of *Pentacrinus* were selected and placed in separate jars bought for the purpose. Three of these were taken to the office of the Consul, in order that through him they might be presented to the Governor General and Secretary General of Cuba. One was taken for the Consul himself, who had incidentally mentioned that a similar favor was extended by the "Albatross" when she dredged pentacrini off Morro Castle. The gentleman who delivered these specimens returned with the report that

Sunday Afternoon on Deck.

the representative of the United States Government had
received this really splendid donation with open contempt,
asserting that the specimens *were not crinoids*. What mental
picture of the crinoid had established itself in the brain of this
official we never discovered, but we left with the conviction
that our representative might ignorantly discredit our attempted
courtesy in the eyes of the Cuban officials. From this time
on an abrupt change was noticed in the attitude of the authorities toward the expedition, which was at least suggestive of
adverse influence. Certain it is that no more superb specimens
of these rare and beautiful forms are possessed by any museum
in America than those which were thus wasted on account
of the misconception of the Consul General.

Our schooner was thoroughly examined by the United
States Examining Physician, who gave a clean bill of health,
but told us that we would probably be quarantined at Key
West, for which we cleared, although this was not the next
station at which we designed to work.

All our empty water barrels were filled at Havana, we
being assured that the water supplied was excellent, as indeed
it seemed to be. A few barrels full were caught during a
heavy rain-squall, when all hands turned to and had a regular
wash-day, resulting in a good clean stock of towels and clothes.

The next morning, May 30th, we left Havana for the last
time, well satisfied with our visit to the "Queen of the West
Indies," and yet anxious to try our fortunes in other fields.
We could not resist the temptation to make one more haul at
the pentacrinus grounds before leaving the region for good,
and sent down the tangles, which came over the rail with five
good "sea lilies" and a number of fine serpent-stars, after
which we set sail for the port of Bahia Honda, situated on a
bay of that name, about fifty miles west of Havana, in latitude 23°, longitude 83° 13'. The wind was very light, although
fair, and the heat more oppressive than it had been thus far
while we were at sea. The deck was newly oiled and the tar,
liquid with the heat and mixed with the oil, made a pasty
stickiness that was anything but a happy combination. That

night we saw numerous large fires along the coast, which we concluded were from kilns of some sort. For a while the wind gave out almost entirely, and it was a question whether we were going forward or being carried back by the current of the Gulf Stream, which is here much less perceptible than off the coast near Havana.

In the morning we found ourselves near an exceedingly picturesque coast, with high mountains towering above the low-lying clouds. Some of the peaks were really imposing, although clothed to their summits with thick forests, with here and there great patches of bare rocks showing in reddish blotches among the green.

No sign of human habitation was to be seen. The shore was as desolate as a Patagonian coast, and we were at a loss to know where Bahia Honda was, having pictured to ourselves a village, at least, to mark the opening of the bay. A small coasting schooner was creeping down from the east, and we decided to hail her, in hopes of securing a pilot acquainted with the channel into the bay, a place of ill repute to naturalists since the "Blake" was run aground there in the attempt to get into the harbor under the guidance of an ignorant native pilot.

The coasting schooner being finally within hailing distance, we found that our port had been passed in the night, and were forced to put back a few miles. Encountering another native vessel, we fortunately secured a pilot who knew the channel into Bahia Honda. He certainly earned his money. The writer was the only person on board with any practical knowledge of the Spanish language, and hence was expected to act as interpreter between the pilot and the crew. Unfortunately, however, although able to get along moderately well under ordinary circumstances, his vocabulary did not embrace a single word of *nautical* Spanish. Not a sail or halliard, sheet, jib, or command of any kind could be name or express or understand in Spanish. The pilot was soon on the verge of insanity, and the mate completely beside himself at the extraordinary commands delivered with apparent assurance by the perspiring interpreter. The more serious the situation, the more utterly incomprehensible the language of the pilot, and the more completely at sea was the mate, until the hapless interpreter saw with consternation that either his reputation or the vessel was to be wrecked, and promptly abandoned the former. The pilot then, thanks to a really good knowledge of seamanship, flew from the wheel to the halliards, back to the wheel, and then sprang with marvelous agility to the fore-sheet, main-sheet, jib-sheet, or what not, and thus ran the vessel by himself with a dexterity which certainly could not be surpassed, and a skill that amazed us all. This acrobatic performance ended in our dropping anchor about noon in a quiet little harbor at the end of a deep bay, affording an excellent protection against storms from any direction except due north.

The scene was one of ideal tropical beauty. To the west were high banks and rolling grassy hills, dotted here and there with tall palms. Eastward was a sombre mangrove swamp, with its mysterious shades and skeleton network of sprawling roots rising from the still water. To the south were undulating hills, with immense sugar plantations, and beyond, the noble chain of mountains, their sharp peaks piercing above the heavy and ominous bank of dark clouds, from which the mutterings of the coming storm could be heard. Soon the rain was falling as if the "windows of heaven were opened," and all hands were driven below to escape a drenching.

As is usual with these fierce squalls, the storm soon passed, and was succeeded by a calm and the Cuban mosquitoes, which came in swarms to sample the blood of the Iowans.

But other matters soon demanded our attention. A small boat made its appearance, with a man who introduced himself as the second in command at that port (there was only one habitable house visible), and politely informed us that our party could not land without a permit from the Captain of the Port, who resided in a village "una legua" distant. Previous knowledge of the Spanish league had taught me that it might be anywhere from two to eight miles, but Captain Flowers and

I decided to visit "El Capitan" at once. Landing at an old dock leading to an abandoned sugar-house, we passed on to an inhabited house and inquired for horses. There were none to be had. We glanced at the road and knew that we were in for an experience with such roads as only Cuba can furnish. The mud was knee-deep in places, but we plunged in and started on a tramp of unknown length, through sloughs and puddles of unknown depth, with just enough concealed stones and jagged rocks to break the monotony of the walk. The mosquitoes enjoyed the excursion, however, and our countenances were soon covered with mud splashes, and blood from the slain insects. Clean collars and shirts were wilted before half a mile was traversed. Our "good clothes" were fairly plastered with mud as sticky as putty, and our good temper was completely gone.

At this juncture a turn in the road revealed a horseman in uniform, who proved to be "El Capitan" himself, who spoke about as much English as we did Spanish. He was extremely affable, but the utmost persuasion, and even an official letter from the authorities at Havana, could not extract his permission to send a land party for the purpose of exploring the fauna of the mountain slope before us. His hands were tied, he said, by strict orders, and it had been reported that a vessel from the United States with three hundred revolutionists on board was expected to land somewhere on that coast, and the unmistakable inference was that he was by no means certain that the "Emily E. Johnson" was not that vessel. The fact of ladies being on board failed to convince him of our innocence. We would be permitted to work on the water or in the water, but not to go more than thirty yards from the shore line. Thus our cherished plan of doing some naturalizing on the Island of Cuba was blocked, and we were forced to content ourselves with the meagre concessions granted. During the whole of our stay the party was under constant suspicion, and subjected to repeated visits by the officials and soldiers, who were always polite, but evidently under orders to scrutinize everything and every one on board the schooner.

Upon our return to the vessel we found all hands engaged in a desperate battle with the mosquitoes. There was little sleep that night, as a number of the party, finding sleep impossible, tramped the deck till morning, making repose out of the question for those who had learned to endure the pests from past and oft-repeated experiences. In the morning all hands, except those whose presence was needed on board, were detailed for work along the shore and in shallow water.

The entomologists and botanists found that the thirty yard strip of land conceded by "El Capitan" well repaid careful exploration. Those interested in Conchology discovered in the mangrove swamp a splendid field for their favorite pursuit, and crustaceans and echinoderms were discovered in considerable abundance in the quiet shallow water near the shore and in the swamp. Only three species of birds were secured before the authorities put a stop to our shooting. *Garzetta candidissima*, the little white Egret, was found breeding in the swamp, several fledgelings being secured and placed in alcohol. *Icteris hypomelas* (Bonap.), an oriole, was found. The body was black, shoulders, rump, lower wing coverts and upper and lower tail coverts bright yellow. The sexes were colored alike, but a young specimen had the black of the lower parts behind breast, and entire upper parts replaced by yellowish green. *Spindalis pretrei* (Less.), a brightly colored tanager, was the only other bird secured.

It was a decided aggravation to one interested in Ornithology to be within sight of the densely wooded slopes of the Cuban hills, imagination peopling the dense jungles with abundant bird-life of new and interesting forms, and still be forbidden by what seemed official stupidity, from exploring the region at all, although we had been informed that the Governors of the provinces had been expressly instructed to permit the landing of parties of our naturalists for just such purposes. The Governor of this particular province, being, we were told, some sixty miles distant, was as inaccessible to us as if he had been at the North Pole.

Mr. Wickham furnishes the following entomological notes:

"Our knowledge of the Entomology of Bahia Honda, as of other branches of shore work, was necessarily confined to the strip of thirty yards' width bordering the shores of the bay. The first attempts were directed toward an examination of an old fallen banana stem. The results were three or four myriopods and a large scorpion. As soon as beating was commenced, however, a little better luck was had, especially in the line of weevils, which form here, as in the Bahamas, quite a respectable proportion of the fauna. This may be owing in great part to the difficulty with which these insects are drowned, and the consequent ease, comparatively speaking, with which they may thus be carried from place to place by currents of water. If we add to this the fact that the larvæ of many of them live in fruits or nuts, or in the stems of plants, all easily transported by the waves of ocean, reasons seem not wanting why they should abound. It is also remarkable that in the West Indies the same species of weevil may be found on many different sorts of plants.

"Among the weevils may be mentioned *Baris chalybea* Boh., a very fine steel-blue species beaten from bushes near the beach; *Baris quadrimaculata* Boh. from a plant resembling our jimson-weed, higher up on the hills which skirt the bay. The latter is a very striking species,— black with two very large reddish yellow spots before the middle of the elytra, and two smaller ones at the tip. A *Lachnopus*, which may be *floridanus* Horn, was found in some numbers, -a black beetle with numerous golden spots on the elytra. Under a log by the beach a number of *Anchonus* were found, but the species has not yet been picked out from the formidable lot described by Suffrian in his papers on the Rhynchophora of Cuba.

"The ELATERIDÆ were represented chiefly by a species of *Monocrepidius*. The CHRYSOMELIDÆ were not especially numerous, but specimens were obtained of two species belonging somewhere near *Metachroma* and of *Luperus malachioides* Chevr. besides a very pretty little halticid with red thorax and green elytra. No Adephaga were found near the anchorage, but near the mouth of the bay, while on a trip for turtles. *Cicindela tortuosa* and *C. olivacea* were both taken.

"Spiders were tolerably numerous, the ATTIDÆ forming a conspicuous feature among them. A few Lepidoptera, chiefly micros, were taken on a little island in the bay."

The most interesting crustaceans were the land-crabs. A large species of *Geocarcinus*, common here, is of a bluish grey color, and esteemed a delicacy by the natives.

The modifications of the crustacean anatomy, to subserve the purposes of an essentially terrestrial life, form an interesting study. The whole structure connected with respiration is specialized for the purpose of making a little water go a long way. Externally we notice the unusally hard and dense shell covering the gill-chamber. Below, the branchial region is covered with a dense spongy mass of matted hairs, excellently adapted to the retention of moisture, and preventing evaporation through the carapace. The openings around the maxillipeds are lined with similar hairy brushes for the same purpose. Opening the branchial chamber, we find it lined with a thick, smooth membrane bearing in texture a remarkable resemblance to India-rubber, and apparently just as impervious to water. The eight pairs of gills are stiff and erect, and do not collapse or mat together when out of the water, as do those of ordinary crabs. A beautiful contrivance exists for keeping these structures moist so long as even a little water remains in the bottom of the branchial chamber. Attached to the third maxilliped is a long thin curved plate bearing a brushy fringe on its edge. This plate is directed backward and fitted perfectly over the outer surfaces of the gills, so that the animal, by a motion of the maxilliped, can dip this curved brush in the water at the bottom of the branchial chamber, and apply it in the most effective manner to the outer surfaces of all the gills. On the inner surfaces of the gills two smaller brushes similarly arranged serve to apply the water. These inner brushes are attached to, and worked by, the second and third maxillipeds, the larger of the two being attached to the first, and the smaller to the second maxilliped.

A small crab belonging to the genus *Sesarma* was very abundant on the pilings of an old wharf and on the sprawling roots of the mangroves. The carapace is an oblong square, wider in front, and with straight lateral and anterior margins the latter being suddenly deflected between the widely separated eyes. The rather small chelæ have bright red fingers, and are haired on their external surfaces. A large number of specimens were secured, but they were all females.

Around the spreading aquatic roots of the mangroves a large assemblage of mollusks finds a secure and congenial abiding place. At low tide our conchologists, Messrs. Drew and Rogers, reaped a rich harvest by exploring the mangrove swamp in one of the boats. The sprawling roots were then above water, and were fairly bristling in places with mollusca of many kinds. Among the gasteropods the following genera were represented: *Murex, Natica, Nerita, Cerithium, Littorina, Potamides, Fissurella,* and *Bulla.*

The Lamellibranchiata were very abundant in individuals, although the species were not numerous. *Arca noæ* and *A. transversa* were secured in quantities. *Meleagrina meleagris* formed large clumps of shells attached to the mangrove roots. We could not learn that they were ever collected by the natives, or that pearls were found in them. A very fine Pinna was abundant with the costæ ornamented with rows of long tubular spines. A species of *Asaphis* was secured which has the umbo colored a delicate pink.

The most abundant echinoderm found here was *Toxopneustes variegatus*, which furnished ample material for our students to undertake a careful study of the echinoid anatomy. Microscopes could be used to advantage while our vessel was floating on the quiet waters of the bay, and the cabin-top proved as good a laboratory table as could have been devised. *Arbacea punctulata* was the only other echinoid found in abundance.

Several species of serpent-stars were found, but these forms seem to prefer purer water than that of this bay.

A few corals of the reef-building species were collected at

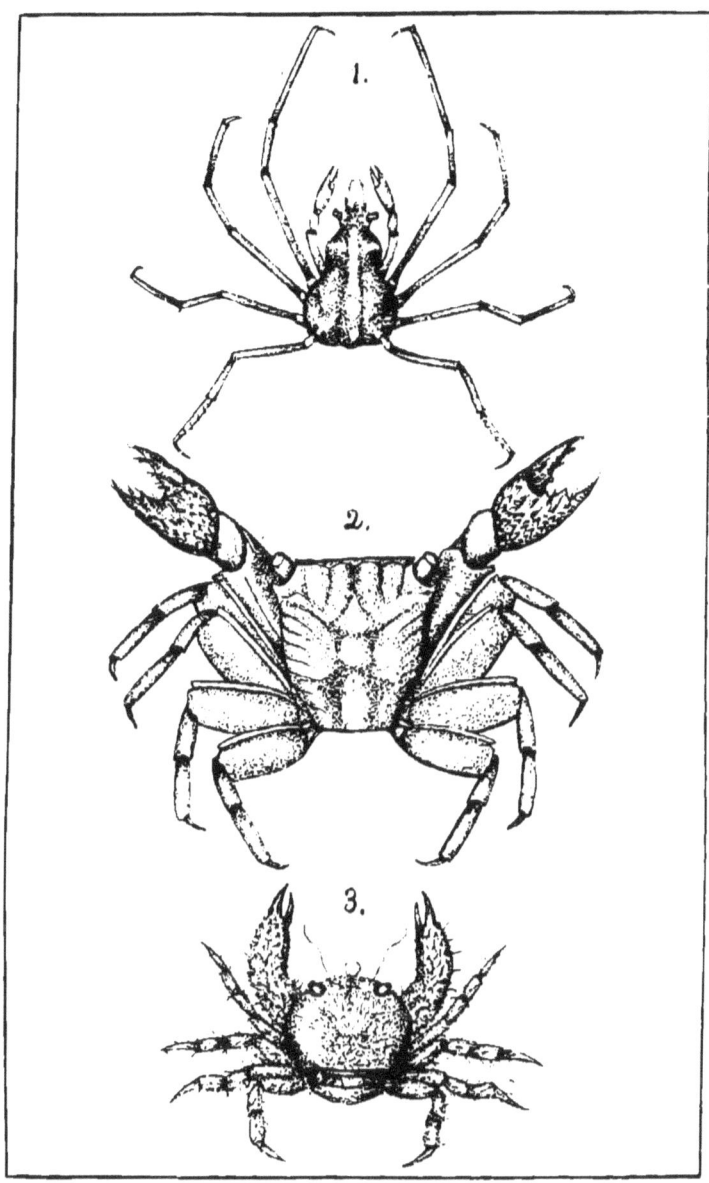

Crabs from Egg Island and Bahia Honda.

Fig. 1. PODOCHELA RISEI. Stimp.
Fig. 2. ARATUS PISONI. M. Edw.
Fig. 3. PILUMNUS CARIBÆUS. Desbonne and Schramm.

this station. *Oculina varicosa, Porites clavaria, Siderastrea galaxea, Meandrina sinuosa,* and *M. clivosa,* were found attaining a respectable size and apparently thriving in water that was very impure, so much so that the occurrence of reef-building corals was a surprise to us.

At night the water was alive with a large and beautiful species of ctenophore. It would be hard to find more beautiful objects than these animals as they appeared in the collecting tubs, with the luminous waves of light pulsating rhythmically along the ambulacral zones. When free on the surface of the waters of the bay these acalephs move with considerable speed, tracing curves and circles of fire which intersect each other in a bewildering maze of brightness.

A large number of very fine actinians were found at Bahia Honda. Indeed these beautiful forms were more abundant here than at any other station at which we collected. Various experiments were made with a view to ascertaining a satisfactory method of killing these animals with the tentacles fully expanded. The best success attended the use of water heated to a point just bearable with the hand. A sudden immersion in this water killed a number of specimens expanded in a very satisfactory manner. One species with exceedingly long non-retractile tentacles was found to have stinging powers much more pronounced than was possessed by any other species. The tentacles not being able to seek safety in retraction, had evidently secured immunity from attack by unusually effective nematocysts.

Miss Bertha Wilson has kindly furnished the following notes on the flora of this region:

" The plants found at Bahia Honda were similar to those secured at Egg Island. Along the shore the sea-loving cocoanut spread its feathery tops, and underneath bristled the Agave or Pita-plants as before, intermixed with the prickly-pear cactus.

" The mangrove swamps are quite extensive, and we were given a good opportunity to study these curiosities, which year by year are stealing the land from the ocean. They grow not only at the water line but in the water itself with their trunks often immersed to some length. Their appropriation of land from Neptune's realm as well as the continuation of the species is accomplished in two ways: *first* — By the growth and spreading of the roots, which issue from the parent trunk even at some distance above the water, and arching downward establish themselves in the mud. Roots also issue from the branches above in the manner of the banyan tree. As a result there is an intricate tangle of slender twisted roots in the mazes of which is lodged ultimately a wealth of mollusks, crustaceans and sea-mosses swept up by the waves. *Second* — By aerial germination of the seed, which pushes down its long radicle before it leaves the parent tree, and is already well started on its career before it finally drops down into the water, and sinks into the mud. The flower is small and pale yellow; the fruit is a bean-like pod.

"The Fan-palms also grow in the tangles along the shore, overshadowed by the round fleshy leaves of the 'sea-grape' with its inconspicuous panicles of greenish flowers. Further inland are the same tall hedges of sage-brush or lantanas, with white moon-flowers and blazing passion-vines trailing over them. A little further from the shore in an old sugar-cane field, we found the small orange-flowered lantana of our green-houses, and the coarse and gaudy *Zinnia* cherished in our old-time gardens. There were several species of Solanums with blue-black berries and flowers varying from a small white star-like affair to a pinkish lavender wheel.

"The Leguminosæ are omnipresent in one form or another, and the showy pea-vine twined in among some wild tomato plants. A species of milkweed with greenish white flowers was common.

"The Compositæ, numerous and showy and, for the most part, low-growing forms, have not yet been identified.

"One peculiar tree noted along the banks had a tough, corky bark and when bruised exuded a milky, resinous fluid. The flowers were fragrant and not unlike those of the orange in general appearance. Unfortunately we did not succeed in satisfactorily classifying this either. On a small island in the harbor was an oleander conspicuous with its load of pink blossoms, and we also found there a single cotton plant, showing every phase of frutition from the curiously shaped lemon-colored flowers to the fluffy cotton seeds. Though both were in this instance probably planted by man, they often grow wild in this climate. The hibiscus also flourishes here. At Havana we saw great bush-like affairs with gorgeous rose-red blooms as large as a tea-cup.

"There are common to this region also, trees remarkable for their gorgeous blossoms and the beauty of their foliage. Possibly the most noticeable is *Ponciana regia*, the common park tree at Havana. It grows about thirty feet high, having delicate fern-like foliage, and is crowned with great masses of flaming scarlet blossoms that make the tree a blaze of color. Another tree, called by the natives the 'Geiger tree,' has clusters of wheel-shaped flowers, vivid orange in color.

"Along the banks at Bahia Honda we also saw the broad, waving, banner-like leaves of the banana, unfolding like a mammoth Indian maize, the leaves sheathing the stem till a stout trunk is formed; and hanging down almost within our reach was a bud-shaped bunch of blood-red leaf-life bracts, a velvet covering for the tiny flowers within, destined ultimately to develop into the yellow bananas of our markets. The plantain is similar in growth. We saw here also the bright green ribbon-like leaves of the sugar-cane, and the 'pines' with their whorl of slender, spiny leaves growing to a height of three to four feet, and a single pineapple at least nestled snugly in their midst.

"A great variety of fruits are common in the island. Mangos were brought us. They grow on a tree from thirty to forty feet high, with dense, glossy, spreading foliage. The fruit is about the size of an apple, a little oblong in shape, and mottled green and brown and yellow or reddish without, and a fine golden yellow within, not unlike a peach. There is often a strong flavor of turpentine, and a relish for them must be acquired. The custard-apples, pawpaws and sour-sops belong to the same family, though the fruits are very different in appearance. The sapodillas are about the size of an apple and russet colored, with a sickening sweetish taste not unlike a pear that has ripened a day too long in the sun. The 'rose apples' are about the size of a large crab, and as I remember them are cream colored, with a rosy flush, and have a strong flavor of rose. The 'mameys' belong to the same family.

"Unfortunately many of the fruits common to the tropic markets we did not have an opportunity to see growing, and so the characteristics of their foliage or their individual peculiarities cannot be described."

CHAPTER V.

THE DRY TORTUGAS.

Between the vicious attacks of the Cuban mosquitoes and the suspicious attitude of the authorities, our stay at Bahia Honda, although profitable from a scientific standpoint, was attended with considerable physical and mental discomfort. A general desire to get out of this deep landlocked bay, and a longing for blue water, instead of the tortuous channel that lay between the "Emily" and freedom, made itself manifest before forty-eight hours had been spent at this port.

During the second day of our stay we received a call from the Captain of the Port of Mariel, about twenty-two miles east of Bahia Honda. This gentleman seemed very anxious that we should visit his bailiwick, and extended the courtesies of the town with a cordial politeness that was tempting, to say the least. Our plans, however, did not include any purely social functions, nor would our appearance at that time among the élite of Mariel tend to impress the Cuban gentlefolk with an adequate respect for the "Americanos." Between exposure to sun and wind, and the bumps and blotches caused by the mosquitoes, our faces had assumed an appearance which could not be regarded as creditable, although it was productive of no little mirth among ourselves. One can hardly imagine until he has seen it, how completely a usually dignified countenance can be transformed by a lump on the upper lip, or a deeply sunburnt and repeatedly peeled nose.

Early in the morning of Saturday, June 3rd, the welcome sound of the clanking anchor-chain proclaimed that we were to make the attempt, at least, to leave this inhospitable bay. The mists of the morning lay heavy on the water, and the threatening clouds indicated squally weather. The pilot who had so efficiently brought us into our anchorage was on hand to take us out again. He brought along two of his own sailors, having doubtless a vivid recollection of his former unpleasant experience while attempting to have Spanish orders understood by an American crew.

The channel is a dangerous one, apparently more so than is indicated by the chart, and I would not advise any future expedition to attempt it. It will be remembered that it was in the effort to get into Bahia Honda that the "Blake" was run aground, and lost several weeks of most valuable time. Those present on that occasion seem to have a distinct impression that the misfortune was by no means accidental.

The Captain of the Port had advised us that he would come aboard to give us our clearance or dismissal, there being no custom-house at Bahia Honda, but finally sent word that we could drop down to the mouth of the harbor and there await the necessary papers. While thus detained, a boat was sent ashore for the purpose of securing some turtles from the fishermen who lived in a little hamlet near the harbor mouth. The turtles, loggerhead and green turtles, were kept in a small enclosure surrounded by a paling or fence. When one was wanted it was killed by cutting its throat with an ax. The boat returned with a fine specimen of each species, and the bleached skull of a loggerhead, which Mr. Wickham picked up on the beach. The turtles had been purchased or rather traded, for a half-barrel of corned beef which had become a little too pronounced in flavor to suit the Iowans, but seemed just to the taste of the Cuban fishermen, to whom beef in any form is a rarity and a luxury. The green turtle was found to be a female, with eggs in all stages of development from little yellow spheres no larger than peas to fully matured eggs with the leathery white membrane. There were such a quantity that we were surfeited with them before they were all eaten. The meat of the green turtle is excellent, and the amount furnished by the large specimen secured at this time was amazing. It can be cooked in various ways, and proved a grateful relief after the long siege of salt meat. Unfortunately we put to sea before the party enjoyed their first meal of green-turtle steaks, and once in rough water the capacity to enjoy anything eatable was completely gone, so far as several of our company were concerned.

One of the most surprising things about these giant reptiles is the smallness of their brain, a specimen weighing over two hundred pounds having a brain no larger than one's finger, reminding one of the diminutive cerebral development of the old-fashioned mammals pictured in our geological text-books. Portions of the viscera were saved in alcohol for future study. One turtle was skinned and the other skeletonized for museum specimens.

It was with no little relief that we finally found ourselves outside the entrance to the treacherous channel into this bay, and turned the pilot and his men adrift with many expressions of good-will toward the man who had not only proved a competent pilot, but a sailor able to manage a one-hundred-and fifteen-ton schooner by himself.

Our main object in visiting Bahia Honda had been to attempt to secure specimens of that rarest of crinoids, *Holopus rangei* (Carpenter). It was here that Prof. Alexander Agassiz had secured a specimen, and he it was who suggested the possibility of our striking a spot rich in this interesting species. We found, however, that the bottom dropped so suddenly just outside the harbor that we could not find it with the two-hundred-fathom sounding-line without going nearer to the reefs than prudence would allow, especially with a sailing vessel. We then put over the tangle-bar and paid out our entire stock of wire rope, three hundred fathoms, but failed to reach bottom. Evening was approaching, the weather looked threatening, and above all there was a fair wind for Key West, and we concluded it was wise to give up the *Holopus*, and set sail for American territory. It took no great discernment to see that the moment the stern of the "Emily E. Johnson" was pointed squarely toward the Cuban coast was one of intense relief to Captain Flowers, whose patience had been sorely tried by the attitude of the officials and the repeated visits of the native soldiery to our vessel. It was no slight ordeal, moreover, to trust one's schooner to a piratical looking Spaniard who couldn't speak a word of honest English even to save a vessel.

On the morning of Sunday, June 4th, Marquesas Buoy was sighted, and the whole day was spent in beating against the wind and current toward Key West. This strong current setting westward was something of a surprise to us, as we had expected the aid of the Gulf Stream at this time. The westward flow is probably due largely to the backset or eddy from the Gulf Stream moving in the opposite direction. This westward, inshore current we found to vary considerably during our stay along the Keys, being greatly affected by the winds and tides. The various channels between the Keys leading from the Gulf to the Atlantic side served to complicate matters, so that the currents became a perplexing problem. The various "rips" caused by these conflicting currents would doubtless afford good collecting grounds for pelagic material. As a general thing these currents flow from the Atlantic to the Gulf side during the rise of the tide, and in the opposite direction during its ebb. Late in the afternoon we made Sand Key Light, near Key West, and stood off and on all night, not being willing to risk running into the harbor during the darkness.

At 8:30 the next morning a pilot came aboard, one that spoke good American and could give us the news, such as there was. The charge for pilotage at Key West is three dollars per foot for the draught of the vessel each way. If the master of a vessel is willing to risk it without a pilot, he can do so by paying one-half the regular pilotage for the privilege. The tariff, therefore, for a vessel the size of ours was eighteen dollars each way, with a pilot, or nine dollars each way without. As we eventually found it necessary to run into Key West a number of times, the pilotage would have been a serious matter to our slender exchequer, had it not been for the generosity of the Pilots' Association at Key

West, which agreed to charge us one full rate and then allow us to run in and out without charge for the remainder of our stay in that region, a courtesy for which we were indeed thankful.

The run into the harbor was delightful, the day being bright, the waters exquisitely tinted over the shoals, and the city, guarded by grim old Fort Taylor, appearing to best advantage in contrast with the desolation of Bahia Honda. But our reception here was even worse than at the Cuban port. The quarantine officer came aboard, surveyed with evident surprise the disreputable looking company, ascertained that we had cleared last from Havana, and then indignantly demanded why we came to Key West. We endeavored to prove our respectability, apparently with questionable success; but the doctor said that there was nothing for him to do but put us in quarantine for fifteen days, according to the law enforced after June 1st against vessels coming from Havana. After further consideration, he concluded to send us direct to the Dry Tortugas to be fumigated, after which we would be detained five days and then discharged from quarantine, provided no sickness occurred on the vessel in the meantime. It must be confessed that our party was not particularly dismayed by this decision, having been informed by the United States Examining Physician at Havana that the Tortugas would probably be our fate upon reporting at Key West. Knowing that these islands, so bleak and repellent to most people, would prove an excellent station for the study of marine biology, we were rather pleased than otherwise at the prospect of a few days' visit in that region, under the protection of the United States government. The doctor was evidently astonished at the equanimity with which we accepted the situation, being doubtless accustomed to loud lamentations, or worse, from those whom duty compelled him to send to the fumigating station.

We remained between the yellow buoys in Key West Harbor until our mail could be brought aboard by the doctor's man. A grewsome feeling came over us at the thought of our absolute isolation in that scene which seemed almost metropolitan after our recent experiences. Our vessel was as completely shunned as if it were the royal barge of "Yellow Jack" himself. Not even a fisherman's boat or a banana-man came within hailing distance. Two of our party had been so persistently seasick that they longed to leave the schooner and go overland to their home, but the doctor, backed by the majesty of the United States law, said "No." The situation, although regarded good-humoredly by most of our party, was a source of bitter trial to others, to whom the mail brought sad news of death and sickness at home, and the utter inability to fly to the afflicted loved ones added cruel suffering to that necessarily caused by the sorrowful tidings.

At half past two P. M. the anchor was shipped and the "Emily E. Johnson" retraced her course without a pilot, passed out beyond Sand Key Light, and bore away for the Tortugas with a good sailing breeze astern, the vessel swinging along with the lazy roll and gentle swish of waters under the bows, indicating that one sail is boomed out to starboard and the other to port, or that she is sailing "wing and wing." By six o'clock the next morning, June 6th, we were anchored safely between the yellow buoys under the guns of Fort Jefferson at the Dry Tortugas, the "Land's End" of the Gulf coast, given over now to the government's unfortunate "Yellow Jack" patients and suspects.

The old fort looked grim enough from the outside, with its row of big guns on the parapet and double row of ports below. We little thought, as we gazed upon the huge structure, how much of comfort and pleasure was stored up there for us, but simply waited to see what the officials were going to do with us next.

After waiting some time, a little sail-boat rounded an angle of the fort and sped across the green water, bearing a gentleman in a somewhat faded uniform, who it seemed, was left in charge of the quarantine station in the absence of the regular surgeon. Having examined our papers and glanced with something of consternation at the motley company on board, he informed us that we must bring the vessel up to the dock for the fumigation. The wind would have been directly in the teeth of a vessel trying to reach the dock by the only visible channel, and we asked for a tug to tow us in. No tug nor steam vessel of any kind was at the station, it seemed. "Well, then," said Captain Flowers, "give us a kedge-anchor and we will ·kedge· in." This also was not to be had at the Tortugas, and we began to think that it was a trifle unreasonable to expect a sailing vessel to get up to that dock, and indeed further reflection has confirmed that idea. During about four-fifths of the quarantine season the wind blows directly ahead for any vessel trying to work up that channel to the fumigating dock. The passage is too narrow to permit any but very small craft to beat through it, and the government insists on all vessels coming to the dock for fumigation, without providing any steam power, or even a spare kedge-anchor, wherewith to make it possible to comply with the regulation.

For our part, we were not at all concerned in hurrying matters, but proceeded to get out our collecting gear, feeling sure that the shores of the surrounding islets, and the extensive sand-flats showing in brightest green beneath the water, would afford entertainment until Providence should send a fair wind, or the government a tug. The boats were lowered, and a party set out for Bird Key, the largest of the uninhabited islets of the group. We were not permitted as yet to land on Garden Key or Loggerhead Key, upon the former of which is the fort, and upon the latter a light-house. Captain Flowers and I took the ship's boat and a couple of the crew, with the intention of enjoying a plunge in the clear water around some low, sandy islands near the fort. Upon nearing the shore, we noticed a number of black objects moving along in the shallow water. We at first thought that they were porpoises, although they did not act like them. A few strokes of the oars brought us right into the midst of the creatures, and we found with wonder, and a touch of consternation, that the shoal was fairly alive with sharks! There must have been at least seventy-five of these ugly animals in the immediate vicinity of the boat, which did not seem to alarm them in the least. They glided under and around us with the utmost unconcern. A number of them were in such shallow water that their backs were uncovered, and several lay belly up, flapping the water with their fins.

None of the occupants of the boat had ever before seen so many sharks together, and the experience was exciting as well as interesting. Unfortunately we had no weapons with us. We tried clubbing the sharks on the head with oar-handles, but one might as well attempt to smash a base-ball with a shingle. The sharks seemed to imagine that the blows came from their fellows, and would savagely attack the nearest companion until we had three or four of them fighting and struggling violently under the boat. This was more than we could stand with any comfort, and so we left the shoals and agreed to be satisfied with a brief dip in very shallow water on the other side of the islet, instead of enjoying the luxurious swim which we had anticipated.

We afterwards attacked these sharks with proper weapons, and found them to be of an entirely harmless species called "nurse sharks" (*Ginglymostoma cirratum*), with small mouths armed with blunt teeth instead of the formidable dental array of the dangerous species. It seems that this was the mating season for the nurse sharks, and they had resorted in large numbers to the shallow waters for purposes of courtship. Two specimens of this huge fish were secured, the largest being eight feet long and very bulky, the head being considerably broader than in any other species of shark captured by us. The skin was wonderfully tough, rendering it quite difficult to penetrate it with the ordinary "grains" which we had brought for such purposes.

The party from Bird Key returned with a quantity of shallow-water material, and were enthusiastic over the richness of the field which they had visited. The ornithologists had secured series of man-o'-war birds, noddy terns and bridled terns. A curious fact regarding the man-o'-war birds is the quickness with which they will desert a favorite rookery after being disturbed. On this occasion the air above Bird Key was fairly black with these birds, but they left the vicinity entirely after a few shots were fired, and did not return at all during our stay at the Tortugas. This conduct is in marked contrast with that of the noddy tern, for instance, which seems unusually slow to realize the danger incurred by the approach of man.

In the afternoon the barkentine "Robert E. Patterson" cast anchor not far from us, and later the pilot boat "Sea Foam" came from Key West, bringing the quarantine officer, Dr. David R. Murray, and another batch of mail for us. Dr. Murray could not relax the stringency of the quarantine laws for our benefit, and insisted politely, but firmly, that we should bring the "Emily E. Johnson" up to the fumigating dock. Through his friendly offices, however, our enforced stay at the dreaded yellow fever detention station was rendered not only comfortable, but delightful. The old fort, no longer used for military purposes but only as a quarantine station, was hospitably thrown open to our party, and no pains were spared to make us comfortable. The ladies of the expedition were furnished with delightful quarters in rooms placed at their disposal by Dr. Goodman, whose family was away. Commodious quarters they were, especially when contrasted with those on the schooner. Real beds with snowy linen proved a luxury, while late periodicals, easy chairs and plenty of cool, fresh water, were appreciated as only those who have been without these comforts for several weeks can understand.

Fort Jefferson is said to be the second fortification in America in point of size. It was built before the war, and was expected to be of service in commanding the entrance to the Gulf from the Florida Straits. We were told that it had cost the United States government fifteen million dollars, and yet not one of the great guns which surmount the parapet and point out of the embrasures below, has ever been fired with hostile intent. No better example could be found of the fruitless cost of war than this colossal and dismantled fort on the loneliest of lonely spots. Everything is going to ruin. The big guns are toppling over on their decaying platforms; the powder-houses and magazines are in ruins; great piles of shot and shell are covered with ivy and overarched with the graceful fronds of cocoanut palms, forming a fit emblem of peace triumphant over war. Large openings have been cut through the walls of the fort to insure the entrance of fresh sea-air for the benefit of the yellow fever victims, who frequently have to fight their battles with the king of terrors within the walls. No call of bugle or tramp of armed men is heard. The troops have long since departed for good, leaving this great monument of a nation's waste to the half-dozen or more persons who are needed to do the work of the quarantine station. It is not probable that a single one of the several scores of big guns will ever be removed, as no one is likely to be found willing to incur the necessary expense for the sake of old iron, however great the quantity. This originally magnificent fort will gradually crumble away and sink with its guns and balls and shells to the sea-level, where the drifting sands will ultimately furnish a grave, and desolation reign supreme.

The members of our party found it delightful to explore the vast ruin, and to pry into its secrets. Wandering within the dimly lit casemates, surrounded by massive masonry, and occasionally sighting along the big guns to the quiet waters without, we at length came to a gloomy cell which had a part in a national tragedy; for here was confined the prisoner Dr. Mudd, who was thus punished for dressing the broken leg of Booth, the slayer of Lincoln. Several interesting stories were told of him. Once, it is said, he crawled into the muzzle of one of the big guns, hoping to hide until an opportunity presented itself for escape. On another occasion, when the dreaded "Yellow Jack" was in possession of the fort and claiming its soldier victims, Dr. Mudd rendered such heroic service in his professional ministrations that he was recommended for presidential clemency, which was ultimately exercised in his behalf. Within each of the bastions is a great cistern of rain-water, enough to supply a good sized army, and in addition there is a large tank of excellent water on the fumi-

The Soldier's Barracks, Fort Jefferson.   G. L. H.

gating dock. Probably the most important structure about the fort is the light-house, which, with its neighbor on Loggerhead Key, saves many a vessel from going onto the treacherous reefs and shallows abounding in the adjacent waters.

The fort is surrounded by a sea-wall enclosing a broad and shallow moat, which we ultimately discovered was nothing more or less than a magnificent aquarium stocked with interesting marine forms. An ample supply of fresh sea-water is brought in with every tide. The enclosed water is smooth and unruffled by the wind, affording a sheltered home for countless animals of the more lowly kinds, and furnishing one of the very best opportunities for collecting and study that we encountered during our cruise.

Almost all of Garden Key is occupied by the fort, and from it can be seen the larger islets of the Tortugas group. A little south of west lies the largest, Loggerhead Key, which appears to be about a mile in length, and supports considerable vegetation, most of which is the result of the thrifty efforts of the light-keepers and their families. There is a comfortable house surrounded by fruit-trees of several kinds. The island is bordered on the inside by extensive shallows. The next largest Key, Bird Key, lies to the south-west of the fort, and is much nearer than Loggerhead Key. It is almost covered with a thick growth of wiry bushes, among which are placed the nests of multitudes of noddy terns and "egg birds," or bridled terns. The birds rise in clouds on the approach of man, having suffered often from the incursions of egg collectors.

Several photographs were taken of these flocks of sea-birds, but the result was a surprise to all who had seen the birds themselves. In one of the most successful of these photographs only about sixty birds can be counted. Those who had seen the flock as it appeared when the exposure was made, would have described it by saying that the birds rose in a cloud; that there were thousands of them in the field exposed to the camera. Any one who has fired with a shotgun at a flock of flying birds has noticed that he is likely to miss bagging any of them unless he picks out a particular bird and aims directly at that. It is probable that the rapid circling of the birds over Bird Key had the effect of creating an optical illusion, whereby their number is greatly multiplied. Again, the eyes not being focused on any particular individual, the apparent number is double the actual number. A very simple experiment will illustrate this principle. Take a white sheet of paper and make a number of perforations in a group with the point of a penknife; then hold the paper between your eyes and the light. If the sight is focused directly on the holes, their apparent number will be twenty. If, however, the sight is directed in a general way toward the surface of the paper, without reference to the perforations, there will presently appear two instead of one group of holes. In other words, their number will apparently be doubled. It is thus evident that the number of flying birds is multiplied first by the optical illusion caused by the motion, and again by another optical illusion caused by the sight not being focused.

On Bird Key we found two or three graves of sailors who had been buried in this lonely spot. There was something peculiarly desolate in the surroundings. The glare of the sun on the white coral sand, the swish of the wind through the low scraggy vegetation, the rustle of the grotesque land-crabs as they scurry away in the grass, and the screaming of the circling gulls and terns, convey an idea of dreariness, intensified by a lack of repose not in harmony with the rude graves with their weather-worn head-boards.

A short distance to the east of Garden Key are a couple of small, bare islets called Garden Key Reefs, while Bush Key lies, almost bare of vegetation, several miles to the northeast. East Key, the only other of the group visited by us, lies almost directly east of Bush Key, and is barely visible from the deck of a vessel at the fumigating dock. There seem to be no indigenous trees on any of the islands forming the Tortugas group. Quite a number of cocoanut palms and other useful trees attain a very satisfactory growth on Garden Key and Loggerhead Key. The islands seem to be composed entirely of sand and rock formed from the skeletons of animals of various sorts, and also from the secretions of corallines. The latter, indeed, are regarded by some authors, e. g., Prof. Louis Agassiz, as furnishing the main material for some of the larger Keys. Of even more interest than the Keys, at least from the naturalist's standpoint, are the reefs which almost encircle the whole Tortugas group. During a heavy gale the breakers are seen to form an often interruped but still quite distinct line around almost the entire horizon, giving one the impression that the form is essentially that of an atoll. These reefs, especially the one stretching to the south and east of Garden Key, were objects of repeated visits by parties from our schooner, affording an opportunity to observe some of the phenomena included in the ever interesting coral-reef problem.

Although no new facts were discovered beyond those mentioned by the older and the younger Agassiz, we found it well worth our while to see some of these facts for ourselves, as they are presented in connection with one of the youngest reefs of the whole system in process of forming an extension of the peninsula of Florida.

We were unable to examine the outer or southern face of the reef, as the breakers came in with great force during the whole of our stay, although at times it was apparently quite calm. We enjoyed the experience, however, of wading around on the top of the reef and seeing the manner in which the debris is constantly being thrown inward and broken into finer and finer fragments, until the bottom some distance in from the exposed face of the reef is covered with a fine sand or mud with only occasional fragments of coral of any considerable size. On these mud-flats we found a few living corals and hosts of serpent-stars, echini and mollusks.

One of our very best collecting grounds at the Tortugas was in the extensive shallows stretching out northward from Bird Key. The amount of coral, especially the madrepores, which we found around these islands was not so great as we had anticipated, on account of a considerable portion having recently been killed by exceptionally low tides.

Two days passed after we anchored off Fort Jefferson before we could get around to the fumigating dock. One of the men employed at the station finally agreed to pilot us through a channel which led around west and south of the fort, and by skillful handling the schooner reached the buoy near the fumigating dock, where she was compelled to wait two days more before the vessel preceding her, the barkentine "Robert E. Patterson," was fumigated and discharged. Our time came, however, on Saturday, June 9th, when Dr. Murray took the "Emily E. Johnson" in hand and put her through the process required by the United States quarantine laws.

First all the baggage, equipment, stores, and in fact everything movable, was taken from the vessel and placed on the dock. Then the baggage, especially clothes exposed during our visit to Havana, and the bedding, including the mattresses, were placed in a car which was in effect an immense iron crate on wheels. This crate, with its load of clothes and bedding, was run into a huge vat through a door which was hermetically sealed by screw-fastenings and clamps. The interior of the vat was heated to two hundred degrees with a dry heat maintained for about forty minutes. Hot steam was next admitted, and the contents of the vat subjected to steam heat for another forty minutes. After this the dry heat was again introduced for the purpose of drying the clothes and bedding. The door was then opened, the car run out again, and its contents spread out for the purpose of completing the drying process by exposure to the sun and air.

All of the bedding and most of the clothes came out of this process without injury, but some of the ladies' dresses were ruined. Brass buttons were corroded, and a rubber fountain pen carelessly left in a vest pocket was bent almost to a semi-circle. It is doubtful if the germs of yellow fever or any other living thing could go through this process and live. It is fortunate, however, that our party possessed very little valuable clothing, as any but rough apparel would be liable to serious if not irreparable, injury. The stores, more particularly the provisions, were not subjected to the fumigating process, but were locked up in the store-room on the dock.

Meanwhile the vessel was thoroughly washed above and below, every article on deck, as well as the entire cabin, galley and hold, being carefully gone over with a solution of mercuric bichloride. The hatches were then battened down and sealed, the cabin doors and windows closed, and quantities of dense sulphur fumes forced into the hold by means of a steam fan. For several hours these fumes were poured in great volumes through a large hose-pipe, after which the hatches were kept down for about eighteen hours. A kettle of burning sulphur was placed in the cabin and another in the galley.

This process would seem to be sufficiently thorough to insure the destruction of any living germs, and yet there are reasons to suppose that there is room for failure. There is no ground for assuming that the bacilli of yellow fever, if such there be, would not find lodgment in the provisions as easily as almost anywhere else, and yet the provisions are necessarily exempt from the fumigating process. Aside from this, however, the fumigation was of real benefit to us, as it resulted in a complete cleansing of the vessel and a renovating of our effects, besides affording us an opportunity to re-arrange and re-stow our stores and collections, a thing which would under other conditions have been almost impossible to accomplish. We had here an ample dock upon which to work, with no hangers-on to molest our effects, as would have been the case at any other available port. We were also permitted to fill all our water casks with excellent rain-water from the huge tank on the dock, from which a hose was passed directly into the hold of the schooner.

On the whole, we regarded the enforced visit to the Dry Tortugas as a decided benefit to us from a sanitary standpoint. It is exceedingly difficult to keep so small a vessel occupied by twenty-eight persons, really sweet and clean while cruising in the heat of the tropics, and our complete freedom from sickness throughout the cruise may be largely due to the kind although enforced ministrations of Dr. Murray and his associates.

The Dry Tortugas is probably the best station on our

southern coast for marine biological work. The richness of the surface and shallow-water fauna is astonishing. Our expedition did no dredging in the adjacent deeper water, but a few hours' work in dredging across the channel on the inside of Garden Key was amply repaid. Here, too, it is possible to study coral islands in their incipiency, as it were, and the comparison of the faunae of the various Florida Keys from Cape Florida to the Tortugas should yield a complete demonstration of some of the fundamental laws of geographical distribution. It would be most instructive, for instance, for a competent entomologist to undertake such an examination, confining his studies, of course, to insects.

I do not think that a single land-bird was seen on the Tortugas, a fact somewhat surprising at first thought, as one would naturally expect that the comparatively short spaces between the various Keys would not serve as an effective barrier to flying creatures.[1] The explanation may be found in the newness of these islands on the one hand and, what is probably more potent, the further fact that the *gales* rarely blow directly from the east so as to carry the birds from the mainland or more easterly Keys to the westward, although a moderate breeze often blows directly from the Marquesas. It is also important to note that there is no migration route down the peninsula of Florida, nearly all of the land-birds taking the route via the Mexican side of the Gulf or else wintering in the southern states. We thus find that no land-birds seem to have established themselves on the Tortugas, although there are a number of familiar species on the Bermuda Islands, which lie about six hundred miles due east of Charleston, South Carolina. The explanation in the latter case is thought to be to the effect that the birds are caught while migrating southward along the Atlantic coast, and carried by northwest gales in the direction of the islands.

Even the sea-birds, although numerous in individuals, were

---

[1] Agassiz says that the Tortugas are visited by a few land-birds, but does not say what species have been found there,—"Three Cruises of the Blake," Vol. I, p. 90.

not represented by many species. The man-o'-war bird, the booby gannet, the brown pelican, the noddy tern, the bridled tern and least tern were about all that we saw. The absence of wading birds was a surprise, as there seemed to be excellent feeding for them on the shallows around the islets where small crustaceans were particularly abundant.

No reptiles were seen except turtles. The small and active lizards so numerous at other places visited during our cruise were not encountered here. Two loggerhead turtles were "turned" one evening on Loggerhead Key. The helplessness of these animals when placed on their backs is pathetic and yet ludicrous. We were astonished at the force with which they throw sand with their front flippers. It seemed, moreover, as if they had acquired considerable accuracy of aim, throwing the sand with stinging force in the faces of those incautious mortals who ventured too near the vanquished yet belligerent loggerheads.

Something over twenty species of fish were collected during our stay at the Tortugas, a much larger number than we secured at any other station. There being no ichthyologist in our party, no special pains were taken to secure a complete series of fish, although all that were caught were carefully preserved. No one, however, could fail to be attracted by the many brilliantly colored fishes, floating as if suspended in air, in the wonderfully clear waters around the fumigating dock. Their vivid hues rival in many instances those of the gaudiest birds, and it was hard for some of us to keep from spending too much time lazily stretched out on the shady wharf, and watching the procession of gorgeous creatures in the still, cool waters below.

A number of species were caught with hook and line, but more, perhaps, were taken in the dredge and meshes of the tangles while we were dredging in the channel. Among the species secured were the following:[1] A "pipe-fish" *Siphostoma*

[1] The following partial identifications were made by the writer, who is far from being an ichthyologist. It is hoped, however, that the list will give a general idea of the facies of the collection, although the species are in most cases not identified.

sp., about five inches long; "goat-fish," *Upeneus maculatus* (C. & V.), a mullet-like species with two long barbels, large ctenoid scales, and three squarish spots on the sides. A small specimen of pompano was marked with vertical dark bands. A very pretty species of *Serranus* or sea-bass was abundant, and an excellent food-fish. It was colored a reddish yellow, and marked by about eight longitudinal narrow stripes or lines of blue. The dorsal fin was emarginate, with eleven spines; anal spines three. Another *Serranus* was characterized by very distinct round spots on sides of head, and was much smaller than the preceding.

Probably the most beautiful fishes secured were the "angelfish," of which there were several species, all characterized by greatly compressed bodies and scaled fleshy parts of the median fins. Two species probably belong to the genus *Pomacanthus*.[1] One of these, apparently *P. ciliatus* J. and G., had the dorsal with fourteen spines, anal with three, eight spines on the preopercle above the very long spine at its angle; anal and dorsal produced into moderately long streamers. The color in alcohol would indicate that the fish was originally yellow. The surface had a peculiar velvety appearance, owing to the ciliate scales. Another closely allied species had longer streamers, one very large flattened preopercular spine, general color black with three transverse curved bands of white or yellow on the body and one on the tail. This may be *P. arcuatus* Lac.

A small, probably immature specimen of sculpin was secured with the tangles, and a curious little sea-robin, *Prionotus evolans* Gill? having a strongly serrated spine on first dorsal and six small spines on the head. Pectorals with upper ray extended into a filament, and three lower rays detached and banded with brown and light yellow. The pectorals reach to the end of the dorsal. A small "swell-toad," *Tetrodon spengleri* Bloch?, had two large teeth in each jaw and pectoral fins resembling ears, giving a curious rodent-like aspect to

[1] The classification and names employed here are those used in Jordan & Gilbert's "Synopsis of North American Fishes."

the head. There were twelve round spots in a row separating the sides from the ventral portion of the body. A small species of flounder, a minute mackerel, an *Antennarius* such as we found in floating sea-weed in the Gulf Stream, and a "midshipman" (*Porichthys*) were dredged in the channel to the north-west of Garden Key. A beautiful little purple striped species was found living a parasitic life among the tentacles of the Portuguese man-o'-war. It was comical to see the evident consternation of these little fellows when their host was suddenly lifted out of the water. One specimen was found dead among the tentacles. It would be interesting to discover whether the fish are immune from the nematocysts with which the tentacles are packed, or whether the *Physalia* derives some benefit from their presence and refrains from using its weapons. That the fish itself finds excellent protection admits of little doubt. Its colors, striped purple and white, or at least light, assimilate admirably with those of the tentacles among which it lives. Almost every *Physalia* that we saw while at the Tortugas had its little company of fish swimming along among the tentacles.

"The insects taken at the Tortugas were necessarily rather few in number of species, since so barren a collecting ground could hardly be very productive. So far as known, some of the more interesting may be thus specified:

"Among the Hymenoptera, *Oxybelus emarginatus* Say is the sole representative of the Aculeata. A number of ants were found, however, in the sand or beaten from bushes, among which Mr. Pergande has recognized *Camponotus tortuganus* Em., *Tetramorium cæspitum* Linn., *Tetramorium guineense* Fabr. and *Pheidole megacephala* Fabr. A little Lycænid was the only Lepidopterous insect at all conspicuous. The Coleoptera were given the largest share of attention and consequently furnish the longest list of species. Along the beach, under sea-weed, were found *Cafius bistriatus* Er., *Actinopteryx fucicola* Allib., *Phaleria longula* Lec. and *Phaleria picipes* Say. The carapaces of two immense turtles which were laid out on the beach of Bird Key to cure, attracted, besides the two species of *Phaleria* above mentioned, a number of *Saprinus ferrugineus* Mars. Beating the scanty brush brought to light a *Scymnus* yet undescribed but common at various points in Southern Florida, a few examples of *Psyllobora nana* Muls. which we also took in Cuba, a *Corticaria* common throughout Florida, and a lot of *Artipus floridanus* Horn, a weevil extremely abundant at various points on the mainland of this state, where it has developed lately into a nuisance by reason of its habit of attacking various cultivated plants for food. On Bird Key a few *Catorama punctulata* Lec. and *Petalium bistriatum* Say would be found in the beating net after going over the bushes, while Loggerhead Key yielded a number of a little *Pseudebaeus*, perhaps *oblitus* Lec. The sea-oats on Rush Key gave shelter, in their heavy tops, to an *Oxacis*, while the sand and rubbish about the roots covered numerous *Blapstinus opacus* Lec. This *Blapstinus* was also tolerably common under the fallen head-boards which mark the site of the old cemetery on Bird Key. *Hymenorus convexus* Casey showed a particular fondness for resting on the castor bean. Hemiptera were numerous in specimens, one green species being so abundant as to seriously interfere with successful use of the beating net, which would be choked and covered with them after a few moments' work, interfering with the labor of picking out more valuable material. *Murgantia histrionica* was twice met with in colonies –once on Bird Key and once on Loggerhead. The others so far as known are named by Mr. Heidemann *Gonianotus marginipunctatus* Wolf, *Paugaeus bilineatus* Say and *Clorocoris loxops* Uhler. Spiders were abundant, but as yet we have none identified."[1]

Here, as elsewhere during our cruise, the Crustacea were among the most conspicuous and abundant of animal types. About thirty species of Brachyura were collected. One of the most interesting was *Leptopodia sagittaria* (Fabr.) a maioid with exceedingly slender legs, armed with sparse, short thorns, and having a rostrum produced into a slender point and ex-

[1] Mr. H. F. Wickham.

ceeding the body in length. Like the ambulatory legs, this rostrum is armed with a row of thorn-like spines on either side. The chelipeds are greatly elongated and equal in size. Numbers of these spider-like crabs were caught on the piling around an old wharf, which seemed to be their favorite resort. Some dexterity was required in their capture, but a skillful use of the crab-net resulted in an extensive series. *Macrocœloma trispinosa* (Latr.), although belonging to the maioid group of crustacea, is as different from the last in general appearance as it well could be, having an exceedingly heavy body and short legs, each terminating in a strong hooked claw. The space between the eyes is very great, and the eyes themselves small and bead-like.

Pericera cornuta cœlata (A. M. E.) has two divergent spines on the rostrum, and the body covered with curved filaments resembling hooklets, doubtless of service in attaching foreign substances to the carapace for purposes of concealment. One species of *Othonia* was secured, with curiously excavated chelæ, and five species of the genus *Mithrax*, the largest being *M. hispidus* (Herbst.) of a rich reddish brown color, with very strong curved spines on the lateral margin of the carapace. *Mithrax forceps* Milne Edw. has very slender fingers to the chelæ, and a peculiar conical tooth on the inner face of the movable finger, in which it resembles *M. coronatus* (Herbst.). The habit so prevalent among maioid crabs of covering themselves with foreign substances for concealment, is well illustrated by our specimens of *Microphrys bicornutus* (Latreille), which has the carapace covered with a dense growth of a filamentous alga intermixed with sand and bits of broken shell.

One of the most striking crustaceans in the collection is *Platylambrus serratus* (M. Edw.), a species widely distributed in the West Indian region. The chelipeds are remarkably developed, each one probably equaling the body in bulk. They are greatly flattened and armed along both edges with sharp spines. The hand especially is greatly elongated, triangular in section, and enlarged at its distal end, upon which are inserted the small black claws. When folded, the spines on the basal part of the hand fit exactly into those on the meros, while the spines of the internal superior edge of the distal portion of the hands fit between similar spines on the anterior margin of the thorax, thus completely disguising the shape of the animal so that no one would think it a crab at all.

Among the Cancroidea, a minute species of *Panopeus* may be noted. One of the commonest and most conspicuously marked forms is *Leptodius floridanus* (Gibbes), with its polished ivory-black chelae terminating in white tips. *Phrymodius maculatus* Stimpson bears considerable superficial resemblance to the last, but the chelae are not so deep a black, shading distally into brown and then white. *Actæa setigera* Stimpson is another species having black chelae. This character occurring among so many genera living in the same locality seems to indicate some peculiar utility in this conspicuous marking. These animals live in shallow water, crawling among the algæ, corals, gorgonians, etc. A large number, perhaps all of them, are protectively colored in the main, or have the habit of covering themselves with sand, bits of shell, or even with living algæ and other organisms. The chelae and eyes are almost the only portions of the body not protectively colored or covered. Any conspicuous marks generally classed under the head of "attractive coloration," for the purpose of attracting other individuals of the same species but of opposite sex, must therefore be placed on the chelae in order to serve their purpose. Such conspicuous markings do not interfere with the effectiveness of general protective coloration, because the chelae are stowed away under the carapace so as to be completely concealed when not in use.

Liomera longimana A. M. E. has a comparatively smooth carapace with short, black fingers, and a long hand which is colored a rich brown, with distinct pits dotted over its surface. Among the most abundant and interesting crabs is *Neptunus spinicarpus* Stimpson, which has a very long, slender, spine projecting forward from the distal end of the carpal joint, and extending beyond the base of the fingers. This spine is furnished with a close-set row of hairs or cilia on the side which comes in contact with the propodite. By the normal motion of the hand this fringe is made to sweep across the inner surface of the propodite. There seems to be much more than the usual freedom of motion between the carpus and the hand. When the cheliped is folded or the fingers brought to the mouth, the spine lies snugly between the hand and the meros. The whole contrivance is so evidently adaptive that one naturally seeks an explanation of the intent of the structure, but I know of no purpose unless it be defensive, and that explanation does not seem entirely satisfactory. When the cheliped is extended, the long carpal spine projects at nearly a right angle with the hand. Another conspicuous character of this species is the long spine arising from the side of the carapace. Perhaps the largest of the Cancroid group secured at the Tortugas was a specimen of *Achelous spinimanus* Latr., which has a spread of about eleven inches. The manus is conspicuously striped brown and buffy, and the fingers or claws armed with prominent nodules throughout the length of their opposed surfaces.

Among the Ocypodoidea are the familiar *Ocypoda arenaria* (Catesby) and the brightly colored land-crab *Geocarcinus lateralis* (Frem.), which is almost always in evidence on the larger islands of the Tortugas group, scuttling around among the dried grass and leaves, and assuming belligerent attitudes when approached, reminding one of very large "fiddler" crabs. These are among the most conspicuously colored of all the crabs secured during the cruise, the chelipeds and dorsal surface being really beautiful in their livery of yellow, and brilliant crimson shading into pink and black. Their life is almost exclusively terrestrial, and they seem to have few enemies, at least on these islands. That they are efficient scavengers was proved by the facility with which they cleaned the skeletons of two large turtles left on Bird Key for that purpose. Several specimens of a tortoise crab, *Calappa marmorata* Fabr., were found near Garden Key, and caused considerable amusement by their peculiar habit of spouting a little fountain of water almost directly upward, the mouth-parts being so arranged that they form a tube just in front of the rostrum pointing upward and a little forward. The chelæ are enormously enlarged, hard and expanded so as to form a complete buckler when folded in front of the mouth-parts.

Very few Anomura were found, the most abundant being a hermit crab, *Cenobita diogenes* (Latr.) which occupied a great variety of gastropod shells, although it seemed to particularly favor a large *Astralium*. A very large hermit, *Eupagurus granulatus*, was also common, and a truly gorgeous object it was, with its brilliant vermilion chelæ beautifully ornamented with symmetrically disposed nodules. The size of these crabs can be imagined when we say that they sometimes occupied the shells of *Strombus gigas*, one of the largest mollusks of the West Indies. *Petrolistes sex-spinosus* (Gibbes) is the only other anomuran found at the Tortugas.

The great disparity in numbers between the Brachyura, or crabs, and the Macroura, or lobster-like forms, at this station is indicated by the fact that not more than a half-dozen species of the latter were secured during our stay, while thirty-odd species of the former have been identified. There were four decapods, including one *Alpheus*. One of the most interesting of all the Crustacea is a Stomatopod, *Gonodactylus chiragra* Latreille, much smaller than its familiar relative, and with the chelæ formed by a slender but exceedingly hard and ivory-like distal joint without spines, which fits into a groove on the upper surface of the joint below, being turned in an exactly opposite direction from that taken by the ordinary dactylopodite.

Not the least attractive group included in the marine fauna of the Tortugas is the Vermes, but unfortunately there was no one in the party who was at all familiar with them. It would be impossible, however, to see the many strange and beautiful worms at this station without becoming interested in their structure and admiring their exquisite coloring.[1]

[1] Mr. H. E. C. Ditzen had charge of the Vermes during the cruise, and has located many of them in their proper genera, although the task was an unusually difficult one, owing to the paucity of the literature at hand.

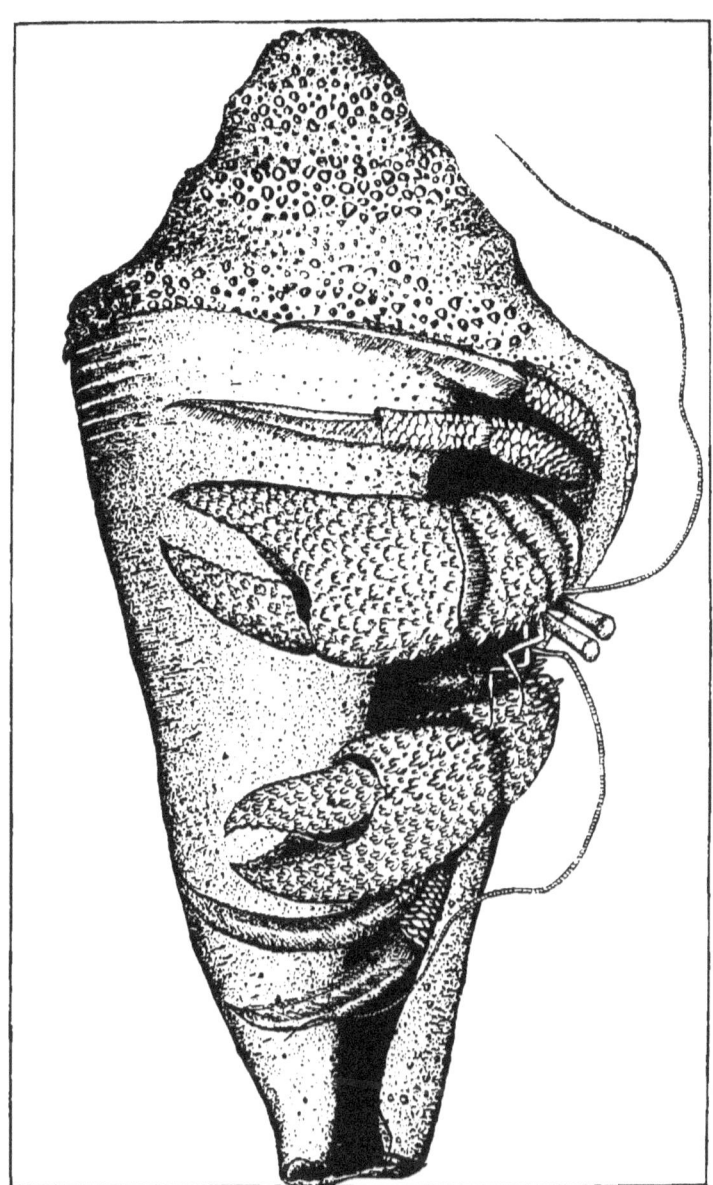

Hermit Crab.
EUPAGURUS GRANULATUS, occupying shell of STROMBUS GIGAS.

Nearly all were Annelids and most of these TUBICOLÆ. Several species of EUNICIDÆ are objects of exquisite beauty, owing to their brilliant iridescent colors, which flash and glow like jewels when the animals are examined in the sun-light. To those persons who regard worms as repulsive objects, such a display is a useful revelation. Like most iridescent hues, these are evidently due to structure and not to pigment. This explains the fact that these species do not lose their brilliancy in alcohol, as is usually the case where pigment is involved. The specimens before me have been immersed in alcohol for about sixteen months, and yet their beauty seems but little impaired. The SERPULIDÆ were especially abundant in the moat around Fort Jefferson, where their tubes were attached firmly to the masonry, and the flower-like tentacles were the objects of delight to the collector, and served as a further illustration of the rare beauty of marine worms. The tubes were so firmly soldered to the masonry, however, that they could not be removed without damage.

Among the Errantia, which do not construct tubes, were some that proved really formidable on account of their severe stinging powers. Several of our party were badly stung by the poisonous bristles that appeared soft and silky, and yet penetrated the cuticle and doubtless conveyed a very severe irritant poison which caused a benumbed feeling in the hand and arm, accompanied by intense burning pain. The species which inflicted this suffering on the incautious collector has not been identified. It is among the larger of the worms secured, and the bristles are in rows of tufts on the sides. They were found among the heads of *Porites* in the shallows.

There is no place, probably, on our Atlantic coast where Mollusca are more abundant and more conspicuous than at the Tortugas. Messrs. Gilman Drew and Arthur M. Rogers, who had this group in hand, had to call others to their aid in taking care of the quantities of "conchs" that were brought in with the return of each boat. The old moat, especially, was a conchologist's paradise, and the walls were studded with various species of gastropods, many of them having the foot and aperture brilliantly colored. A species of *Octopus*, or devil-fish, was quite common in the shallow water. It would be difficult to imagine a more utterly repulsive animal than this. It is so slimy! There is something so stealthy and insinuating in the crawling, gliding motion of the long and snake-like tentacles, that even the naturalist, who has for years contemplated without special repugnance all sorts of animals, can hardly repress a feeling of aversion while handling these creatures. The power of adhesion possessed by the suckers is very great, sufficient, in fact, to permit of the suckers themselves being torn from the arms before their hold is released. A favorite resort of this species seemed to be the closely branching heads of *Porites* so abundant in the shallows around the islands.

A great majority of the mollusks were gastropods, of which twenty-odd species were secured. Many were among the largest known, e. g., *Fasciolaria gigantea* Kiener. When alive, this species is rendered very striking by the brilliant red color of its immense foot, which is very conspicuous when the animal is fully expanded. Several other species collected here were similarly marked. It is significant that, so far at least as I have observed, these brilliant colors on the fleshy parts of mollusks are possessed only by members of those groups which have functional eyes, a fact which would indicate a definite connection between the possession of sight and brilliant coloration and suggest, at least, an application of the principle of sexual coloration. It will be remembered that most strikingly colored mollusks are among the Prosobranchiata, which have separate sexes.

The following genera of gastropods were represented in the collection from the Tortugas: *Murex, Fasciolaria, Columbella, Strombus, Cyprœa, Trivia, Cyphoma, Cerithium, Tectarius, Peloronta, Livonia, Fissurella* and *Strophia*. Probably the most conspicuous and abundant of all was *Strombus gigas*, Linn., the common "conch" of the West Indies. The exquisite hues on the lip and aperture of these shells would cause them to be eagerly sought after for cabinet specimens were they less common. These animals are used for food by the Bahamans, who make them into a sort of chowder. They are undeniably tough, however, and we did not regard them as particularly palatable on the one occasion when an experimental dish was prepared. Candor compels the confession, however, that this may have been due to the fact that our cook used *condensed milk* in the preparation of the chowder.

We were greatly astonished at the toleration exhibited by some of these gastropods to immersion in alcohol. On one occasion a number of small operculate specimens were left for several days in moderately strong alcohol and then spread out on the deck to dry. In a short time they were crawling around apparently not one whit the worse for their long soaking. It is probable that the operculum fits so tightly as to exclude the alcohol, but it still remains a mystery how the animals got air for respiration. Possibly they became narcotized from the fumes of the alcohol, and were thus in a state of suspended animation, as it were, during which the breathing was practically reduced to nothing. That the alcohol does not actually enter the shell is shown by the fact that when small species of operculate gastropods are plunged into alcohol and kept there, they are almost sure to decompose,—presumably from the fact that the preservative does not come in contact with the soft parts of the animal. Mr. H. F. Wickham informs me that he has noticed that non-operculate forms protect themselves when immersed in alcohol by throwing out a large quantity of mucous, which seems to be impervious to the fluid. A similar process may aid in protecting the operculate forms.

The Lamellibranchiata were much less abundant here than at Bahia Honda, although quite a respectable number were collected, including *Chione cingenda* Dillwyn, *Avicula margaritifera* Linn., *Arca velata* Sowb., *Cardium isocardium* Linn., *Pecten ornatus* Lam., *Lucina tigerina* Lamk, besides several unidentified species.

The sub-kingdom Echinodermata was represented by a splendid series of forms. Perhaps the greatest surprise was when we found a magnificent crinoid with a spread of about twelve inches growing in water less than three feet deep. These specimens were of a rich golden brown color, which has not faded in alcohol, and belonged to the genus *Actinometra*. The mouth is even more eccentric than usual in this genus, and the pinnules are long and slender. The arms appear to be more brittle than in other crinoids, and the ultimate ramifications are twenty-four in number. This is probably the handsomest species of free crinoid secured during the cruise, and the unexpectedness of the discovery added to its interest.[1]

Only two species of star-fish were found. One is an *Asterina*, which is quite small, not exceeding an inch in diameter. It is a very robust species, almost pentagonal. The dorsal surface is covered with imbricating plates with a dermal papilla peeping from the upper edge of each. One specimen is four-rayed and almost perfectly square in outline. Star-fish seem to be much more apt to have additional rays than to have less than the typical number of five. By far the most abundant species at this station was a species of *Astropecten*, which came up in great numbers when we dredged across the channel near the quarantine buoys. At no other spot did we find star-fishes so abundant in individuals as here. Like others of the ASTROPECTINIDÆ, this species is partial to a clear, sandy bottom. We greatly admired the arrangement of paxillæ, whereby these animals were able to keep their dermal tentacles constantly bathed in fresh sea-water without the channels becoming clogged with sand. So far as my observation goes, it would seem that species with true paxillæ always live in sand or mud, and are as a rule flat, not vaulted, and thus especially apt to be covered with sand.

The serpent-stars were unusually abundant in this region, the genus *Ophiura* being represented by some half-dozen species. The most abundant of these is the *Ophiura cinerea*

---

[1] Professor Alexander Agassiz informs me that he has found large *Comatula* in shallow water at the Tortugas. Whether it is the same species as ours or not I do not know.

Lyman. This serpent-star, like many others, is extremely variable in coloration, the specimens from the Tortugas being darker and less decidedly gray than those from the Bahamas. In *O. lævis* Lyman, the radial shields are evident in the adults, but are covered in the younger specimens, the full grown animals closely resembling *O. cinerea*. Another somewhat doubtful species is *Ophiura appressa* Say, which has the radial shields and side mouth-shields covered, and nine arm-spines. This species is considerably smaller than *cinerea*, and some specimens are strikingly colored, the disk being pure white marked with dark olive-green blotches. Another specimen is considerably larger, the mouth-shields are oblong oval, the side mouth-shields are uncovered, and the radial shields covered. One of the prettiest species secured at this station was *Ophiura rubicunda* Lyman, which has the disk beautifully mottled with lake-red and grayish, the arms being banded with the same colors. This seems to be the variety mentioned by Lyman as "a so-called variety of this species which may be said to have the under side of *O. cinerea*, and the upper side of *O. rubicunda*."[1] This statement almost exactly expresses the facts in regard to our specimen. The familiar *Ophiocoma echinata* Agass. is very abundant here, and is the largest Ophiurian secured at the Tortugas. It is a form admirably adapted to demonstrate the mouth-parts of the serpent-star before classes. *Ophiocoma riisei* Lütken is characterized by having slender arm-spines, oval mouth-shields, and a single tentacle-scale. It seems to grade into *O. echinata* in many particulars. *Ophiocoma* sp. is of a very light yellowish brown, banded with darker brown in about equal proportions, and is characterized by having one tentacle-scale, four arm-spines,—the third and fourth the longest,— disk finely and evenly granulated, and mouth-shields almost round. I am unable to place this specimen in any species described by Lyman. *Ophionereis reticulata* Lütken has the upper arm-plates furnished with supplementary plates, and is of a yellowish brown color reticulated with fine lines of reddish brown.

[1] Illustrated Catalogue Mus. Comp. Zoöl. No. 1, page 31.

the arms bearing distant annulations. *Ophiothrix orstedii* Lütken is the most beautiful as well as most abundant species of Ophiuran at the Tortugas. The body color is green or blue, the arms being crossed by pure white lines, disk beset with long glassy spines, and the spines of the arms bearing the characteristic spinelets of this genus. *Ophiomyxa flaccida* Lütken is also common. The rays are shorter than in typical specimens, and annulated with dark olive and light buffy in several of our specimens from that locality.

A species of basket-fish was collected here: *Astrophyton costosum* Seba is of a purplish brown color, with very prominent radial ribs bearing rounded nodules or blunt spines. The branching of the rays is not truly dichotomous except the first few basal forkings. After this the main branches run straight outward, giving off branchlets from time to time that are themselves truly dichotomous. Twenty forkings can be counted in one specimen, and this would give, according to the method of computation adopted in the famous communication from Gov. John Winthrop to the Royal Society, about 21,000,000 terminal tendrils or branchlets. Of course a vast majority of these are usually lacking in museum specimens, but there are still enough to hopelessly entangle the mass. The arms are closely and evenly granulated throughout, and do not have the appearance of segmentation so strongly marked as does *Astrophyton agassizii* of Lyman. Radial dark, almost black blotches are symmetrically placed between the radial ribs, and there is a large black blotch at the centre of the disk.

The sea-urchins were numerous individually, but the number of species was not remarkably great. *Cidaris tribuloides* Bl. was found principally on the mud-flats just inside the reef. The symmetrical disposition of the spines of this species and the well marked tubercles make it an excellent one for class use in a preliminary study of the Echini. By far the most conspicuous echinoderm was *Diadema setosum*, Gray which was abundant on the sand-flats near Garden Key. The spines of this species attain a length of seven inches, and are literally as sharp as needles. Although they appear to be as brittle as glass, they are capable of piercing not only the human cuticle, but even strong leather shoes, a fact several times demonstrated by our collectors while working in the shallows. The wound is quite severe, and as painful as a wasp's sting. The tip of the spine is usually broken off in the wound, and a dark crimson or purple fluid is injected. The spines and test of the animal seem covered with this fluid in life, giving a bloody appearance. Whether this secretion is poisonous or not, the wound is so painful as to suggest it. Several of our party suffered severely from this cause, especially while trying to get hold on the under side of coral heads, when the hand would often come in contact with scores of these long, cruel spines. Almost the only profanity that I heard during the trip was wrung from some of our best young men by the unbearable pain inflicted by the spines of *D. setosum*.

When the animal was undisturbed, resting on the bottom, the long black spines were symmetrically arranged radiating in all directions. Upon being touched, the points of the spines would converge toward the disturbing object. It seemed to several of us that the urchin had the power of imparting a true thrust to the spines. The writer experimented by placing his finger as lightly as possible against the tip of a spine, and received a sting like that of a hornet. At the base of each spine is a considerable mass of muscle fibres, but a somewhat hasty examination does not reveal any circular muscles which might give a thrust to the spine by compressing the bundle of longitudinal fibres.

Echinometra subangularis Desml. was common on the mudflats, together with a very large species, probably *Hipponoë esculenta* A. Ag., with short white spines and a much larger test than is found in specimens of this species in the Bahamas. *Toxopneustes variegatus* A. Ag. is also found here, but all of the specimens were of the variety having thick reddish-brown spines, and would have been considered a distinct species from those collected at Bahia Honda were it not for the emphasis laid by Agassiz on the extreme variability of this urchin. *Echinanthus rosaceus* Gray was found in limited numbers, and a portion of the test of a *Metalia* was picked up near Bird Key.

The corals were of course the best represented group of Cœlenterates. We were told that most of the branching forms had been killed a few years previous to our visit, probably by unusually low tides. The following reef-building forms were collected:

Siderastræa galaxea Ell. and Soland., *Manicina areolata* Linn., *Isophyllia dipsacea* Dana, *Diploria cerebriformis* Lamk., *Meandrina clivosa* Verrill, *Meandrina sinuosa* Lesr., *Porites astræoides* Lamk., *Porites furcata* Lamk., *Porites clavaria* Lamk., *Agaricia agaricites* Pall., *Orbicella annularis* Dana., *Oculina varicosa* Lesueur. Of these, the two species of branching *Porites* were by far the most abundant, growing inside the reefs and fairly covering considerable areas of the bottom. Only one specimen of *Madrepora cervicornis* Lamk. was found, although we were told that they were formerly very abundant.

Millepora alcicornis Lamk. was the only hydroid, if it be a hydroid, found at this station, a fact that surprised us greatly. Of course we did no dredging in deep water, and thus were unable to investigate the fauna outside of the reefs.

Only two species of Medusæ were found. - *Linerges mercurius* Haeck. and *Polyclonia frondosa* Agassiz, the latter being very abundant in the old moat, where it rests on the sandy bottom with its tentacles turned upward. In spots they are closely packed together, and the waving, leaf-like tentacles give them a semblance to a thick growth of algæ. *Physalia arethusa* Agassiz is the only Siphonophore found by us at this station. It was abundant, and as before indicated, is almost always accompanied by a little group of parasitic fishes.

On Tuesday, June 13th, the boats were sent for the turtle skeletons which the land-crabs had cleaned for us on Bird Key, and the corals which had been put to bleach on Bush Key. A strong wind was blowing, but abated somewhat in the afternoon, and the "Emily E. Johnson" left the fumigating dock with her passengers unanimously of the opinion that Dr. Murray and his associates had put the expedition under great obligation by their attention not only to the comfort and health, but also to the pleasure of the entire party. For once, at least, in the history of the Dry Tortugas, people left the domain of the yellow flag with genuine regret.

The vessel remained at anchor that night within the harbor, or rather channel, off Garden Key. A heavy gale blew from the S. S. W. all night, raising a sea that sent the waves dashing high over the sea-wall against the old fort. Not wishing to leave our safe anchorage in such a gale, we busied ourselves in doing odd jobs about the vessel and in reading. The next day a high sea was still running outside, and we concluded to try a few hauls of the trawl and tangles across the channel. The bottom must have been actually paved with a species of *Astropecten*, as the tangles were fairly crowded full of them. The trawl could be used to advantage on this smooth sandy, bottom, and we thus secured quite a number of small fish that would otherwise have been missed.

On the morning of Friday, June 16th, we finally bade goodbye to the Dry Tortugas, but were glad to see Dr. Murray on board to accompany us to Key West. This gentleman has probably had more experience with yellow fever than any other American physician, and we were greatly interested in the tales of the pestilence which he could so graphically relate. His opinion was that the disease is not nearly so terrible as generally supposed, and that with proper treatment there is no necessity for a mortality greater than two per cent. The doctor was evidently skeptical concerning the existence of the yellow fever bacillus.

CHAPTER VI.

KEY WEST AND THE POURTALÈS PLATEAU.

On Saturday, June 17th, we again put into Key West, tying up to the government wharf, where a berth was secured for the "Emily E. Johnson" through the kind offices of Dr. Murray.

It was really a relief to be again allowed to mingle with our fellow men, and not bear the stigma which Uncle Sam had so promptly put upon us when we entered the port before. Being tabooed by one's kind is doubtless sometimes for the general good, but it makes the victim feel as if there were some moral obliquity involved, and tends to decidedly diminish one's self-esteem. Being pronounced once more fit for contact with American citizens, we welcomed the advent of the numerous parties who were willing to supply us with fruits, provisions, curios, clean linen, etc., with a cordiality which must have seemed unduly emphatic, and patronized ice-cream saloons and soda-water fountains with a zest unknown since childhood.

Key West is a Spanish city, with a strong Bahaman flavor, placed on American soil. Its main industries are sponge-curing, cigar-making, and the hatching of Cuban rebellions. If the Spanish authorities could swoop down on that city some night and exterminate its inhabitants of Spanish blood, it would be safe to insure Cuba against revolutions for a generation to come. This city, of twenty-odd thousand inhabitants, is an anomaly. The only thing about it that is American is the coral rock upon which it stands, and a few of the government officials. One can enter store after store without being able to transact his business in English, and when he does find a man who speaks English it isn't American English, but Bahaman English, a curious *patois* composed of negro dialect and the language of the London cockney, in which the h's are misplaced with consummate adroitness.

The city itself lacks the picturesqueness of the Spanish city, the cleanliness of the Bahaman village, and the push and vim of an American town. The only really handsome building is the custom-house and post-office combined, a substantial structure of stone and brick, overlooking the harbor and embellishing an otherwise unattractive water front. Some distance further to the south is the U. S. marine hospital, where we found a formidable accumulation of mail for our party. Still farther down and separated from the island by a causeway, Fort Taylor adds a bit of romance to the scene. The beach is lined with cocoanut palms, trees which seem graceful and picturesque at first, but grow commonplace and monotonous on long acquaintance. The shops of the town are mostly wooden structures, sadly in need of paint, and a majority of the signs are in Spanish. One of the most pretentious buildings is the Masonic building, which is three stories high, and contains a public library and free reading-room. A horse-car line runs along the principal business streets, but the horses pulling the cars usually walk. The streets themselves have the virtue of being wide. The residence part of the city is much more attractive than the business portion, and contains quite a number of sensible and homelike houses, with commodious verandas and abundant shade.

A new industry has been inaugurated at Key West in the shape of a canning factory for pine-apples. This enterprise was started two or three years ago by Martin Wagner & Company, of Baltimore, who ship the pine-apples from the Bahamas to Key West and can them there, instead of transporting the fruit to their factories at Baltimore, as in times past. The misfortunes to which sailing craft are subjected were well illustrated by a schooner that arrived during our stay at Key West, consigned to Martin Wagner & Company.

This schooner had left Eleuthera three weeks before, had been becalmed in the Florida Straits, and carried by the Gulf Stream clear through the straits and around north of Abaco, which is further from its destination than was the starting place. Of course the load of pine-apples had rotted down and was completely ruined.

At this place two members of the expedition were compelled to leave us, owing to constant seasickness, and proceeded by steamer to Tampa, and thence home to Iowa by rail.

We remained at the wharf over Sunday, but noticed an intolerable stench arising from the hold. Our search for the source of this foul odor was at first unavailing, but we finally discovered that it arose from some of the potato barrels. These were taken on deck and opened, disclosing a serious state of affairs. The potatoes had suddenly commenced to rot, and several of the barrels had their contents reduced to a disgusting, putrid mass, which we hastily pitched overboard. Then all the other barrels were brought up and opened, and the potatoes picked over, the small remnant of sound tubers being spread out on the deck to dry, after which they were again stowed below. This was a serious loss, as potatoes were too expensive at Key West to permit of our stocking up there, although we did get a few bushels of sweet potatoes. We also discovered at this time that our corned beef was beginning to spoil, but succeeded in trading off some of our superfluous coffee and flour for hams, bacon, eggs, and vegetables, on a basis that showed that the good people of Key West knew how to drive a hard bargain when they had their customers in a tight place. Our experience would go to prove that about the only kind of provisions that are sure to keep well without ice, on a long cruise in the tropics are the various kinds of canned goods. I do not remember that anything put up in this way spoiled, even the butter remaining sweet and good to the very last.

That evening we left the dock, and dropped down to near the entrance to the harbor, in order to get a good start for the dredging ground in the morning. One of the most important undertakings which our expedition had in view was a somewhat thorough exploration of the famous "Pourtalès Plateau," perhaps the richest field in the Western Hemisphere for the marine zoölogist. Outside of the line of reefs known as the Florida Reefs there extends southward a gentle submarine slope reaching out toward the trough of the Gulf Stream. "This rocky plateau with a very moderate slope begins a little to the westward of Sand Key, and stretches to the northward and eastward until it reaches its maximum breadth, of about eighteen miles to the eastward of Sombrero. It then diminishes in breadth, and finally ends between Cary's Foot Reef and Cape Florida. . . . The plateau begins at a depth of about ninety fathoms, and ends at about three hundred."[1] The bottom is limestone composed of the debris from the adjacent reefs, cemented into a sort of conglomerate. We have here the most favorable condition for a profusion of animal life: –a gentle slope leading off from a continental mass, for the real outline of the Florida Reefs include the whole line of keys and reefs, bathed by a constant and powerful current.

Acting on the advice of Professor Alexander Agassiz, we did all of our dredging on this plateau between Sand Key and Sombrero Key. Taking our bearings from Sand Key Light, American Shoal Light, and Sombrero Light; and frequently getting cross-bearings from two of these, we were able to know nearly our exact position during the whole time. With some interruptions due to calms and a run into Key West for a spar, we worked eleven days on the Pourtalès Plateau, making forty-four hauls of the dredge or tangles. When the weather permitted our dredging all day, we made six or seven hauls daily. A comparison with our record while dredging off Havana will show that practice considerably facilitated our work. We also found that the labor was much less trying when we became used to it, although the heat was considerably greater than we found it during our dredging off the Cuban coast. Of course the comparative absence of sea-

[1] Three Cruises of the Blake, vol. I, p. 286.

sickness had a great deal to do with making our Pourtalès Plateau work seem pleasanter, and the health of the party had been improved by our stay at the Tortugas. Practice also increased the efficiency of each one in that particular work which fell to his or her share, so that the material was more quickly cared for and more intelligently disposed of. A certain familiarity with the different groups of animals began to make itself evident on the part of the students, showing that the educational value of the expedition was assuming the proportions hoped for by its projectors. Not only was each person able to recognize at a glance the animals falling within his particular province, but every one was able, in a general way, to sort out the material into the proper classes as it was dumped from the dredge or picked from the tangles. The educational value of the mere handling and assorting of a miscellaneous heap of material is perhaps greater than can be realized in the same time in any other way, and when the work is done where there is ready resort to the general literature of the subject, and also to the microscope and laboratory tools, it will be seen that our young people were enjoying unsurpassed educational facilities along biological lines, although there was comparatively little of the time when they were consciously studying.

We soon found that there was little use in dredging inside of about the sixty-fathom line, the slope from the reefs to that depth being singularly rocky and barren of animal life, although fairly good spots were occasionally encountered at less depths. The first hauls we made after crossing the one-hundred-fathom line directly south of Sand Key Light were a revelation, at once demonstrating the exceeding richness of the fauna and the vast difference between it and the reef fauna, and the difference between both of these and the fauna of the opposite slope of the Gulf Stream off the Cuban coast. No more instructive lesson on the geographical and bathymetric distribution of marine life could well be found. But few species, so far as yet determined, were found common to either two of these three faunæ, and the general facies of each was remarkably distinct from that of either of the others. The trough of the Gulf Stream seems to be a most effective barrier, fully as potent as a range of mountains on the land, while a difference of a few score fathoms in depth zoölogically divides the Pourtalès Plateau from the reef region as effectively as thousands of miles difference in latitude does the terrestrial forms.

Taking it all in all, this was the most profitable part of our cruise, both from a scientific and an educational standpoint, although it was characterized by almost continuous work and considerable discomfort from the heat, as well as a certain degree of danger. The latter element came in, as usual, in a manner and at a time entirely unexpected.

On Monday, June 19th, just when we were rejoicing over the first splendid haul from below the one-hundred-fathom line, and most of the party were eagerly picking the harvest from the tangles, a serious accident happened. The large oyster-dredge had been lowered and was dragging nicely on the bottom, when it suddenly caught firmly on some object, and with scarcely a moment's warning the tremendous pressure on the iron rope, caused probably more by the current of the Gulf Stream than the passage of the vessel through the water, created havoc unparalleled during the entire cruise. The mate and Mr. Larrabee, who were watching the dredge rope, were seated on the windward bulwarks just forward of a break in the rail. A number of others were on the opposite side of the vessel picking over the tangles after the preceding haul. The first thing to give way was the two-and three-fourths-inch Italian hemp rope which guyed the dredging spar in position while dredging, thus bringing a longitudinal strain on the dredging spar which swung aft; next the rope securing the throat of the spar to the foremast parted like so much yarn; then the rope which secured the heavy iron pulley-block to the deck just aft of the galley broke at both ends. The spar fell to the deck with a crash, breaking in two as it struck, and the pulley fell, barely missing the head of a young woman working over the tangles. The iron rope then came to the deck, swept along the bulwark, and almost caught the two men, in which case they would have been cut in half against the break in the rail. The rope began sawing through the rail, and the dredging machine seemed about to be torn from its bolts and taken bodily overboard, which would have ended our dredging once for all. All of these disasters occurred within eight or ten seconds,—so suddenly that we were fairly dazed, giving us the impression that everything aloft was falling about our ears, and that the fearful strength of our iron rope was going to wreck the vessel.

By this time the schooner was firmly anchored by the dredge, and the danger would have been over were it not for the strong current of the Gulf Stream and the terrible strain caused by the rolling of the schooner. Captain Flowers was equal to the emergency, however, and with the help of some of his men and our boys, managed to get the rope under control again, after which we succeeded in breaking the dredge from the bottom, and finally reeled in all the rope without the loss of a single foot of it, nor so much as a serious kink, which is nearly as bad as a break. When the dredge came up it contained what appeared to be fragments of badly corroded iron plates, evidence that it had caught on a sunken wreck. The dredge was fouled many times during the cruise, but on no other occasion did it catch so firmly and suddenly as then. The coral rock and conglomerate on the Pourtalès Plateau would have yielded more promptly to the strain.

It is the unexpected that happens, and no better illustration could be found than in our experience. Who would have thought that the only really serious dangers encountered during our cruise would have been a mad dog on deck and an old forgotten wreck a hundred fathoms below the surface on the Pourtalès Plateau?

That evening we ran into Key West for a new dredging spar. The broken spar had cost two dollars in Baltimore, but at Key West they wanted fifteen dollars for a fifteen-foot pole without irons. Captain Flowers pronounced this pure robbery, and said that we would mend our broken spar, which although it was somewhat heavier and not nearly so comely, he did, making it fully as useful and even stronger than before.

It was during this time that we experienced great discomfort from heat. For several successive days there would be a little breeze early in the morning, which died out when the sun got well above the horizon, after which a dead calm would set in and last for the rest of the day. Although the middle of the day was actually the hottest, we found the time from seven to eight in the morning as uncomfortable as any, from the fact that the sun would get into our faces under the largest hats or bonnets, and the reflections from the water would add very materially to the glare which hurt the eyes and burned the face. At this time no shade was afforded by the sails, the nearly horizontal rays passing under the booms and even under the awning, when the latter was up. But when the sun reached the zenith, the tar would actually boil from the deck, and the awnings would only slightly modify the heat, which struck through them so forcibly that little relief could be secured. Below it was simply stifling, and the merciless glare of the deck, unrelieved by a particle of breeze, seemed to sap all ambition and vitality from even the strongest members of the party. The thermometer registered 135 on the deck, and well into the nineties under the awning. The lot of our cook was, at this time, certainly far from enviable. He had to spend the greater part of the day in the seven-by-seven galley, with a large range and a roaring coal fire, which made the deck seem cool in comparison. Here poor Smith had to cook three meals a day for twenty-eight people, whose appetites were, to say the least, not delicate. One afternoon when the fire was going down after dinner the thermometer registered 143 in the galley. Under these circumstances, there is little wonder that our cook lost flesh with startling rapidity, and that, whereas he came on board a rather sleek and portly darkey, he left us at Baltimore, an emaciated and aged man. His general health seemed little affected, however, and, let it be said to his credit, his patience and good nature proved inexhaustible. I doubt if any white person could have endured staying in that galley for half an hour during the hottest times.

On several such days, seeing that the breeze was about to fail us, we used what remained in getting to an anchorage inside the reefs. When this was done, collecting parties could be sent out in the boats after corals and shallow-water forms, and any serious loss of time prevented. At such times we found great relief from the heat by going overboard and swimming in the crystal clear water on the shady side of the schooner. These swimming parties were greatly enjoyed by all who participated in them, and a number both of young men and women learned the delightful and invigorating art of swimming. An extra spar was hung over the side, in addition to the boarding steps and several lines, and we had a natatorium which could not be surpassed either in cleanliness or convenience. When a novice desired a lesson, a rope was attached to his or her belt, and the aspirant for natatory accomplishment was persuaded to jump overboard in preference to being thrown overboard. The end of the rope was held by some one on board. After a few such lessons, almost every one who tried was able to float or swim without assistance, although the line attachment was never omitted, in the case of the young women at least, several of whom became quite able to float or swim, much to their delight and profit. It was a novel and interesting sight to see the bulwarks lined with a row of these young men and women, who, at a given signal, jumped or dove into the cool, clear depths together. This healthful exercise served to break up the oppressive monotony of the calm weather, and doubtless had a good deal to do with the continued good health of all on board. When the calm caught us at sea, we tried our hands at fishing. The sharks appeared to be quite numerous, and could be seen from the deck, gliding around the vessel some distance below the surface. On one occasion a very large "hammer-head" was seen from the cross-trees. It was, apparently, the largest fish observed during the cruise, but it is difficult to estimate

the size of objects in the water, which may account for the
large proportions of fish stories. The commonest shark in
these waters was the blue shark. *Carcharhinus glaucus.* (T.)
Jor. and Gilb. This is one of the so-called man-eating sharks.
It was hard to repress a feeling of repugnance while watching these huge brutes cruise around and around the "Emily
E. Johnson," as if they were treading a regular beat for business purposes. At such times the boys lost their desire to
jump overboard, and conceived a still more intense longing to
catch sharks. Captain Flowers eagerly aided and abetted
them in this purpose, and their efforts resulted in the capture
of a number of the man-eaters. The largest of these seemed
enormous as we hauled him aboard, and almost any of us
would have said that he was fifteen or twenty feet long. He
measured, however, just twelve feet, a good-sized shark after
all, although specimens are rarely mentioned in the literature
of adventure which are less than twenty-five feet long. The
vitality of this great fish was wonderful. It was shot several
times through the head before being hauled aboard, but gave
an occasional flap of its tail for a long time afterward. The
heart kept up its pulsations long enough for us to make a dissection, affording an instructive demonstration of the gross
anatomy of the circulatory system. The lance-like sharpness
of the teeth was learned from the most practical teacher,
experience, by several of those who were engaged in the dissection. This specimen seemed to have the power of everting the stomach out of the mouth, a considerable portion of
that organ being in the mouth when the animal came aboard.
Some of our party conceived the idea that the flesh of a
young shark would be good eating, and tested their theory by
a gastronomical demonstration. They reported the flesh quite
palatable, as, indeed, it doubtless was.

Probably the best sport in the fishing line was dolphin
fishing. These were the *fish* and not the mammal known by
the same name. A school of these beautiful creatures was
seen swimming around the vessel during a calm, and all hands
got out hooks and lines for a try at this novel sport. Shark

meat was used as bait, and for a long time it seemed as if the attempt were doomed to failure. The dolphins appeared to be tempted, but would sheer off again in the most exasperating manner. Finally one adventurous fish swallowed the hook, and soon lay on deck, a mass of changing hues. Another and another followed suit, and soon the dolphins were biting ravenously, and being hauled aboard in the most gratifying numbers, until nearly all had paid the penalty of their rashness. They proved excellent eating, and we much enjoyed the store of good fresh fish thus so opportunely secured.

The far-famed colors of the dolphin are not exaggerated. Indeed they could not be, so vivid and exquisite are they. One specimen was a monster of its kind, being four feet long and having the frontal prominence greatly developed,—so much so that the eye appeared to be in about the middle of the head. A broad band running from the forehead nearly to the tail was a real glittering gold, just as true a gilt as could be made by laying on gold leaf. This is the largest surface covered with this rare metallic color that I have seen in nature. The dorsal fin was a rich blue, the under surface was white dotted with small, regularly distributed "polka dots" of blue. Yellow, red and green also entered into the coloration of this gorgeous creature. The changing of hues while dying consisted in flushes of color passing rather slowly from one to another. It did not seem, however, to be so brilliant at any time while dying as it was immediately upon coming out of the water. In a few minutes all the richness of color was gone forever, and nothing remained but a very ordinary fish. A good cast of this creature made after the modern method and colored correctly, would be a most attractive object for a museum, although most of the visitors would doubtless consider it highly unnatural and impossible, a criticism often made by the ignorant in the presence of faithful reproductions of natural objects.

Of course the absence of ice on board the schooner was something of a hardship to those who had never before been called upon to do without it during hot weather. It would have been impossible, however, to have carrried along a sufficient store to keep through the cruise, and the hardship would have been all the more severe had we taken a supply from Baltimore, which would inevitably have failed us after we got into a hot climate, making it necessary to go suddenly from ice-water to the comparatively warm water of the water casks. As it was, the water grew warm so gradually that there was no sudden transition. We found great relief, moreover, in the Cuban water-jars, or "ollas," as they are called. These are almost globular jars made of a very porous white clay, with a handle on one side, a short spout on the other, a ring on top, and an aperture for pouring in the water. Such a jar is filled and then hung out in the air and sun. The evaporation going on from the damp outer surface cools the water very perceptibly, making it quite palatable and really better for drinking purposes than ice-water. Several of these ollas were always kept hanging from the stern davits. They were filled every morning from the water casks. After we learned to utilize these very sensible contrivances, which were bought at Havana, there was little complaint so far as the drinking water was concerned. From a sanitary standpoint there is little doubt that the use of the ollas is far better than dependence upon ice.

Most of the fishes secured in this region were not taken from the Pourtalès Plateau proper, but in the shallower water between the reefs and the one-hundred-fathom line, by far the greater proportion coming up on the trawl or tangles from a depth of about fifty fathoms. The assemblage of forms as a whole was characterized by the grotesqueness of shape so often found in aberrant groups. Of course there were few typical deep-sea forms, the deepest haul producing fish being one hundred and twenty fathoms. It is impessible to tell whether even these came from the bottom or were caught at intermediate depths by the ascending trawl or tangles. One species, however, a flounder, can be reasonably assigned to that depth.

Among the more interesting forms secured may be mentioned a species of sea-horse, *Hippocampus*, one taken from a depth of sixty fathoms and others from shallow water in the Key West channel. The rapid vibration, resembling ciliary action, of the fins is unlike that observed in any other fish that we studied. The resemblace of these curious little animals to the knights of the chess-board is rendered very evident when the fish are erect, in their normal attitude. Another striking form was probably a "flute-mouth," *Aulostoma* sp.? which was taken from the stomach of a dolphin and is about four inches long, with sides covered with brilliant silvery scales. The jaws, as the name implies, are very long and tubular, with a small terminal mouth. The dorsal portion of the animal is covered with scales edged with blackish, and there are several dark blotches on the sides. Two small species of sculpins were secured, both apparently belonging to the genus *Scorpæna*. One was dredged at about one hundred and five fathoms. The scales are ctenoid, without flaps; dorsal spines twelve; preopercular spines five; there are five spines on the ridge over the eye. We noticed that this, as well as other specimens from comparatively deep water came up with the mouth open to its widest capacity, as if the fish were suffering from strangulation. The other sculpin was taken from a depth of sixty fathoms, was four and one-half inches long, and had some of the ctenoid scales armed with conspicuous fleshy flaps. The fins were barred with brown, and the lower part of the sides marked with small, sharply circumscribed black or brown spots. A fish belonging to the "eel-pout" group (ZOARCIDÆ) was taken from a depth of one hundred and twenty fathoms, and was eight inches long, the anal and dorsal continuous, and the ventrals jugular, reduced to two long, rather fleshy filaments. A row of eight light or white spots ornamented the sides, and there was a broad somewhat truncated muzzle projecting over the mouth. The eyes were very large. From the same depth a codling, *Phycis regius* (Walb.) was secured, a long, slender fish with barbels on the chin, and ventrals reduced to two long filaments. The first dorsal is very small, lobate with black edgings. Both dorsal and anal are long and low. Two vertical series of dark brown or black spots are on the sides of the head. This is the largest species dredged on the Plateau, being nine inches long. "Said to exhibit electric powers in life." (Jordan & Gilbert.) Another specimen from this haul is a much mutilated flounder, which is not in a condition for even approximate identification, as is indeed unfortunately the fact in regard to several specimens from this station.

An interesting species of *Antennarius* was secured from about fifty fathoms, and differed considerably from the others seen by us. The first dorsal spine was modified into a "fishing-rod," which is exceedingly slender, bearing a small trifid "bait" on the end. The body is covered with sharp trifid spines, which bear considerable resemblance, superficial of course, to the calcareous spicules of some of the flexible corals and sponges. These spines impart a velvety appearance to the surface when dried, but it feels much like sand-paper. The lateral line is armed with clumps of spines, the series extending over the eye, where it is greatly accentuated. The second and third dorsal spines are much thickened, fleshy, and covered with the minute spines. There is a large oval black spot surrounded by a narrow white edging just below the middle of the long dorsal. The abdomen is greatly dilatable, it being possible to blow up the alcoholic specimen. The pectoral fins are placed far back, giving a ludicrous resemblance to hind legs, while the ventrals are much more widely separated than in the *Antennarius* which inhabits the Gulf weed.

Another strange form belonging to the order Pediculati and dredged from a depth of one hundred and twenty fathoms, is such a curious combination of characters that it cannot be placed in any family defined in the only systematic work on fishes at present accessible to the writer.[1] The gill-openings are far above and considerably behind the upper axils of the pectorals, being situated further back than in any other fish that I have seen. They are longer and more conspicuous than in the species just described. The animal has the gen-

[1] Synopsis of the Fishes of North America, Jordan & Gilbert.

eral contour of the fishing-frogs, LOPHIIDÆ, but the position of the gill-openings would exclude it from that family as defined by Jordan & Gilbert. The head is enormous in proportion to the rest of the body, and notably depressed. The mouth is wide, opening vertically. The first dorsal is represented by a peculiarly modified spine, which is short and fleshy, hinged like the "fishing-rod" before described, and fits nicely, when not erected, into a distinct oval pit between the eyes The whole surface of the body is covered with prickly spines. There is a curious system of lines of pores, more extensive than in any other fish that I have examined, reminding one somewhat of *Porichthys*. One line borders the upper lip and curves rather abruptly backward at the corners of the mouth, until it joins a transverse line to be described presently. A pair of lines start from the middle of the upper lip, embrace the pit containing the first dorsal, diverge back of the eyes, until they attain the level of the eyes and then pass directly backward, curving down over the gill-openings until they reach the lower margin of the tail, along which they run as far as the base of the tail-fin. A third series of pores starts from the middle of the lower jaw, forming a horse-shoe with the ends away from the jaw, and connected by a short line of pores. At each end of the horse-shoe a line extends outward and backward to nearly the centre of the body, or just a little in front, but much above, the ventral fins. At this point a transverse line passes over the back across the dorsal lines, and meets its fellow in the centre of the back. The ventral line extends almost directly backward from the origin of the tranverse line, and ends on the proximal joint of the pectoral fin. The body of this strange fish is capable of great inflation, being almost all mouth and stomach. The soft dorsal begins above the pectorals and almost reaches the caudal. The anal is much shorter; the ventrals are very small. There are no fleshy tags on the surface of the body except on the first dorsal spine. The specimen is three and three-fourths inches long and one and five-eighths inches broad, and one and three-eighths inches in height when moderately distended.

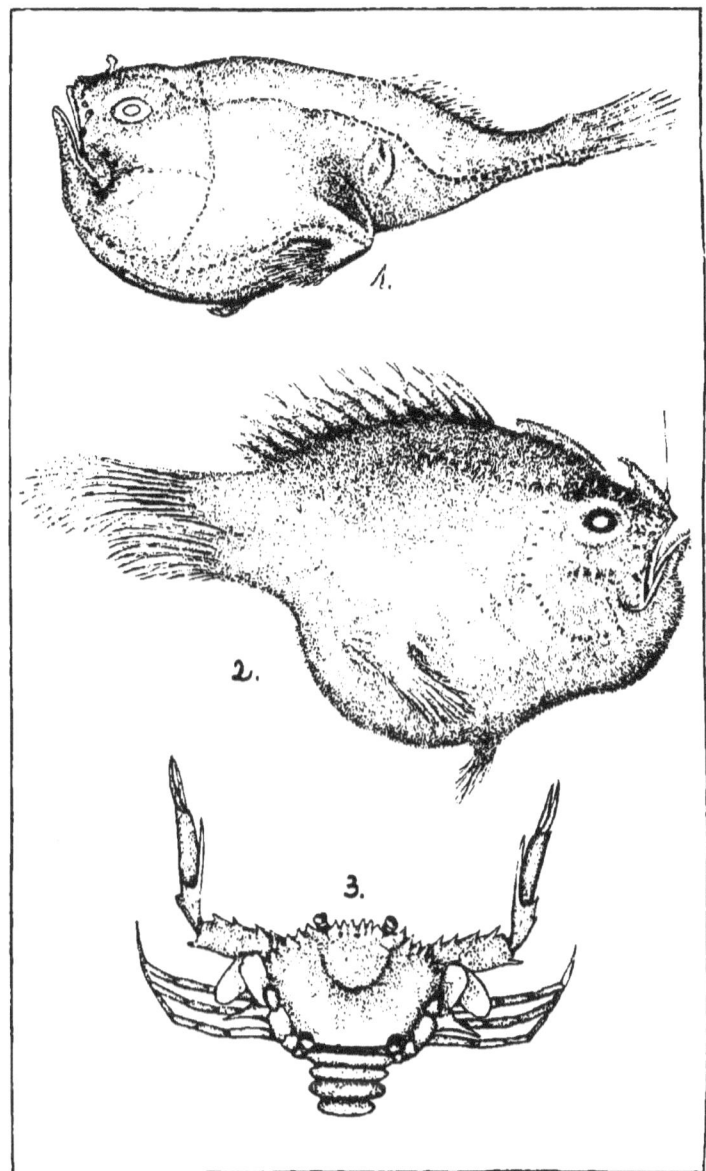

Fig. 1. A strange pediculate Fish. Pourtalès Plateau.
Fig. 2. ANTENNARIUS sp. Pourtalès Plateau.
Fig. 3. NEPTUNUS SPINICARPUS, Stm. Dry Tortugas.

The distance between the eyes is one-half inch, and the width of the mouth three-fourths inch.

Of course it is altogether probable that the ichthyologist will recognize in this a well-known form, but to the laity it is one of the strangest of the strange fish collected by our expedition.

Among the most grotesque forms were two species of "bat-fish" secured from a depth of sixty fathoms. One of these (*Malthe* sp.) was less than two inches long, with a strong, conical rostral process, which was one-third as long as the distance from the mouth to the base of the caudal fin. This process imparts a most ludicrous expression to the profile of the fish, giving a comical resemblance to a human face with large eyes and an enormous nose. The head is much deeper than the body, and its top is ornamented by two series of conical spines which unite at the centre of the back. Similar spines are conspicuous on the margins of the body and on the tail. The pectoral fins greatly resemble the legs of a frog, and the ventrals are small and rather widely separated. The other species belongs apparently to the genus *Halieutichthys*. It resembles a ray in general outline, being exceedingly flat with greatly expanded sides, the width of the body nearly equaling the distance from the mouth to the base of the tail. Total length three inches; mouth small; rostrum not produced. The body is marked with a reticulate pattern of brownish lines, and covered with blunt spines.

But the most remarkable species of all was a worm-like creature which came up with the bat-fish just described. At first sight we could hardly believe that it was a fish at all. The animal was twelve inches long and only three-sixteenths of an inch in diameter. It was scaleless, being as smooth to the touch as an earth-worm. The head was not differentiated from the body, and was produced into a short, pointed snout. The eyes were large, the mouth inferior, and opening some distance behind the end of the snout. The upper jaw was armed with four large, sharp, slightly recurved teeth, passing in front of the lower jaw when the mouth is closed.

The gills open laterally. Color in alcohol, uniform light brown, with no markings of any description.

"At Key West, as with most of the other land stations, the entomological work was confined chiefly to Coleoptera, and only passing notice given the other orders. Attention was at first naturally attracted to the beach, which here proved much less productive than usual, the only species of note thus found being two species of *Cicindela* (*marginata*, Fabr. and *tortuosa* Dej.), and a few examples of *Trichopteryx* (sp. incog.), *Dryotribus* and *Macrancylus*, *Phaleria* being almost entirely wanting. Later on, when opportunity offered to go into the thickets which cover that portion of the key lying behind the city, the insect life was found to be much more abundant and varied than at first supposed. The two species of *Cicindela* already mentioned were not uncommon in the roads and paths which run through the brush in all directions, and under loose pieces of bark lying near pools were taken a few specimens of *Bembidium contractum* Say and of a *Tachys* near the Californian *T. vittiger* Lec. Beating yielded *Chilocorus cacti* Linn., *Psyllobora nana* Muls. (a smaller form than that taken in the Tortugas), and an undescribed *Scymnus* as representatives of the COCCINELLIDÆ, while the CRYPTOPHAGIDÆ were represented by *Loberus impressus* Lec., and the DASCYLLIDÆ by *Scirtes tibialis* Guér. Wherever the herbage was more than ordinarily thick, or a clump of fresh sprouts had sprung from an old trunk, we were pretty sure to find one or two *Monocrepidius lividus* De G.; in the inner recesses of the thickets, where vines and bushes, matted together, overhung the narrow pathways, a few of the little Ptinids, *Hemiptychus similis* Lec. and *Eupactus viticola* Sz. were shaken from their leafy shelters. SCARABÆIDÆ were by no means common, and seemed confined to two species, —*Trichius delta* Forst., which was seen flying about flowers, and is rendered conspicuous and easily recognizable by the triangular yellow mark on its black thorax; and *Canthon lævis* Drury, which was found but once, in cow-droppings. This last species ranges from Canada and New England to Florida and the south of California, and varies in color from green and blue to bronze or black. Those taken at Key West were of the blue form ordinarily found in the south. The CHRYSOMELIDÆ, though few in species, were common enough in individuals, the little *Metachroma pellucida* Cr. being one of the most plentiful species on the island. *Griburius larvatus* Newm. and *Chelymorpha (argus?* Licht.) were rare, the latter occurring on a convolvulaceous plant near the beach. The Cistelid *Hymenorus convexus* Casey, so common in the Tortugas, was occasionally beaten from leaves here, and one of them was taken from the mouth of a large Asilid fly. The flowers of one tree, unknown by name, were swarming with *Oxacis* of apparently three species, none of which can be identified with those already known as members of our fauna. The Rhynchophora were moderately numerous. *Artipus floridanus* Horn and *Lachnopus floridanus* Horn being the most common, while a few *Anthonomus julichii* Dietz were found clinging to the under surface of leaves.

"In the streets and on vacant lots there were a few beetles noticed that did not come to hand in the wooded part of the island. These were *Blapstinus opacus* Lec., which was common on sandy spots under old boards, rags, or anything in fact that offered shelter from the burning sun; *Zophobas morio*, a large black Tenebrionid only lately received as a member of our fauna; a pretty Buprestid of the genus *Polycesta* and the unwelcome but common *Dermestes vulpinus* Fabr. which on one occasion came aboard our vessel in swarms while we were lying at the wharf. In the dusk they flew about our hatches, no doubt attracted by the smell of the large collections stored below, like carrion-flies about a carcass.

"A passing mention of some insects of the remaining orders must suffice for the present, most of the few obtained being still unidentified. Of Hemiptera we have the names of *Thyanta custator* Fabr. and *Euschistus crenatus* Fabr. and also took a species of *Lygaeus* and one of *Holymenia*. Of Diptera, various energetic mosquitoes were numerous, and a large Asilid was not uncommon, being found chiefly at rest on fences, and easily taken by hand without the aid of a net. Two specimens of *Eristalis vinctorum* Fabr. were captured, one of them being taken from the clutches of the Asilid mentioned before. Of the Hymenoptera, we might mention *Stizus hogardii* Latr., a very fine wasp, reddish in color, with smoky wings, the tip of the abdomen black; a small species of *Pompilus;* a female example of *Sphærophthalma ferrugata* Fabr., which occurs also as far north as New England; and a female *Evania appendigaster* Linn., a curious insect of a deep black color, the small subtriangular compressed abdomen appearing out of all proportion to the heavy thorax."[1]

The following interesting account of pelagic Hemiptera is quoted from an article by Mr. Wickham that appeared in "The Entomological News," February, 1894:

On the second of July, while at anchor near the Sand Key Light, a few *Halobates* were seen near the vessel between three and four o'clock in the afternoon. By getting into a boat which was lying alongside, no difficulty was experienced in capturing two or three that came within reach of the net. The next day, while the vessel was under way with quite a pleasant breeze, they were seen again, before seven o'clock in the morning, skimming about the bows. Two or three were again taken by sitting in the chains under the bow-sprit and "jabbing" at them with a crab-net lined with bolting cloth, as often as one crossed our course. By eight o'clock they were less numerous. With the aid of the Report, previously mentioned, they were determined as *Halobates wüllerstorffi* Frauenf. a name afterwards verified by Mr. O. Heidemann, of Washington.

The following day more of them were seen in Lat. 24° 24´ N., Long. 70 49 W. Immediately after dinner, when the water was still, except for a smooth swell, a specimen was caught in a crab-net and turned loose, without being touched by the fingers, into a tub of salt water on the deck. The insect at once commenced to scud around on the surface with movements so rapid that the eye could not follow them, and any observations on the *mode* of locomotion were out of the question. In a few minutes partial exhaustion succeeded these violent exertions, and it was then seen that the long middle pair of feet did nearly all the work of progression, the anterior pair being carried folded up (nearly) and projecting forwards, a little to each side of the head. The antennæ point forwards and outwards, forming a **V**. When the bug tires, the muscles at the insertion of the legs appear to weaken first, and the body is let down on to the water. It there rests in very much the position shown in Mr. Walker's figure in the "Entom.

[1] H. F. Wickham.

Monthly Magazine" for October, 1893, though my sketches, made on the spot, show sharper angles at all the knee joints. The same position is not always maintained, however, by different specimens.

The movements of a tired specimen were as follows: In making a stroke the middle legs were brought forward until the tips were about on a line with the head. They were then rapidly brought back so as to nearly touch the tips of the hind pair, which were moved comparatively but little. The posterior feet seem to be used to steer with rather than as an aid in progression. The four legs work in unison, not alternately, *i. e.*, the middle legs keep time with each other and with the hinder pair. The tips of the legs rest on the water, and are not immersed in it so that the little hollows near each, caused by the weight of the insect, can plainly be seen. With captive specimens sunlight acted as a stimulant, and evoked activity, which was lessened by shade.

One *Halobates* was then placed in a tightly corked bottle, filled, when immersed, so as to make certain that no air was enclosed, except the thin film which invested the insect. This was done at 1:22 P. M., and at 1:30 was witnessed what was then supposed to be the final struggle with death; after the expiration of four minutes this recommenced, and was continued at irregular intervals until 1:43, after which no more were seen until 1:48, at which time a tiny bubble of air made its way from the cork, and at 1:58 another of these bubbles evoked a feeble struggle, the last. When finally removed to the alcohol bottle, not a movement could be detected, and the insect was undoubtedly drowned. This would appear to antagonize the theory that they stay beneath the surface in stormy weather. I also noticed, with several specimens, that they could (or would?) only dive after being wet so that "skimming" was impossible, but this does not agree with the observations of other naturalists, and I recognize its practical worthlessness as purely negative evidence.

This was by far the richest field for Crustacea that we encountered during our work. The Brachyura were, as usual, the most abundant forms and a never-failing source of interest to the students, who were constantly discovering some grotesque shape or special protective modification. Between forty and fifty species of Brachyura were secured here, hardly a haul coming up without its quota. This collection will be systematically treated in a forthcoming report by Miss Mary J. Rathbun, of the Smithsonian Institution, and it is to her kindness that the identification of these forms is due. By far the greater number belong to the Maioid group, commonly called "sea-spiders." Three species of *Podochela* were found, the first, *P. gracilipes* Stm., having the first true walking leg very greatly lengthened, being about twice as long as the next leg. It came from a depth of about sixty fathoms. *P. lamelligera* Stimp. is much larger, very hairy, and has the carapace almost completely covered with bits of shell, coral, sand, etc. *Inamathia crassa* A. M. E. was by far the largest species of Crustacean collected, some specimens being considerably over a foot in "spread." They were bright red and yellow, and the two largest specimens had the body and appendages covered with a species of barnacle. Two stout processes like horns extend forward from the rostrum, and two very long, sharp spines extend laterally from the margin of the carapace. A single specimen of *Inomalothic furcillatus* Stm. was dredged from a depth of one hundred fathoms. It has a very long body, which is produced forward into an immense rostrum bifurcating into two divergent horns. *Lispognathus thomsoni* Norman came up from a depth of two hundred fathoms, and is characterized by having much larger and longer chelipeds than most of the other Maioids. *Arachnopsis filipes* Stm. has three long cylindrical spines on the median line of the carapace. It seems to be rather common, as we took it at six different stations. *Inasimus latus* Rathb. is represented by a young specimen with very slender chelae. *Pyromaia cuspidata* Stm. also came from a depth of two hundred fathoms, and is aptly named from the two curved lateral spines which project from the lower side of the long, strong rostrum like the canine teeth from below the snout of a pig. *Pelia mutica* (Gibbes) is from shallow water near Key West, and is much stouter and shorter-legged than the preceding. Three species of *Macrocaloma* were secured. The largest, *M. septemspinosa* Stm., has a very stout body, armed, as the name indicates, with seven spines, three median, two lateral, and two in a line connecting the opposite lateral ones. The rostrum is produced into an expanded plate, bifurcated near its distal end. *Pericera cornuta caelata* A. M. E. was common, being secured at several stations. Some specimens of this species were so covered with sponge that their shape could not be distinguished, and their antennae must have been practically useless. The chelae are unusually small in this

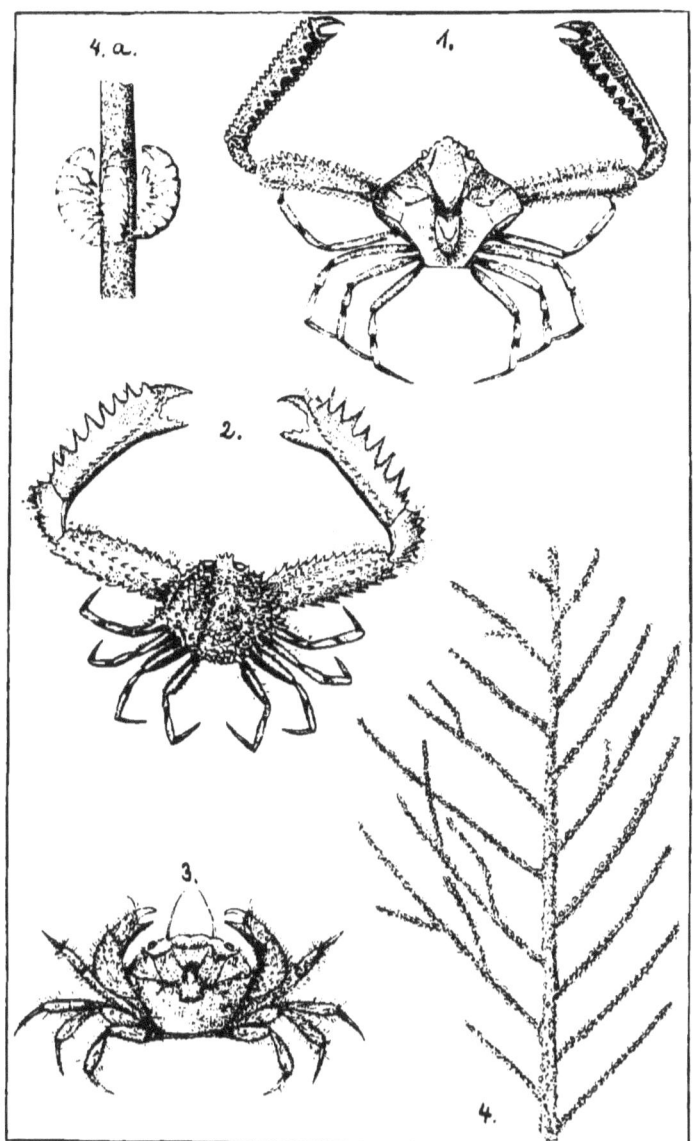

Crabs and Gorgonians from Pourtalès Plateau.

Fig. 1. SOLENOLAMBRUS TYPICUS. Stm.
Fig. 2. PLATYLAMBRUS SERRATUS. M. Edw.
Fig. 3. PILUMNUS GEMMATUS. Stimp.
Fig. 4. Gorgonian.
Fig. 4a. Magnified calicles.

group, but one would think that the formidable spines would render concealment rather a superfluous protection from most of its enemies. Three species of *Mithrax* were secured from comparatively shallow water. Indeed this genus is not represented in our collections from deep water.

The family PARTHNOPIDÆ is represented in the West Indies by numerous species of *Lambrus* and its allies, most of which are characterized by peculiarly shaped chelipeds, the hand being trigonal and greatly elongated, and the fingers very short. The old genus *Lambrus* has been divided by Milne Edwards into at least ten genera. *Platylambrus serratus* (M. E.) was found in shallow water both here and at the Tortugas, while *Lambrus pourtalesia* Stm. was found in abundance on the Pourtalès Plateau proper, and also in deep water off Havana, being one of the few species secured on both sides of the Gulf Stream from deep water. *Lambrus agonus* Stimp. has very long and slender chelipeds, and is one of the numerous species secured by Count Pourtalès during his memorable explorations of the Gulf Stream. The same is true of *Lambrus fraterculus* Stimp., with shorter chelipeds and a carapace longer than broad. The genus *Solenolambrus* was separated from *Lambrus* on account of its smooth, polished carapace and other more technical characters. Our specimen of *Solenolambrus typicus* Stimp. differs from all the other Maioids in the collection in being colored a bright blue, this color covering the whole of the body and appendages, with the exception of parts of the chelipeds. The hand has ten very regular and conspicuous scallops on the upper edge, and the edges of all joints of the chelipeds are beautifully crenulated. It came from a depth of about fifty fathoms. In the original description of this species, the color is not given. If our specimen is normal, we have here a very unusual coloration for a comparatively deep-water Crustacean, (this species having been taken in depths of from fifty to two hundred and forty-eight fathoms.) Almost all the other Crustacea secured by us from a greater depth than twenty fathoms were either lacking in bright color or were a deep, pure red,[1] a few having yellow markings. I have no recollection of any other species with any considerable amount of blue. *Cryptopodia concava* Stimp.[2] is found both on the Bahama Banks and on the Pourtalès Plateau.

About a dozen species of Cancroid crabs were collected here, representing as many genera. The largest species was *Bathynectes longispina* Stimp., which derives its name from the long spine projecting from the lateral angle of the carapace. Four smaller spines are found between it and the eye, and each of the last four joints of the chelipeds bears a spine on its upper front margin. A minute species of *Calappa, C. angusta* (M. E.), was dredged in about eighty fathoms not far from Key West. *Osachila tuberosa* Stimp. is peculiar in having the entire lower surface of the body and mouth-parts covered with irregular pits, giving a honey-combed appearance. Probably the most abundant crab on the Pourtalès Plateau is the little *Cyclodorippe nitida* A. M. Edw., which came up by the score at nearly every haul in the Gulf Stream. The general color is bright red, varied with white, and the surface is smooth and glossy. It is one of the species discovered by the "Blake." *Cymopolus asper* A. M. E. is another "Blake" species, with an exceedingly hispid surface and a considerable portion of the abdomen visible from above.

But three species of Anomuran crabs were collected in this region. One was the hermit crab *Cenobita diogenes* Latr., almost omnipresent on the sandy keys, especially Sand Key proper, where a bucket full was collected in a short time. The exposed portions of these animals are most brilliantly colored, the large claw being a clear dark blue, while the other exposed feet are bright red. Their favorite habitation seems to be the shell of *Astralium caelatum* Gmel., which is abundant here. This is, in fact, a hermit crab which has adopted a terrestrial habit almost, if not quite, as complete as

---

[1] Professor Verrill thinks that the red color, on account of the actinic properties of the pale-green light at great depths, is protective, only appearing bright when exposed to daylight.

[2] See p. 51.

that of the true land-crabs of the Bahamas. Those from Sand Key were most of them collected under the loose boards of the floor of an outhouse, where they fairly swarmed. It is a curious fact that these crabs are passionately fond of offal, which will so attract them that the vicinity will quickly be swarming with the hermits disporting themselves much after the manner of "tumble-bugs." Another hermit crab, *Eupagurus discoidalis* A. M. E. was brought up from a depth of two hundred fathoms.

The Macroura of the expedition have not yet been named, but the collection, though small, contains some striking forms. One species closely resembles the *Munida* figured on page 43 of "Three Cruises of the Blake." The chelipeds are greatly elongated, the fingers slender, and the back covered with transverse corrugations. The rostral spine is very sharp, and is flanked by a much shorter spine on each side. The abdomen seems to be habitually flexed, while the last walking leg is carried over the back. A number of specimens were brought up from a depth of about eighty fathoms. Another species apparently allied to this had a central rostral spine with two long sharp spines on each side. There is a row of anteriorly directed spines on the edge of the carapace, and one on each side of the first abdominal segment. The last pair of walking legs are very minute, and appear at first glance to be lacking. A further investigation shows, however, that they are tucked away out of sight under the flexed abdomen. The chelipeds are much more spiny than in the last species. Specimens of this form were dredged from one hundred and two hundred fathoms.

Perhaps the most beautiful Macrouran secured from the Pourtalès Plateau was a *Nematocarcinus*, which was of a brilliant red color. It differs from *N. ensiferus* S. I. Smith mainly in the much longer rostrum. This feature seems, however, to be quite variable both in length and curvature. In one specimen the rostrum is two and one-half inches long, more than half the length of the thorax and abdomen combined. In another it is very gracefully curved, and only an inch long. In each case it is strongly serrated on its upper edge. The antennae are enormously lengthened, projecting fully nine inches beyond the end of the rostrum and nearly a foot beyond the eyes. The walking legs are also greatly elongated, and are furnished with tufts of hair which are said to aid the animal in resting on the soft bottom. This species may be identical with *Nematocarcinus ensiferus*, but our specimens came from much shallower water than those secured by the "Blake," which were found in from eight hundred to fourteen hundred fathoms. Ours were taken from one hundred to one hundred and twenty fathoms.

Quite a number of specimens of the genus *Alpheus* were secured, belonging apparently to more than one species. Most of them were dredged from a depth of over one hundred fathoms, although all the specimens secured by the "Challenger" came from depths of less than sixty fathoms. On a previous page I was unable to explain the clicking noise made by the large chelae of these animals. Since that passage was in print, however, I find that Professor W. K. Brooks offers the following explanation: "The claw or dactyl is provided with a plug which fits into a well or socket in the other joint, and probably serves to prevent dislocation. When the forceps are opened the dactyl is raised so that the plug just rests in the mouth of the socket. As soon as the claw is released it is suddenly and violently closed, as if by a spring, and the solid, bony points striking together produce a sharp metallic report something like the click of a water-hammer, and so much like the noise of breaking glass that I have often, when awakened at night by the click of a little *Alpheus* less than an inch long, hastened down to the laboratory in the fear that a large aquarium had been broken."[1] In speaking of their pugnacious habits, the same writer says: "Watching its opportunity, it springs suddenly upon its enemy, instantly closing its claw with a violent snap and a loud report, and cutting a vertical sweep with its sharp edge. I have often seen *Alpheus*

[1] The Embryology and Metamorphosis of the Macroura, W. K. Brooks and F. H. Herrick, page 329.

heterochelis cut another completely in two by a single blow, and the victim is then quickly dismembered and literally torn to fragments."

Among the more aberrant forms of Crustaceans may be mentioned a *Gonodactylus* found in shallow water near Key West. A number of specimens of PYCNOGONIDA were collected, a group characterized by exceedingly elongated legs which are eight in number, and thus approach the spider type. Attempts have been made to homologize the different appendages with those of the ARACHNIDA, but this is considered impossible by Mr. Edmund B. Wilson, who has studied this group.[1] Several of our specimens show the egg-sacs attached to the ovigerous legs of the male. They all came from comparatively deep water, eighty to two hundred fathoms, and the eyes in all are either rudimentary or at least not well pigmented. To the non-specialist there appears to be three or four species in our material from the Pourtalès Plateau, one of which is probably an *Ascorhynchus*.

Four or five species of barnacles were secured from this region,—two of the *Balanus* type and two of the *Lepas* type. One of the former seemed specially addicted to attaching itself to the spines of a sea-urchin (*Dorocidaris papillata*). A very large *Lepas* was dredged from a depth of one hundred and twenty fathoms. Another and smaller form was found to be very abundant on the body and appendages of the largest crab taken in this region, *Anamathia crassa* A. M. E.

Very few worms were taken from the Pourtalès Plateau, and these were small, tube-dwelling forms. A number of large Brachiopods were dredged from a depth of about one hundred fathoms. They were apparently of two species, one belonging to the genus *Terebratula* and closely resembling the figure of *T. cubensis* Davidson. It is by far the less abundant of the two, at least in the series secured by us. The other species appears to be *Waldheimia floridana*. The admirable joint formed by the apposed margins of the two valves in this species is shown by the fact that a specimen will hold alcohol

[1] Bulletin Mus. Comp. Zoöl., Vol. VIII, No. 12, page 241.

without any perceptible leakage, and a long soaking in that fluid is necessary before the Brachiopod will become filled. Another interesting fact is the extreme thinness of these shells in comparison with those from shallow water.

About twenty species of mollusks were found here. Probably the most striking fact concerning them is the great preponderance of the Gastropods over the Lamellibranchs, only two species of the latter being found, and one of these (*Chione cingenda*) was a dead shell taken from shallow water near Key West. The only living species was a small *Arca*, from a depth of sixty fathoms, and hence not from the Pourtalès Plateau proper. With the above exceptions, all the specimens were Gastropods. A species of *Terebra* has a beautifully sculptured shell in the form of a greatly elongated cone, ornamented with revolving ridges with crescentic cross markings between. Among the rarities may be mentioned two specimens of *Voluta junonia* Chemn., which Tryon in his "Marine Mollusca of the United States," published in 1873, calls "the most rare and valuable American marine shell." Neither specimen was living, however, but one contained a hermit crab. A small and highly ornate *Fusus* (*F. eucosmius* Dall?), is characterized by fine revolving ridges and swollen varices. While the colors of these deep-water mollusks are seldom brilliant, the sculpturing and ornamentation of form renders them more beautiful, it seems to me, than their shallow-water representatives. A small species of *Columbella*, for instance, looks as if covered with regularly disposed rows of pearly beads, while superficial ornamentation would seem to reach the limit of extravagance in *Murex cabritii* Bernardi, which is found in shallower water and has the added beauty of a delicate pink color. This elegant mollusk has the anterior portion greatly elongated into a slender, straight spine beset with long, curved, horn-like processes which project at right angles. Similar spines ornament the varices of the shell. The species was found by the Blake as deep as one hundred and sixty-four fathoms. Three other species of *Murex* were secured, all having conspicuous spines. They seemed to be *M. nodatus* Reeve, *M. fulvescens* Sowerby, and *M. pomum* Gmel.[1]

The class Scaphopoda was represented by a beautiful *Dentalium*, probably *D. laqueatum* Verrill. This is a white species, less curved than many of the genus, and marked with deep longitudinal fluting.

A remark made by Dr. Dall, to the effect that hermit crabs which inhabit straight shells are themselves bilaterally symmetrical, is illustrated by a little hermit which had taken up its abode in one of these tube-like structures of the *Dentalium*. Upon removing the crab, it was found to be as straight and symmetrical as any normal Crustacean.

The reason for the beautiful surface ornamentation of many of the deep-water mollusks is not plain. It seems unlikely that the light produced by phosphorescence or otherwise could make it possible for these beauties to be seen, even if the molluscan eye were capable of such discernment. A certain beauty is of course imparted to these shells by their very delicacy, but the purely superficial lines and bead-like ornamentation is beautiful, aside from any quality of texture. Perhaps the best suggestion bearing on this point is made by Dr. W. H. Dall in the admirable discussion with which he introduces his report on the Mollusca of the "Blake." He says: "Much of the sculpture which is presented by the deep-sea species is particularly beautiful from its delicacy. There seems to be an especial tendency to strings of bead-like knobs, revolving striae and threads, and delicate transverse waves. It is particularly notable that many of the deep-sea forms, among all sorts of groups indifferently, have a row of knobs or pustules following the line of the suture and immediately in front of it. The representatives of the rock-purples, or Murices, a group which in shallow water frequent the rocks and stony places, and are then strongly knobbed or spinous, retain a similar character in the deeps, but the processes in question are extremely delicate or foliaceous, instead

---

[1] The author is here, as elsewhere, indebted to Mr. H. F. Wickham for the preliminary and approximate identification of *Mollusca*.

of being stout and strong. This is probably a reminiscence of the time when their distant progenitors were shallow water animals." [1]

The opinion seems quite general among those who have studied the animal life of the deep sea, that it has been peopled in a general way by a gradual invasion of forms which, originally adapted to the conditions of littoral surroundings, have encroached more and more upon the unoccupied territory in deeper water, where they were, for a time at least, free from the fierce competition to which shallow water forms are subjected. We can account, on this principle, for the ornamentation of the deep-water Mollusca by regarding it as merely the remnant of more conspicuous characters which have been of use to the ancestors of these forms before they retreated from the shallow water, where the structures forming the ornamentation were of use either as protective contrivances or as a means to attract the opposite sex.

The broken shell of an *Argonauta* (*argo?*) was all that we obtained during the cruise to represent these exquisitely delicate and beautiful animals. Indeed, it was the only Cephalopod found on the Pourtalès Plateau. The whole great group of Pteropods is also unrepresented in our collections, although we had expected surely to encounter some of them in this region.

Great numbers of Crinoids were collected here, but the species were comparatively few. The two common West Indian genera were represented, but none of the rarer forms were obtained. We especially regretted our failure to secure specimens of *Rhizocrinus*, a genus which is represented by abundant individuals in certain definite spots on the Pourtalès Plateau.

That there are portions of the sea bottom covered with as dense a growth of crinoids as any that flourished in Paleozoic seas, has been proved more than once by recent deep-sea explorations. We had ample demonstration of this fact on several occasions, notably when the tangles came up after a

[1] Bulletin Mus. Comp. Zoöl., Vol. XII, No. 6, page 184.

haul at a depth of one hundred and twenty fathoms.[1] As the bar neared the surface and the tangles themselves could be seen rising through the blue water, we noticed that a stream of brownish objects was trailing after it, as if innumerable mossy bits were floating away from the hemp strands. When the tangles came on board we found them literally covered with a mass of crinoids, all of one kind and quite small. We estimated that at least five hundred specimens came up in that haul, and it was evident that hundreds or thousands had washed off during the ascent of the tangles from the sea bottom. This was probably the greatest number of individuals of any one species obtained at a single haul during the entire cruise. The bottom must have been actually packed with them in spots. It appears that other expeditions secured almost as great numbers of *Rhizocrinus* at a single haul, and over a hundred specimens of *Pentacrinus* came up at once on the tangles while the "Blake" was working in the Caribbean. When we remember that these forms all seem to occur in isolated colonies where the individuals are very numerous, and that great areas of the sea bottom have never been touched by dredge or tangles, it becomes evident that the Crinoidea form a much more important element in the fauna of the great deep than most people, even zoölogists, suppose. This fact is still further emphasized when one examines the splendid volumes of the "Challenger" Report which are devoted to the Crinoidea and finds that over two hundred and fifty species of the COMATULÆ and some thirty species of the PENTACRINIDÆ are therein described and figured.

Probably no group of animals secured on the Pourtalès Plateau contained more that is of interest to the general naturalist than the class *Asteroidea*.[2] None of the star-fish were

[1] The bearing of this spot, as near as we could get it, is Sand Key Light, fifteen miles distant, bearing N. by W. ¼ W.

[2] The following approximate identifications were made mainly with the help of the "Challenger" Report on the *Asteroidea*, by W. Percy Sladen, F. L. S.

very large, but many were of unusual beauty. Several species of *Astropecten* were secured. One was a rather small species with a series of spines on the supero-marginal plates and several closely crowded rows on the infero-marginals. The abactinal surface was covered with paxillæ, with their beautiful radiating spinelets, resembling the spokes of a steering-wheel. Another *Astropecten* was about as large as the last, but had very few spines on the supero-marginal plates, and four very small lateral spines set in an oblique series on the infero-marginals. The paxillæ were crowned with a dense cluster of partially coalesced vertical spinelets. This species came from a depth of one hundred and ten fathoms. The interesting genus *Luidia* is represented by *L. alternata* (Say), a large, slender-rayed form bristling with long, marginal spines, which are chocolate brown basally and pure white distally. The paxillæ have each a stout, vertical spine set in its centre. The two lateral rows of paxillæ are without this spine. Quite small specimens are white throughout in alcohol, while larger individuals have the spines colored as in the adult, but the disk white, as in the young. Other specimens, possibly of a distinct species, have all the paxillæ bearing comparatively short, blunt spines. Like others of the genus, these specimens exhibited an aggravating tendency to shed their rays, so that a really complete specimen is hard to find. They came from shallow water near Key West.

The family GYMNASTERIIDÆ is represented by *Poronia* sp., a small pentagonal form with the lower inter-radial spaces nearly bare, there being only a few isolated spines on the smooth plates. The marginal plates bear a very beautiful ornamentation in the shape of two series of fan-shaped tufts of spines, giving very much the appearance of the peculiar scallops resulting from the use of the old-fashioned pinking-iron on cloth. There are two series of interambulacral spines. The single specimen of this pretty star-fish came from a depth of about one hundred and ten fathoms. A species which I take to be an *Anthenoides* has gracefully tapering arms and very conspicuous marginal plates, the upper series of which are contingent on the outer portion of the ray. The entire dorsal surface of the animal is covered with a pavement of polygonal plates closely set with granules.

The order Cryptozonia was instituted by Sladen to include the star-fishes with inconspicuous marginal plates. It contains most of the prizes among the Asteroidea from the Pourtalès Plateau. An *Ophidiaster*, resembling *O. tuberifer* Sladen has the dorsal plates arranged in regular longitudinal series alternating with eight rows of spaces for dermal tentacles or papulæ. On the actinal surface of the rays just outside of the spines is a row of very peculiarly modified pedicellariæ, which are large and sessile with holes countersunk in the plates on either side. The rays are very slender and the disk small, giving the animal a striking resemblance to *Zoroaster ackleyi* as figured in the narrative of the Blake. Coming to the family Solasteridæ, we find several remarkable forms. One looks like a five-armed *Crossaster*, but probably belongs to the genus *Lophaster* of Verrill, characterized by two rows of marginal paxillæ which are long and crowned with dense tufts of spines. The whole dorsal surface is covered with similar but smaller tufts. Another specimen, which may be a young individual of this same species, has only four rays, making a cross. This seems to be normal and not the result of mutilation. The interambulacral spines bear clusters of minute spinelets on their summits. Several specimens of a species probably belonging to the genus *Korethaster* were dredged near the one-hundred-fathom line. They are small, pentagonal specimens, with a highly vaulted disk resembling that of the last species. The actinal surface, however, was quite different, being covered with long, flat spines. The paxillæ are very long and apparently composed of agglutinated spines whose tips are separated. It differs from the type of the genus in having dermal tentacles on the dorsal surface. Species of this strange genus were found by the "Blake" at a depth of two hundred fathoms.

It was among the Asteridæ, however, that the most striking forms of star-fish were found. The most abundant, perhaps, was a little six-rayed species with rays unsymmetrically developed, giving the appearance of immature specimens. The largest was not over three-fourths of an inch in diameter. There were two rows of interambulacral spines. The most beautiful of all was a species closely related to *Asterias volsellata* Sladen, which was discovered by the "Challenger" near the coast of Japan. Our specimens were small, the largest being about two and one-half inches in diameter. This superbly ornamented star-fish has eleven arms which are very slender and abruptly differentiated from the disk, reminding one of the serpent-stars. Each ray has two lateral and a dorsal series of long, stout spines, and around the middle of each spine is packed a globular cluster of pedicellariae, as if a white bead were strung on each spine, giving an exceedingly elegant and graceful style of ornamentation. Another row of these spines, likewise ornamented with the globular clusters of pedicellariae, is placed between the dorsal and lateral rows on each arm. The dorsal surface bears a large number of dermal tentacles. The interambulacral plates bear two series of long spines. The ambulacral feet are large and greatly protruded in our specimens. One individual had twelve instead of eleven arms, and another had lost nine out of its eleven, but had evidently not given up the fight, as nine new arms were sprouting in their proper places around the disk. Another specimen, perhaps representing a separate species, had but ten arms and each globular bundle of pedicellariae was borne on the summit of a spine, giving an exceedingly elegant effect. Indeed this particular specimen is the most beautiful star-fish that we secured during the trip. Another *Asterias* belonging, as did the last, to the sub-genus Stolasterias, has but five rays. The spines are ornamented with the little globular bundles of pedicellariae. There is a well marked median dorsal row of spines, two lateral rows and two between the dorsal and lateral rows. On the ventral surface there are two rows of interambulacral spines pointing at right angles to each other. Next there is a row of simple spines without pedicellariae, and then comes the lateral row

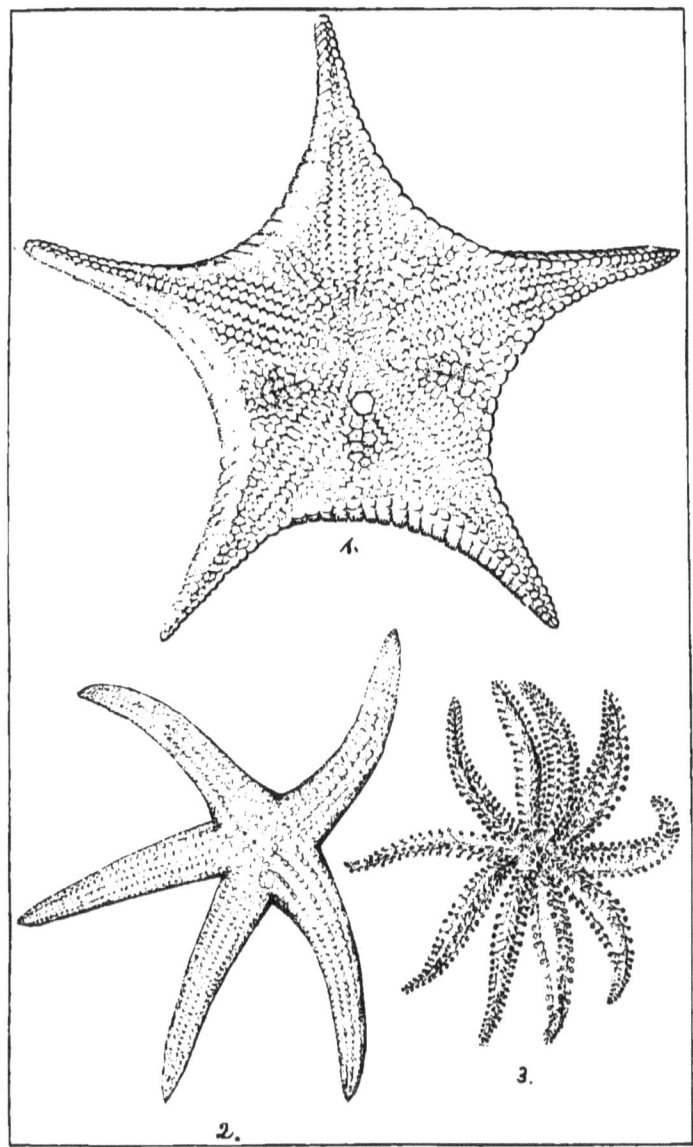

Starfish from Pourtalès Plateau.

Fig. 1. ANTHENOIDES (?) sp.
Fig. 2. OPHIDIASTER (?) sp.
Fig. 3. ASTERIAS sp., near VOLCELLATA Sladen.

bearing a half globe of pedicellariae, on their upper surfaces. At the bases of these last are very large sessile pedicellariae. These specimens were about four inches in diameter, and came from a depth of seventy to eighty fathoms.

A species belonging to the PENTAGONASTERIDÆ agrees in almost every detail with the unusually complete description given by Sladen for the genus *Leptogonaster*, although it also agrees superficially with the figure given of *Anthenoides piercei* (Perrier) secured by the Blake. Our specimen has no pedicellariae on the dorsal surface; the disk is large; the arms taper gradually to a slender point; the upper surface is covered with polygonal plates, between which numerous papulæ appear; there is a well marked ridge on the supero-marginal plates; the infero-marginal plates are armed on their external edges with a row of spines; the actinal surface is covered with granulated plates; the interambulacral plates are armed with fan-shaped groups of spines, immediately outside of which is another series of larger and stouter spines, and outside of these a row of very large, procumbent pedicellariae; diameter about five inches; depth eighty fathoms.

One of the most noticeable things about the OPHIURIDÆ was their tendency to appear in great quantities of individuals belonging to a single species, as if they lived in definite spots of the sea bottom which were densely crowded with certain species to the exclusion of others. Professor Alexander Agassiz has noted this peculiarity of the fauna of the Pourtalès Plateau, and his observation was amply confirmed by our experience, more particularly in connection with the serpent-stars. The number of species was not very great, but the individuals were in surprising quantities. The most extensive colony of any one species of Ophiuran that the writer has ever seen was not here, however, but in the Bay of Fundy, where in dredging the channel between two islands, the dredge came up time after time filled to the top with *Ophiopholis bellis* Lym, and a species of coralline.

Among the OPHIURIDÆ or serpent-stars, probably the most abundant species was a small white *Ophioglypha*, with the disk covered with scale-like plates, large, triangular, radial shields, a fringe of scale-like genital plates extending around over the bases of the arms, and very long arm-joints. The actinal surface was peculiar in the round, scale-fringed pores for the tentacles, the very large mouth-shields, the slender side mouth-shields, and three curiously shaped mouth-papillæ. There were three very short arm-spines, the middle one being the shortest. Another species closely allied to the last has much longer arm-spines and differently shaped arm-plates. They came from comparatively shallow water. A small species of *Amphiura* has two mouth-papillæ, one tentacle-scale, and six unequal arm-spines. Depth about one hundred and thirty fathoms. The genus *Ophiocoma* is represented by a single species and a single specimen. The disk is closely covered with stumpy nodules or blunt spines, there are two tentacle-scales, five or six arm-spines, five mouth-papillæ, and very numerous, closely set, tooth-papillæ. The mouth-shield is very large and roughly heart-shaped. A species of *Ophiocamax* dredged from near the one-hundred-fathom line shows an approach to *Astrophyton* in its spiniform mouth-papillæ and tooth-papillæ, although in other respects it is a typical serpent-star. The disk is symmetrically studded with spinulose stumps, and the radial shields are small and triangular. There are nine long arm-spines which bear spinelets over their entire surface instead of along the sides only. A still nearer approach to the basket-fish type is found in a species of *Ophiomyxa*, which has four arm-spines that are larger and sharper than in *O. flaccida*. Our specimens came from a depth of twenty to sixty fathoms.

But the greatest surprise revealed by our dredges and tangles while working on the Pourtalès Plateau was the great quantity of ASTROPHYTIDÆ, both simple-armed and branched. As in the preceding group, we were constantly struck with the tendency on the part of single species to occur in great numbers on definite spots of the sea bottom. Especially was this true of the simple-armed forms, a group which none of us had seen before our experience off the Cuban coast. On

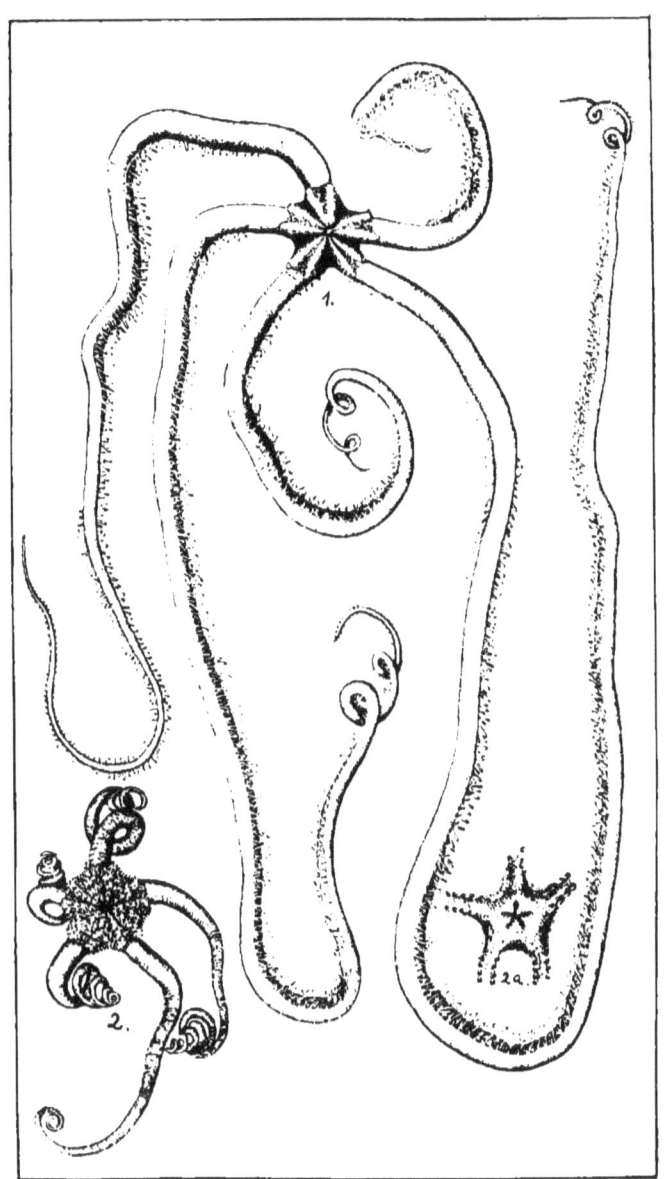

Simple-armed Basket Fish from Pourtalès Plateau.

Fig. 1. OPHIOCREAS LUMBRICUS, Lyman.
Fig. 2. ASTROGOMPHUS VALLATUS, Lyman.
Fig. 2a. Disk of same, ventral view.

the Pourtalès Plateau some of these forms came up by the hundreds, and proved that they were even more abundant than the regular serpent-stars. The most common and striking species of this interesting group was *Ophiocreas lumbricus* Lyman, in which the sharply defined radial ridges run nearly to the centre of the disk. The spine-like tentacle-scales are in pairs, the lower being about twice the length of an arm-joint. The whole animal is covered with a smooth skin, and the long arms look like earth-worms; hence the name,— "lumbricus." Alcoholic specimens give no adequate idea of these striking forms. They were very conspicuous as they came up on the dredge or tangles, being of a bright orange color. The rays of the largest specimen were fully two feet long, making a spread of *over four feet* for the entire animal. This is the largest measurement that I have heard of for any Ophiuran. The disk itself is not over one inch in diameter, seeming ridiculously small in proportion to the length of the rays. It can easily be imagined that we were somewhat excited when the first deep-water haul in that region brought up a dozen or so of these brilliant creatures. It was no easy matter, however, to extricate the long, snake-like arms from the tangles and from each other. In fresh specimens there is no indication of the arm-joints, giving a particularly smooth and even polished appearance to the arms. This species formed the type of the genus *Ophiocreas* described by Lyman from specimens brought back by the "Blake." We secured a large series from depths varying from ninety to two hundred fathoms. Indeed this seems to be one of the most characteristic forms of the plateau. Another extremely abundant simple-armed basket-fish is *Astrogomphus vallatus* Lyman, another generic type yielded by the investigation of the "Blake" material. This species, although not so conspicuous, is even more numerous in individuals than the last. The arms are much shorter in proportion than in *Ophiocreas*, and the entire surface is strongly hispid. The disk is armed with radiating lines and concentric circles of stumpy, thorny spines, while the arms are annulated with rings of thorny granules and roll in a vertical direction, a true trade-mark of the ASTROPHYTIDÆ. A very prominent row of stout papillæ reaches between the bases of adjacent arms, separating the upper from the lower surface of the disk. The mouth-papillæ and teeth are all spiniform. The tentacle-scales are usually four in number, and are crowned with a clump of spines. There are minute hooklets on the granules on the dorsal surface of the arms. This species is corn-color in life, and has the most rigid arms of any Ophiuran with which I am acquainted, and its numerous spines, together with a habit of rolling the arms up into a tight coil, made it exceedingly troublesome to extricate from the tangles.

Coming to the typical basket-fish, i. e., those with branched arms, we have first to notice a magnificent specimen that came up on the anchor one morning near Sand Key. This was *Astrophyton costosum* Seba, the same species as that found at the Tortugas; but this particular specimen was a remarkably fine one, and richly deserved our thanks for its thoughtfulness in climbing onto our anchor and being hauled aboard. This species does not appear to be so brittle as *A. agassizii* Stimp. Another species was from much deeper water, and was quite common below the one-hundred-fathom line. This is *Astrophyton mucronatum* Lyman, and is characterized by high radial ribs, each bearing an irregular double row of conspicuous thorny spines. The center of the disk is depressed and crowded with similar but smaller spines. The proximal portions of the arms are also ornamented with spines and marked with cross-bars of brown, the general color of the animal being a light, buffy yellow. There is but one madreporic body, and the tentacle-scales are considerably smaller than in other species. The granules on the distal branches of the arms bear hooklets resembling those found on *Astrogomphus vallatus*, with which it was frequently associated. This species was brought up clinging to deep-water gorgonians.

About fifteen species of Echinoidea were secured. These, also, were found in definite spots where there were innumerable individuals of certain species, apparently to the exclusion of others. This was particularly noticeable in the case of *Dorocidaris papillata* A. Ag., which repeatedly came up on the tangles by the hundred, and became a sore trial to our patience, the serrated spines being especially difficult to disengage from the tangles. Indeed, this labor became one of our main occupations while on the Pourtalès Plateau. *Dorocidaris bartletti* A. Ag. is a beautiful species with the spines banded with red and white. *Dorocidaris blakei* A. Ag. is regarded by its describer as "perhaps the most interesting of the recent CIDARIDÆ." All of our specimens, unfortunately, were without the peculiar fan-shaped spines or radioles which constitute the most striking peculiarity of the species. The characters of the test were well marked, however. *Cidaris tribuloides* Bl. was also secured.

Cœlopleurus floridanus A. Ag. was probably the most beautiful of the true sea-urchins collected at this time, some specimens being considerably larger than those secured off Havana. Not only are the long, slender spines brilliantly colored with carmine and white or orange, but the test itself is equally striking with its alternate chocolate and orange zones, making it resemble the gorgeously colored balls in which children delight. The largest sea-urchin secured during the entire cruise came from a depth of one hundred and five fathoms. This was a huge specimen of *Asthenosoma hystrix* A. Ag., a representative of an ancient group of Echini, with flexible tests and overlapping coronal plates. This specimen was seven inches across the test, and was swollen out, when it came on deck, to the regulation outline for a sea-urchin, although Agassiz says that the Challenger specimens in alcohol were "as flat as pocket handkerchiefs, and were naturally regarded as flat sea-urchins, although, of course, endowed with great mobility of test."[1] Our specimen gave us a good idea of the temperature of the bottom, for it was inflated with water which had not yet been warmed by the surface heat, and felt icy cold to the hands. We soon discovered, however,

[1] "Three Cruises of the 'Blake,'" Vol. II, p. 94.

that it was not an animal to be handled with impunity, as its spines, although small, were exceedingly sharp, and inflicted a wound so painful as to suggest some poisonous properties. The specimen was of a dull vinaceous color.

A few specimens of *Echinometra subangularis* Desml. were found in comparatively shallow water. Two representatives of the sculptured sea-urchins such as flourished during tertiary times were secured. One was *Temnechinus maculatus* A. Ag., characterized by a single large anal plate and radiate excavations around the primary tubercles, and the other, *Trigonocidaris albida* A. Ag., having four large, unequal anal plates and the test beautifully ornamented with radiating ridges as if a thread had been wound around and around the test between the spines. The pedicellariae are more conspicuous than in most species, and the buccal membrane is set with large, apparently imbricating plates. Both of these sculptured species are very small in comparison with the others collected by us, and are light colored, the former being light green and the latter a buffy white. They are abundant on the Pourtalès Plateau from eighty to two hundred and fifty fathoms. *Echinus gracilis* A. Ag. is another abundant species, which is much more conspicuous than the last, being brightly colored and the largest species from this region excepting *Asthenosoma hystrix*. It is almost globular in form, and the test is a vivid green with vertical series of sharply defined, diamond-shaped white markings. The spines are white, short, and somewhat sparse. Next to *Dorocidaris papillata*, this was the most abundant species of sea-urchin found on the plateau.

Only two species of Clypeastrids were collected here. *Clypeaster subdepressus* Ag. is a flat species with the centrodorsal region somewhat abruptly raised into a dome-shaped eminence. This species is particularly interesting from its unusual distribution, being found on the African coast and off the coast of Florida. I have not heard of its occurrence between these widely separated localities. It was dredged from a depth of about sixty fathoms. *Palaeotropus josephenae* Loren is the only representative of the Petalosticha that we secured.

This is a small form with two genital openings and sparse spines. It has also been found near the Azores. We found it in depths from one hundred and ten to two hundred fathoms.

The Cœlenterates, with the exception of the hydroids, collected by us in this region, have not as yet received more than passing attention. It is evident, however, that the group is richly represented in the collection, and contains many striking forms not ordinarily found in the museums of educational institutions.

Among the Alcyonaria perhaps the most common form is a beautiful species which I take to be a *Caligorgia* perhaps *C. gracilis* M. Edw. Some specimens attain a height of two feet. They branch in a palmate manner, the main stem giving off alternate pinnæ which may again divide in the same plane, forming a graceful flabellate structure. The calicles are arranged in whorls of three to seven or eight, and are bent inward at their summits and covered with beautifully marked scales. The color of the colony is a buffy light yellow, but when dried it is pure white and exceedingly brittle. The little whorls of calicles appear like small white beads strung at regular intervals along the branches. Another common gorgonian seems to belong to the genus *Platycaulus* Wright. It is much smaller than the last, of a bright red color, and flabellate in shape. The branching is very irregular, and the branches occasionally anastomose. The calicles are on the sides of the branches, leaving the front and back bare. The polyps are protected with spicules and retract into verruciform calicles. This species is a very brilliantly colored one, and came from our deeper dredgings in considerable abundance.

Some very beautiful specimens of *Isis* were taken from a depth of about one hundred and twenty fathoms. This coral is peculiar in having a jointed appearance, owing to ivory-white joints composed of limestone, alternating with shorter brown, corneous, or horny joints. The whole colony attains a height of about two feet, and the terminal branches are exceedingly slender and erect, giving an appearance of unusual delicacy and grace. Another very strange form came up in the shape of long, harsh, hair-like filaments which were unbranched and seemed to have a spiral twist. They looked so much like horse-hair that some one facetiously ventured the suggestion that they were hairs from the sea-horse's tail. This is one of the Antipatharian corals, a group characterized by having a flexible, horny axis beset with thorns, while the polyps have the unusual primitive number of six tentacles. Our species would belong to the genus *Cirrhipathes*, according to Milne Edwards' arrangement. Some of these specimens attain a height of nearly three feet, and came from a depth of about sixty fathoms. Another species belonging to this family is quite different in shape, having numerous pinnately disposed branches, which are very long in proportion to the height of the colony, about three inches. It came from deeper water than the last, and does not seem to be so abundant.

Passing now to the regular corals, we find that a number of the simple corals of the Cyathophylloid type are included in the collection. They cannot, however, be even approximately identified with the literature at hand, unless we except *Rhizotrochus fragilis* Pourtalès and *Haplophyllia paradoxa* Pourtalès.[1] Several species were secured in considerable quantities. One of these, probably a *Thecopsammia*, was a bright red when it came up in the dredge.

We were greatly surprised to see a number of specimens of *Oculina*, perhaps *O. arbuscula* Lesson, come up in the dredge where the soundings indicated a depth of eighty fathoms. The specimens were fresh, and had evidently been in place when caught by the dredge. Several cyathophylloid corals came up at the same time. I have seen no record of reef-building species being found at such a depth. It does not seem possible that there was an abrupt elevation upon which the *Oculina* was growing, as this would have been perceptible by the feel of the dredge rope.

[1] The writer wishes to take occasion to acknowledge the great aid he has enjoyed in his work by constant reference to the many excellent figures in Alexander Agassiz' "Three Cruises of the 'Blake.'"

Among the Hydrocorallinæ were several very beautiful forms originally described by Count Pourtalès. *Pliobothrus symmetricus* Pourtalès was dredged from a depth of one hundred fathoms. Agassiz says that it was found by the "Porcupine" north of the British Islands at a depth of six hundred fathoms. *Distichopora* sp. is another form which assumes a flabellate outline and is often as symmetrical as the last. Many specimens of this latter were of a beautiful deep salmon, or even red, color, and still retain an exquisite flush. Our specimens have the calicles placed in furrows which run along the edges of the fronds between two small ridges. The front and back are ornamented by peculiar swollen nodules. Another species, which I take to be *Allopora miniacea* Pourtalès, grows in foliaceous masses of considerable size. There was another specimen, apparently of a separate species.

Several kinds of anemones were secured, some from considerable depths. We were only partially successful in preserving these beautiful, but untractable, forms. Repeated attempts at narcotizing them with tobacco and alcohol met with very indifferent success, and the several methods of injecting with hot chemicals were no better in their results. Even those that came out comparatively well had lost all the glory of their brilliant colors long before they reached Iowa.

Owing to causes already referred to, we were unable to do any satisfactory work in surface collecting while the vessel was at sea, and this probably accounts for the almost complete absence of medusæ and Siphonophores from our collection. On one occasion, however, while hauling in the dredge from a considerable depth, we noticed a long string of pellucid, club-shaped bodies wound around the iron dredge-rope. On attempting to disentangle them from the rope we received severe stings from the nematocysts with which the creature was armed. This we took to be *Pterophysa grandis* Fewkes, a Siphonophore which was caught in the same way by the "Blake." We estimated that the entire colony must have been twenty-five or thirty feet long. The appendages were eight to twelve inches apart. In the alcoholic specimen the central cord is so shrunken and twisted that the "tasters" are usually less than one-half inch apart. Other sets of appendages are doubtless tactile organs and reproductive persons. The anterior end of the colony is furnished with a float containing a bubble of oil or gas. A microscopic investigation showed that the nematocysts are after the pattern found in the Portuguese man-o'-war, being almost globular and having the thread coiled in a regular spiral. The thread-cells in the *Pterophysa* were considerably larger, apparently, than those of the *Physalia*. Their sting seemed to be felt more quickly, but the pain did not last so long. It was also noticed that they could not effect the palms of the hands, but were quite severe when applied to the opposing lateral surfaces of the fingers, or back of the hand.

A rich harvest of hydroids was secured here, twenty-three species, many of them new, or otherwise of special interest, being noted in the collection.[1] Indeed nearly half of these species are apparently new, a fact which will indicate the real importance of this part of our work.

Halecium filicula Allman was secured at depths of from fifty-six to two hundred fathoms, and two new species were added to this genus. One of these was a particularly beautiful form, having the margins of the hydrophores gracefully reflected, and showing the mysterious circles of brilliant dots like necklaces of jewels, an ornamentation as beautiful as it is inexplicable. Another new species of this genus is still more striking, having very large cylindrical hydrophores with numerous margins which are abruptly rolled outward and have very brilliant "necklaces." The hydranths are unusually large and capable of great expansion. An elegant new form of branching Campanularian, probably an *Obelia*, has very thin, glassy, sub-conical hydrothecae, the upper parts of which are thrown into longitudinal folds or pleatings, which,

---

[1] The author wishes to note the very faithful work of Professor S. Stookey and Miss Margaret Williams in attending to the Hydroida during the cruise. The really superb collections of these forms are due largely to their painstaking care and perseverance.

with the deeply serrate margins, impart a particularly ornate appearance. The genera *Hebella*, *Cryptolaria* and *Grammaria* were each represented by new forms.

The SERTULARIDÆ was but poorly represented, their being only two species, *Sertularella gaya Var. robusta* Allman, and *S. distans* Allman.[1] The PLUMULARIDÆ, however, came up in quantities, and constantly elicted exclamations of surprise and delight at their exquisite grace and beauty. Some were of monstrous size for this group, reaching a height of two feet or more. Among the more notable prizes were two species of Allman's genus *Schizotricha*, a genus hitherto unrepresented in the West Indian region. The name is descriptive of the fact that the pinnæ are divided or split into two branches. I am inclined to believe that one of these branches is merely a modified phylactogonium, a specialized branch for the protection of the reproductive organs. Two species of *Plumularia*, *P. attenuata* Allman and *P. geminata* Allman, were collected from rather deep water. The beautiful genus *Aglaophenia* was represented by three species originally described by Allman, *A. apocarpa*, *A. gracilis* and *A. rigida*. There has been considerable discussion regarding the validity of the last two species. They were described originally with the reproductive portion or gonosome of *A. gracilis* unknown. Afterward, Dr. J. Walter Fewkes seems to have found the gonosome of the latter, and considered it the same as that of *A. rigida*, and seemed inclined to regard the two species as identical. Our specimens, however, show the gonosome to be quite different from that of *A. rigida*, the corbula having about ten pairs of entirely free leaflets with a row of nematophores on both sides of each leaflet. The trophosome has been compared with specimens in the Museum of Comparative Zoölogy at Cambridge identified by Clarke, and they were found to agree. A new species of *Aglaophenia* secured by us has a very large and ornate corbula which varies greatly in length in different specimens. The leaflets are numerous, twelve

---

[1] This name is preoccupied, having been used by both LaMarck and Lamouroux early in the present century.

or more, and are greatly expanded, the front edge of each extending forward and upward over the one in front. Each leaflet has a row of nematophores along its free margin, a strong double process at its base, and a series of distinct narrow ridges leading from these nematophores directly toward the base of each leaflet, giving a remarkably beautiful radiating style of ornamentation, making this the most ornate corbula in the collection.

Two species of unusual size represent the genus *Cladocarpus*. The first, *C. paradisea* Allman, is well named. It is hard to keep from using extravagant language when describing these surpassingly graceful and striking forms. The other species was described by Allman under the name *Aglaophenia sigma* from specimens destitute of the gonosome. Our series shows the gonosome, and demonstrates the fact that it belongs to *Cladocarpus*, having the typical gonosome of that genus. Both of these species attain a height of about two feet.

One of the prizes encountered among the hydroids is a species of *Idia* dredged from shallow water near Key West. Only one species has hitherto been known which was so unique that it was made the type of a new family by Allman. The original form was found near the Philippine Islands and off Bahia. The characteristic urn-shaped gonangia were well shown in our specimens. They are among the most beautiful of all the various structures developed for the protection of the reproductive zoöids among the hydroids.

No attempt has as yet been made to study the deep-water sponges of the collection, nor can the general zoölogist hope to do anything with this difficult group. Judging from the figures in Professor Alexander Agassiz' "Three Cruises of the 'Blake,'" it appears that we secured among others the following species of silicious sponges belonging to the HEXAC-TINELLIDÆ: *Eurete facunda*, a species formed of anastomosing cylinders of the most delicate lace-work; *Aphrocallistes bocagei*, with an equally beautiful network of silicious spicules forming series of prominences like finger tips; *Tisiphonia fenestrata*, which usually assumes a more or less globular form, with long, sharp, needle-like spicules radiating from the surface; *Phakellia tenax*, a flabellate form strangely resembling some of the sea-fans, with freely anastomosing branches covered with projecting bristles or spicules, giving the appearance of a fur or felt. The color of this species when fresh is brown, but this color fades out to a gray after long immersion in alcohol.

This ends our hurried survey of the assemblage of animal forms secured from the Pourtalès Plateau, and the shallower water between it and the reefs, a region of surpassing interest to the naturalist, or to any one else who can be interested in Nature's handiwork. This was probably the most profitable part of our cruise, although there were no such striking novelties as the Pentacrini. The collection as a whole was of greater scientific interest than any secured from other localities. The amount of labor involved in bringing up these thousands of specimens from the sea bottom, and caring for them after they were secured, was at times calculated to destroy the enthusiasm of any but the most persistent workers. But our young men and women labored most faithfully day after day in the intense heat without complaint, and with cheerful compliance with every reasonable demand made upon their energies. The time was emphatically well spent, and the educational value of constantly handling and observing so many and varied animal types was incalculable.

CHAPTER VII.

HARBOR ISLAND AND SPANISH WELLS.

On Saturday, July 1st, our vessel cleared from Key West for the port of Harbor Island, Eleuthera, British West Indies, after having all the water casks refilled with good water at a cost of one cent per gallon. The customs officials at Key West were extremely courteous, and facilitated our affairs so far as the law would permit. We were given a hint by one of them that would probably have saved us many a dollar had we been able to act upon it at the proper time. We were told that a "yachting license" could have been secured before starting, which would have rendered it unnecessary to enter and clear at the various ports at which we desired to touch, and thus saved a really serious source of delay and annoyance. We had, indeed, inquired at Baltimore if there were not some way to simplify matters, but were told by the brokers that we would have to be treated exactly as any trading or passenger vessel. Our informant was not an entirely disinterested party, however, and I should advise anyone who, in the future, desires to charter a vessel for a purpose similar to ours, to make every effort to find a way to avoid a part, at least, of the endless red tape, which is doubtless necessary for the interests of the merchant marine, but a useless farce for a scientific expedition. As it was, life was made a burden to some of us while in port by the exactions of the custom-house regulations, which seemed to us to bear a very close resemblance to the procedure in the "circumlocution office," so well depicted by Dickens.

In the evening we dropped down the channel, but were becalmed before passing Sand Key Light, and anchored for the night. A boat was sent to take off a lot of coral, principally *Madrepora palmata* Linn., which had been left to bleach about ten days before on a little sand key near the Eastern Dry Rocks. The storm of the preceding Saturday had raised a sea, which broke clear over the little islet, and buried most of the coral under the sand. We found that many of the specimens were uninjured and beautifully bleached. One in particular was a perfectly symmetrical corallum of *M. palmata*, with numerous broad fronds rising in whorls one above another. This superb but fragile specimen was the prize cabinet coral of the whole collection, and the object of much solicitude. We hardly dared hope to succeed in getting it to Iowa City intact, but our care was rewarded by success, and the specimen is now in the museum, a flawless, symmetrical type of what is really one of the most beautiful of all West Indian corals, although the fragments usually exhibited in our museums would fail to indicate any grace or beauty. The "long boat," as we called the largest ship's boat, originally built for the navy, was placed on the deck and braced right side up on an even keel. It was then filled with the branching corals, which were thus comparatively safe and in an excellent place to complete the bleaching process. The plug was taken out of the boat, and the corals drenched with salt water several times a day, and then exposed to the full force of the sun.

On Monday, July 3rd, light head-winds were encountered, but some progress was made with the aid of the Gulf Stream, which we were now crossing for the third time. Had a calm set in, we would doubtless have been carried through the Florida Straits to the north of the Island of Abaco. Most of this day was spent in packing that part of the coral which was fairly well bleached. Several of the largest heads of *Madrepora* were carefully wound with strands of Italian hemp rope, so that each branch was fully supported by several others. The specimens were then crated separately, each being slung in its crate by ropes so that it could not touch the wood at any point. This method had the further advantage of furnishing a certain degree of spring to the support, so that any sudden jar to the crate would be greatly lessened before it was communicated to the coral. The effectiveness of this method of packing was demonstrated by the excellent condition in which these large heads arrived at Iowa City, after a journey of about twelve hundred miles by sea and a thousand miles in a freight car. Such specimens as were not too large we packed with hay in barrels, using great care and not permitting one specimen to be in contact with another.

While under way, the alcoholic specimens which had been in the tanks for several days were taken out and placed in the pans, which were soldered together, as described on page 56. Two members of the party always attended to this soldering, at which they soon became quite proficient, and it was surprising to see the amount of material that could be safely disposed of in a couple of hours. The result showed that specimens preserved in this way were even safer than those kept in alcohol. Should the alcohol be a little too weak, as is sometimes the case, the specimens are irretrievably ruined. As a matter of fact, none of the material in the pans was injured, save a few specimens that were spotted with rust.

During the whole of our cruise the evenings were delightful almost without exception. No matter how hot the day, there was no discomfort from heat in the evening nor during the night. The "dog-watch" (from six to eight P. M.) was our time for social enjoyment, and then the whole party would usually be seated on the top of the cabin and on the quarter-rail, engaged in singing and story-telling. The hard work of the day made this evening hour all the brighter, and every one was then good-natured and happy. At such times we were at peace with the world, and often sat late into the night in the stern-sheets or on the "lazy-board," either in quiet conversation or in silent communion with the spirit of Old Ocean, watching the flashing of the phosphorescence in the wake of the schooner, or listening to the hissing of the waters along the side. Then each would roll up in his blanket and stretch out on the cabin top, gazing upward at the moon or watching the sweep of the main-gaff between us and the starry heavens, until we were lulled to sleep by the swinging of the schooner as she "rocked in the cradle of the deep." The writer has been to sea in various craft, but believes that on a sailing vessel alone can the real delights of sea-life be found. What does a passenger on a modern Atlantic liner know of the poetry of the world of waters, or of the spirit and moods of the wind and sky and ocean?

The morning of July 4th, found us at sea, with no land in sight. As good patriots we decided that the day must be appropriately celebrated. At breakfast the ladies had a surprise in the shape of pretty souvenir cards with designs in water-colors, and original verses. Each wore the national colors, secured by cutting up an old flag, and the steward was appropriately decorated with a red, white and blue cap. Coming on deck we found "old glory" at the mast-head, and under it the old gold pennant of the State University of Iowa. Every gun on the vessel was brought up and the flag and pennant saluted with a volley each. Cheering was indulged in "ad libitum," and the sweet familiar strains of "America," "Star Spangled Banner," "The Red, White and Blue," etc., brought the tears to many eyes. It may well be doubted whether a profounder love for country was felt by any American citizens that day than stirred the hearts of the members of the "Bahama Expedition." At dinner we were regaled with the chief remaining luxury on board, i. e., a meat pie with canned turkey as its main ingredient.

At noon a calm set in, and we experienced some of the most intense heat met with during our voyage. It only lasted about two hours, however, after which a light breeze sprung up, which proved a head-wind, and of course less welcome on that account.

That night a sudden squall struck the schooner after we were all asleep on the cabin top. The wind did not seem particularly violent, but it suddenly ceased altogether, and the schooner rolled more outrageously than at any other time during the voyage. The heavy main-boom "slatted" so violently that it broke loose and came near doing serious damage before we again had it under control. Below could be heard the smashing of crockery and glass-ware. Investigation showed that very little damage had been done, although we feared the loss of a considerable portion of the jars and dishes which were stored in racks.

On Wednesday, July 5th, the wind was at last in our favor, and the schooner was able to hold her course across the Bahama Banks. The clear light green of the water on the Banks extending to the horizon on every side, forms a marine view which is almost unique in its coloring. Again we noticed the rich purple effects in the clouds which were so conspicuous when we crossed the Banks the first time. Dr. L. W. Andrews, of the State University of Iowa, suggests that this effect is to be ascribed to the fact that the sensitiveness of the optic nerve to the green color becomes exhausted by the constant contemplation of the vivid green water, and that purple, the complement of green, appears in place of the blue of the sky. If this were true, it would seem that prolonged contemplation of green trees and grass would also make the sky appear purple. The actinic power, however, of the green reflections from the water is shown by the fact that such water appears almost white in a photograph. Stirrup Key Light was sighted in the afternoon, and we once more anchored on the eastern edge of the Banks.

The next day was spent in beating against a head-wind, the west side of Abaco being made about noon, after which a long tack to the southward occupied the rest of the day until we sighted the lights of Nassau, N. P., when we came about on the other tack for the remainder of the night. Many of the party would have been glad to visit the city of Nassau, which is the metropolis of the British West Indies, but our time was getting short, and we were not on a pleasure excursion. The comparative idleness of the last two or three days had made the young men so frisky that more than the usual amount of skylarking was indulged in that night, including an impromptu concert, that was not greatly appreciated by those who desired to sleep.

Early in the morning of Friday, July 7th, our old friend Egg Island was sighted. The wind was still ahead, and it took us nearly all day to beat along the coast of Eleuthera to Harbor Island. When opposite the town of Spanish Wells, a small boat came out with a pilot, who proved to be an old acquaintance of mine having been my boatman and general factotum in 1888. He agreed to pilot us into Harbor Island. A little boy of perhaps eight years, his nephew, had come out with him in the sail-boat, and it was with no little surprise that we heard Philip, the pilot, order the little fellow to take the boat back to the port, some ten miles away. No wonder the Bahamans make skillful boatmen, when little boys who would, with us, scarcely be out of the kindergarten, are competent to handle a sail-boat with judgment and confidence.

The entrance to the harbor at Harbor Island is about as forbidding a looking channel as we saw during our trip. At one place there seemed barely room for the vessel to pass between the great masses of black rocks, where the tide was rushing like a mill-race. The vessel got through about sunset, and her passengers were just congratulating themselves on getting into harbor all right, when the schooner went hard and fast aground on a sand-bar inside the harbor. Although getting aground is always a serious matter with a vessel the size of the "Emily E. Johnson," it would have been hard to select a better place than the one where she rested that night, the keel being supported throughout its length on fine coral sand. Captain Flowers was naturally exasperated at the pilot for his inexcusable blunder, but did not fly into a passion, as most skippers would have done, so that our admiration for him was increased, if possible, by the incident. It was flood tide again at 2 A. M., but the schooner did not budge, and there was nothing to be done but occupy ourselves in collecting until the high tide in the afternoon.

The bottom of the harbor was dotted with magnificent specimens of *Pentaceros reticulatus* Linck, perhaps the most conspicuous of American star-fishes. A large number of these were brought on board, and a class organized under the leadership of Professor Arey for the study of the anatomy of these huge Echinoderms. In spite of its apparent rigidity, this star-fish is able to turn its rays over its back until the tips of opposite rays meet above the disk.

Others of the party took boats and went collecting around the rocks on either side of the harbor entrance, where they secured quite a quantity of mollusks and gorgonians, some of the latter being afterward killed with the polyps nicely expanded, by plunging the whole colony into hot, but not boiling water.

As might have been expected, the morning light revealed the white sails of numerous boats, all speeding toward the "Emily E. Johnson." It is safe to say that the occupants of every one of them would not have been greatly disappointed at an entire failure to get the schooner off the sand. From the earliest times, a wreck has been regarded as a special "God-send" by the natives of the West India Islands, and they can hardly be blamed for looking at the matter in that light. They are almost without exception poor men who have a hard struggle for their daily bread. A wreck often means comparative affluence to a whole community, and men in more favored countries are frequently only too glad to profit by the misfortunes of others, and are often willing to bring disaster upon others just as truly and criminally as the man who runs a vessel on the rock. Most of the little boats that gathered around the schooner had something to sell in the shape of fruits or vegetables. Their occupants were nearly all negroes of the regular Bahama type, great talkers with any amount of time to spare, and no fools when it came to bartering.

In the forenoon a number of us went to the town of Harbor Island to attend to various items of business. The island itself lies north and south a little way from the main island of Eleuthera, and is about three miles long by half a mile wide. On the east a range of high sand-hills separates the town from the sea, which here breaks upon a beautiful sand-beach said to be the finest in the Bahamas. The west side of the island is low and much of it wooded. Here the town proper faces the harbor, and presents an unusually picturesque view. Some of the finest cocoanut palms that we saw in the West Indies are found here. The quaint old houses, white like the coral rock streets over which wheeled vehicles or horses seldom pass, seem plunged in a perpetual sleep. At one time this was one of the most important West Indian ports, but now the pine-apple trade has largely departed to the east coast of Eleuthera, and with it has gone the main industry of Harbor Island. At the time of my former visit, a canning factory for putting up pine-apples was in full blast, but the "pine" season was over now, and the inhabitants did not seem to be very actively engaged in anything in particular, except in showing a friendly interest in the crowd of young Americans that had so suddenly and unexpectedly dropped down among them.

The town of Harbor Island is considered one of the most healthful spots in the West Indies The drainage is excellent, and the people look as if they lived better than most of the Bahamans. A path leads from the town over the hills to the beach on the east side, where there are a number of "wells," that is, holes dug in the sand at the bottom of which is water rising and falling with the tides. The native women do most of their washing here, beating the clothes with a sort of paddle, and managing to get them beautifully clean in the process. A great deal of water for household purposes is carried over the hill in buckets and small tubs on the heads of the women. Even the poorest houses are scrupulously clean, the floors being white with frequent scouring. I was told that the floors are often scrubbed with the skin of a species of *Balistes* or filefish, which is covered with closely set spines, giving it the feel of sand-paper.

The people seem to be almost universally polite, greeting the stranger with a smile and pleasant word, and offering him their best if he enters the door. Not only the houses, but their clothes and persons are clean. Their garments may be scant and tattered, but the meanest negro of them all would feel disgraced if he or his clothes were anything but clean.

The magistrate who dispenses justice to this and neighboring communities, Mr. Solomon, is an old man now, having served his queen for over a quarter of a century, and is a type of the old-time English gentleman worthily discharging his not unimportant duties, and held in respect by the whole community, and in wholesome fear by the evil-doer. He made our official business with him a pleasure instead of a disagreeable task. Some of us were allowed to inspect the jail, which, as is usual, was guiltless of prisoners, and contained nothing more terrible than some clothes which malefactors are compelled to wear. The place had an air of habitual desertion that was an index of the law abiding character of the people.

There are two churches in Harbor Island, one, the largest, being Methodist and the other Episcopalian, these two being the only denominations which have obtained any considerable foot-hold in the Bahamas. On the island of San Salvador, or "Cat Island" as it is more generally called, I once attended service in an Episcopalian Church where the preacher, choristers, and entire congregation with the exception of the visitors, were negroes of the purest African type. As to the morals of these negroes, from the information obtained by me—whether reliable or not I can not say—it appears that they are intensely religious, but as a writer once said concerning them, "they are not *immoral*, but *unmoral*," a distinction that is often not made, but is nevertheless a fundamental one.

The United States agent, Mr. Monroe, was exceedingly attentive and courteous during our stay, entertaining a number of our party in a very delightful manner, and giving a good deal of interesting information about the place. From another source and upon a previous visit to these Islands, I heard of an instance of the working of our diplomatic service in obscure places that was, and for aught I know is yet, a disgrace to the United States Government. At that time the United States had an alleged representative at a place called "The Cove" on the other side of Eleuthera, who kept a low doggery in the town, and was so illiterate that he was unable to make out his official papers. An entirely amicable arrangement was understood to exist between this man and the British representative, whereby the latter made out all the official papers of the American "Consul," who reciprocated by supplying whatever liquor was needed for the personal consumption of Her Majesty's representative. This story I believe to be true, having seen and conversed with the parties interested. The American representative was certainly as ignorant and degraded in appearance as any man that I encountered in the West Indies. The idea that such a person should have power over the liberty and property of American citizens who traded in that port to the extent of scores of thousands of dollars annually, was enough to disgust any one who knew of the situation. The writer has seen a good many of the representatives of our government in out-of-the-way places, and is of the opinion that they are usually a poor reliance in case of difficulty, as the policy of the government is to pay them so little that they are obliged to engage in some other pursuit, thus compelling them to have a personal business interest in keeping on the good side of the authorities where they reside. It is, of course, out of the question for an American to secure justice under such circumstances, if justice conflicts with the wishes of the local government.

At 1:30 P. M. the schooner floated off the sand-bank and was brought up opposite the town, greatly to our relief, and the rest of the day was spent in visiting our friends ashore and securing fresh fish and fruit. It was with no little delight that we found a goodly number of watermelons, which were a decided treat under the circumstances.

Early the next morning we started with a new pilot for Spanish Wells, which we had obtained permission to visit, although it is not a port of entry. We took what is known as the "inside passage," a narrow and winding channel between the rugged coast of Eleuthera and the line of reefs, a passage well calculated to make the skipper and his passengers hold their breath. The water was, as usual around these islands, wonderfully clear, making the dangers all the more apparent, and revealing the ugly black heads of rocks appearing on every side, as the schooner doubled and turned in her course under the skillful guidance of the pilot, who seemed to be perfectly self-possessed and confident, although a single false turn of the wheel might have ended the cruise and the schooner. At times it seemed that there would hardly be room for the vessel to pass between the rocks, and at others we were apparently rushing right on to the sunken masses, which turned out to be many feet below the surface.

Had we been less nervous about the vessel, this run would have been a most enchanting one. The crystal clearness of the water made it possible to see the wonderful "sea-gardens" over which we were passing,— gardens of waving plume-like gorgonians, and patches of anemones rivaling the brightest flowers in their conspicuous coloring. Great heads of coral seemed to glide by or under us, and so clear was the sea that they appeared just beneath the surface. Out to the right were the patches of barrier reef, while beyond them, the intense blue of the deep water added its pure and white-flecked beauty to a superb marine view. On the left the coast of Eleuthera, one of the largest of the Bahama group, was at times within a stone's throw of the schooner. At first the coast was low, but later it became more rocky. A short distance inland the country was rugged with limestone hills, water-worn at times into fantastic shapes. On the face of one of these cliffs a hole could be seen, which we afterward found to be the mouth of a cave. At the water's edge the limestone head-lands were being undermined throughout their extent, the material thus broken up being carried along the shore and built up into the sand beaches that gleamed dazzling white in many a sheltered cove. Finally a ruggeder headland than any yet seen came into view, and disclosed in profile the outline which gives it its name of "Ridley's Head." Rounding this, the palm-embowered village of Spanish Wells, with its white beach and pretty harbor where all the boats were drawn up or at anchor in Sabbath repose, was welcomed as the last station at which we intended to spend any considerable time.

The town of Spanish Wells is on the first of a chain of islands which border the mainland of Eleuthera on the north, and extend to Egg Island on the west. The island itself is probably not more than a quarter of a mile broad, but extends two or three miles east and west. There are no hills, the greatest elevation being not over fifteen or twenty feet above high water. On the north side a beautiful sand-beach runs almost if not quite the length of the island. Here one can see the process of converting coral sand into rock in almost every stage from the loose sand to the hard limestone rock. For a considerable distance the sea is undermining some high banks of partially solidified sand. The entire island is made up of this sand and rock. On the south a narrow channel divides this island from Eleuthera, and affords an excellent refuge for small boats. The harbor itself is east of the island, being protected on the east by a high point of Eleuthera. The channel to the harbor is very narrow, and at the time of our visit was partly blockaded by a wrecked brig, which was allowed to remain directly in the centre of the channel. Here, as elsewhere in the Bahamas, the largest trees are the cocoanut palms, which line the beach on the north and form quite a respectable grove to the west of the town. This grove is noticeable from the fact that most of the trees lean to the east or north-east, a reminder of a hurricane that swept over the island some years ago.

The town itself consists of a number of houses, set down with almost no regard to the points of the compass, and jumbled together in what appears to be the most hap-hazard confusion. They are mostly frame houses, as square as a box, with low, pyramidal roofs. Very few of the windows were glazed, most of them being without sashes, but protected by heavy storm-shutters. The house itself is almost always raised about two feet above the ground on low posts. Back of each residence is the oven, a sub-conical structure, about eight feet high, and whitewashed on the outside. There is a good-sized church, built of coral rock, where a devout congregation assembles to worship after the manner of John

Wesley, and hard by is the cemetery, a desolate enough looking enclosure, where the irregularly disposed mounds of coral sand, surmounted by white head-boards, are unrelieved by any sign of grass or turf, although some shrubbery with brilliant scarlet blossoms gives a touch of beauty. Upon inspection, one sees that the graves are fairly riddled with holes made by land-crabs, and can hardly repress a shudder at the repulsive thought of these ugly, crawling scavengers, whose presence attests the fate of the bodies entrusted to this cemetery. After all, however, this is no more repulsive than the accompaniments of all civilized burial. Perhaps, indeed, less so, in that the process is more rapid here than elsewhere.

But the thing which impresses the stranger as the most peculiar about this interesting town is that it has no streets in the part where the houses are most thickly aggregated, although there is a wide and tolerably straight path leading from the western part of the village toward the west end of the island. A little reflection will show us, however, that streets are entirely superfluous in a town which is *without a single wheeled vehicle of any kind.* In its early history this community, like others in the West Indies, was liable to hostile incursions from piratical crews, and this may account for the manner in which the houses are huddled together, when there would appear to be abundant room to spread out comfortably. It looks for all the world like a covey of quail bunched together in fear of the dogs.

It was the privilege of the writer to spend some months in this unique community during a previous visit to the Bahamas, and thus to obtain something more than a superficial knowledge of the life of these people. I speak advisedly in using the word "unique," for here is a community of some five or six hundred souls, nearly all of them white and descendants of Englishmen, which seems to me to be more isolated from the world than any other community of like character and size that can be found. Here are adult men, speaking the English language with a maltreatment of the h's equal to that of the most approved London cockney, some of whom,

Scene in Spanish Wells. G. L. H.

if I am informed correctly, have never seen a horse or a cow or a wheeled vehicle; whose personal knowledge of the Mammalia is confined to man, pigs, dogs, cats, and rats; to whom not only the locomotive, electric light, telegraph, and phonograph are matters of hearsay, but also the threshing machine, self-binder, and even the common plough. Here are people who never saw a river, mountain, two-story house, or field of grain, and, until recently, were guiltless of a practical knowledge of a pane of glass, a lamp, or an iron stove.

It is hard to imagine the effect of such a life upon naturally intelligent people, but intercourse with them will show strange and unexpected glimpses of the results of this environment. For instance, I remember that while talking to a bright young man, who was head scholar and assistant teacher in the school, we got onto the subject of panthers. He seemed to have a good idea of the size, agility, and ferocity of this animal, but upon being asked for a more particularized description, replied that he thought it was *like a large lizard!* Now, as a matter of fact, the largest wild animal that this youth had ever seen was the iguana, a large lizard, and his mental picture of the panther was simply a greatly exaggerated and particularly ferocious lizard, a perfectly natural result of his circumscribed experiences.

Physically, many of the men are up to the average in most respects, except in an appearance which would indicate an insufficiency of food. They are tall, well-formed, straight-limbed, with bright, kindly faces, indicative of a clean moral and physical habit, but their youth departs altogether too soon, and a really well-fed man or woman is a rarity. They have enough to eat to satisfy hunger, probably, but they appear as if physiologically starved for all that; and no wonder! Except in the pine-apple season they have very little fruit indeed. Their principal vegetables are yams and a scant supply of bananas and plantains. The flour that they have is poor in quality, and they can afford to buy but little of that. Fresh meat is rarely obtained, and then usually in the shape of green turtle. Salt beef and pork they greatly prize, but do not always have. Fish are plentiful in the surrounding waters, but no one seems to make a business of securing them for general consumption, and even when a good catch is made, they will attempt to sell them. A sort of soup or chowder is made of the " conch," *Strombus gigas*, but the meat is exceedingly tough and about as savory as India rubber. Land-crabs are caught in a hap-hazard, spasmodic way, as are the spiny lobsters, which they call "craw-fish." Milk and butter are only occasionally obtained by the sick. Eggs are bought and sold singly, and are so small that one seldom sees enough at any one time to satisfy a man with a reasonably good appetite. The only things that can be regarded as staple articles of diet are yams, flour and conchs, the other edibles mentioned above being more properly ranked as luxuries and dainties.

Our good doctor was regarded as a special Providence by these people, and faithfully ministered to them and their little ones during our stay at Spanish Wells. She studied these people with some care, and came to the conclusion that the women and girls were in worse condition than the men and boys, not receiving the benefit of the out-door life enjoyed by the latter. Most of the sick children and infants were suffering greatly from lack of proper nourishment, but she also noticed so many cases of malformation and monstrosities of various sorts, that another cause seemed at work. This, she thinks, is found in the almost unbelievable extent to which the people of the settlement have intermarried. In her own words: "As an explanation of this we would give the constant intermarriage of near relatives, which has a tendency not only to deteriorate the family by diminishing fertility, but reaches the inevitable result of ill-balanced offspring. A very good illustration of this degeneracy came under my observation. Among the twenty or more patients treated, I have but three surnames on my case-book. With the exception of two, all were of the same name. This family have lived here generation after generation, marrying and intermarrying until there is not a family on the island with more than two or three living children, and many of these are ill-formed, delicate, rachitic, or scrofulous. The girls told sad stories of their sufferings, and the married women of protracted and painful maternity. The young ladies were trained to the idea that it was a hazardous undertaking to marry any young man not a native of this particular island. In this village I met three little "midgets," all women and cousins, but of what degree I am unable to say, as they seemed to have little idea of degrees of relationship. The smallest of these is a woman thirty-four years old, twenty-seven inches high, and weighs forty-five pounds. A male dwarf that we saw in Key West is a cousin of these Spanish Wells midgets, making four in one family."[1]

In spite of all these drawbacks, the citizens of Spanish Wells are by no means an unhappy people. Indeed as I look back to my residence among them, they seem to have found considerable enjoyment in life. The young men and women were as light-hearted as the most fortunate of their cousins across the water. They have their social gatherings and games. I well remember being an interested spectator one moonlight night, when they assembled down on the pure white coral beach and played the old-fashioned "kissing games" to the tune of "King William was King George's son, and he the royal race did run," each verse ending up in a manner which was evidently much to the satisfaction of the parties immediately concerned. The Spanish Wells young folks are celebrated throughout the islands for their excellent singing. The grand old hymns of John Wesley are sung by the sabbath congregation with a volume and swing that is refreshing to hear after much of the emasculated congregational singing in the North. The time is perfect and the parts well sustained, and there is a quaintness in the lining out of the leader, followed by the ready volume of response that makes the coral structure fairly quiver. One evening the school-teacher brought his pupils on board the schooner to

[1] Dr. Leora Johnson.

sing for us, and we never heard children sing with more vim and fidelity to tune and meter. They sang "God Save the Queen" and "Ring the Bell for Little Nell," and several old-fashioned rounds in excellent style, and there was more singing to the cubic inch of child than we would have deemed possible. Then the young men and women came aboard and showed the fruitage of such training in a delightful extemporized concert, and won our hearty applause as they made the shores of Eleuthera resound with the grand and quaint melodies of "Somebody's Dyin' Every Day" and "The Old-Time Religion is Good Enough for Me," and a score of other favorites brought over a century or more ago from Old England. These young people were perfectly willing to admit the superiority of their vocalistic powers, and one of them confided to me with perfectly serious conviction that he "reckoned" that he "was about the best bass singer in the world." And so he was, in *his* world, and that person would be heartless indeed who would impair such naïve confidence.

These people are intensely religious, and take more comfort in their religion, which is of the strictest Wesleyan type, than do most people. It has a reality and vitality that I have seldom seen elsewhere. Immorality is exceedingly rare, and the graver social sins appear to be almost inconceivable to most of them. Their shortcomings are more of the nature of peccadillos, and such crimes as serious theft, burglary, arson, or murder are probably as nearly unknown as anywhere else on the globe.

The advent of a schooner-load of young folks from unheard of "Iowa" was an event from which to date lesser happenings for a decade to come. They were self-contained, however, and did not divulge their opinion of us. Perhaps that was best. One of the leading men of the place, an old acquaintance, informed me that he had gone so far as to tell the folks that there were "some good people even among the Americans." The most important occupation engaged in by the Spanish Wells men is the culture of the "pine," or pineapple as we call it. It seems that many years ago the Queen gave to this colony a certain amount of land on the mainland of Eleuthera to hold in common. Each person could claim as much land as he cultivated, and keep possession so long as the land was under cultivation. This system of land tenure, although it would seem almost ideal, was, as a matter of fact, about the most unsatisfactory that could have been devised, and gave rise to innumerable quarrels and lawsuits. The main point of difficulty was the definition of terms used in the grant. Some indolent or tricky individuals claimed that land once held by them remained theirs so long as even a single banana stalk or pine "tree" was growing on it, while others claimed that all of the area must be in bona fide cultivation before the terms of the grant could be held as complied with. And so this quarrel has become a traditional one, and is a pregnant source of strife among the colonists. When one comes to look at their "farms," his chief wonder is what there is to quarrel over. There is not a spot on the whole plantation where a plow could be run for a single yard. The whole surface is not only rocky, but is solid coral rock, with here and there a little accumulation of earth in the hollows. Wherever a little soil has lodged, a pine-cutting is set. In spite of the hopeless appearance of things to a man from the Iowa prairies, they do manage to raise considerable quantities of pine-apples on just such land as this. Most of the fruit is bought by Baltimore firms and shipped to Baltimore or Key West to be canned. The amount of money realized by an individual worker in the Spanish Wells plantation must be pitiably small. Indeed I imagine that not many of these men see more than twenty-five dollars in cash in a year. So far as I know, the school-master receives the highest regular salary of any one on the island. His pay is fifty pounds, or two hundred and fifty dollars per year, and with this he lives better, and dresses better, and supports a family in better style than most of his fellows even in fortunate America. In spite of their poverty, the people are almost without exception thoroughly self-respecting, God-fearing and honest, and among them are some of the best types of sterling Christian manhood that I have ever known.

Our main object in going to Spanish Wells was to give the students a further opportunity to study the wealth of animal life about a typical coral reef. It will be remembered that at the Dry Tortugas we were unable to study the outer face of the reef on account of its exposure to the swell, which would have been dangerous to small boats. Moreover, most of the Madrepores had been killed by unusually low tides. My previous experience at Spanish Wells had shown what could be seen of the reefs there, and given confidence that a visit by our students would be of great educational value. About a mile to the west and a little north of the entrance to the harbor, is a rocky mass known as "Pier Rock," and around this the water is shallow, although the rock itself has been excavated at the water-line into various shelves and crannies and cool retreats suitable for occupancy by a great variety of marine forms, especially gorgonians, mollusks, sea-anemones and tube-dwelling worms. Although we did not expect to find any great zoölogical rarities, we did expect, and rightly, that there would here be excellent opportunity to study a number of these animals at home in their appropriate surroundings.

About a mile to the north of Spanish Wells is a patch of genuine coral reef growing most luxuriantly and protected from the wind during a greater part of the time, so that it can be visited safely by small boats, in which one can cruise along the outer face of this reef and study the ever enchanting forms of life in a leisurely and satisfactory manner.

Both men and boats were very cheap at Spanish Wells, and we found it better to employ the natives with their sail-boats than to use our own, and thus secured a greater degree of real comfort in our work than at any other station. We had long since discovered that the romance of pulling at the ponderous oars of a ship's boat was terminated by the first real experience, and were more than ready to employ the native sail-boats and their owners, who are all skillful boatmen, thoroughly acquainted with the surrounding coast and reef.

I doubt if anything else during our voyage was enjoyed by

the students more than these trips to the outer reefs. With
the aid of the "water-glass," which is nothing more nor less
than a glass-bottomed bucket, every detail of the sub-marine
scene could be discerned almost as clearly as if one were looking into air rather than water, so exquisitely transparent is
the sea around these islands. The bottom of the water-glass
is sunk just a little beneath the surface, the bucket being
held right side up. All the ripples are thus destroyed, with
their attendant confusing reflections, and every object is as
sharply defined as in the upper air. The scene thus revealed
is one of such surpassing beauty that a poet, rather than a naturalist, should undertake its description. Great heads of
massive coral rise almost to the surface, covered with living
and expanded polyps. Miniature trees in the form of branching madrepores, with fantastically spreading fronds, often
appear attached to the coral heads. Here and there patches
of sandy bottom reveal clumps of yellow and red sea-fans,
nestling in sheltered nooks. Long, graceful sea-feathers and
sea-whips wave their flexible branches in answer to the gentle
undulations of the water. Old masses of coral rock, carved
into fantastic similitude of castle and arch and grotto by the
action of waves and a host of rock-boring animals, are the
homes of innumerable animal and vegetable forms, draped
with the fronds of algæ until they resemble some great rock-
ery overgrown with ferns. In and out of these caverns, and
through the silent groves of madrepores and sea-fans, glide
troops of strangely shaped and brilliantly colored tropical
fishes. Surely Solomon in all his glory was not arrayed like
one of these! The most vivid reds, yellows and blues in
sharpest contrasts of bands and stripes and blotches, reveal
the very abandonment with which Nature lavishes adorn-
ment on her finny tribes. In sheltered nooks, between coral
masses, the anemones fairly revel in gorgeous mimicry of daisy
and dandelion, pink and aster and chrysanthemum, of the
upper world. In this strange realm even the worms take
shapes of grace and loveliness, rivaling the anemones in the
beauty of their flower-like whorls of tentacles. In this water-

world, as in that above, forms of beauty are strangely mingled with repulsive and uncanny shapes. The cavities of the coral fairly bristle with the cruel black spines of sea-urchins (*Diadema setosum*). —spines seven inches long and sharp as needles. Great spiny lobsters creep among the roots of the gorgonians, and repulsive sea-spiders lurk in the recesses and among the algae.

Another more prosaic but still good collecting ground was a flat bar which lay between the anchorage and the mainland of Eleuthera to the east, and was nearly bare at low tide. This proved a good place for mollusks, especially *Pinna*. Here also were great quantities of sea-urchins, particularly *Hipponoë esculenta* A. Ag. The mainland of Eleuthera itself proved an excellent collecting ground for the entomologists and botanists. The ornithologists found that the birds were much the same as those collected at Egg Island. On one occasion a party visited a cave some distance from the shore, securing a number of interesting bats.

The islanders themselves were good collectors, and we availed ourselves of the opportunity to buy a number of the more showy specimens, such as the king and queen conchs, and nicely prepared specimens of *Pentaceros reticulatus* which these natives know how to preserve in excellent shape for cabinet specimens. The most enterprising dealers were from the Current, a few miles to the west of Spanish Wells, and they carried on a brisk trade with our party, succeeding in selling pretty much all they brought to the schooner. We found them sharp at bargaining, and they could apparently spare any amount of time in a transaction involving only a few shillings. We soon ran out of change, and were forced to abandon further negotiations, as it took but a short time to use up all the silver and copper that we could secure from store-keepers in the village.

The collection drawn from these various sources grew to be quite an imposing one before we left this locality, and the deck of the schooner was usually piled high with a miscellaneous mass of zoölogical and botanical specimens.

The only mammals collected during the whole cruise were some specimens of *Macrotus waterhousii* Gray secured by Mr. Wickham in a cave on the island of Eleuthera. This is one of the "leaf-nosed" bats belonging to the family MEGADERMATIDÆ. The ears are enormous, their bases meeting at the top of the head, and having conspicuous tragi. A fleshy appendage projects upward from the nose, resembling the horn of a rhinoceros in front view. The tail projects slightly beyond the interfemoral membrane, which is supported by a very long calcar or accessory ossicle. The dental formula is m. $\frac{5}{6}$, c. $\frac{1}{1}$, i. $\frac{2}{2}$. The animal is about the size of our *Atalapha noveboracensis*, or perhaps a little smaller.

The following list of the birds of Eleuthera is made up partly from species secured at this time, and partly from a collection made by the writer at the same place in the summer of 1888:

Larus atricilla Linn., laughing gull; *Gelochelidon nilotica* (Hasselq.), gull-billed tern; *Sterna maxima* Bodd., royal tern; *Sterna antillarum* (Less.), least tern; *Sterna anæthetus* Scop., bridled tern; *Anous stolidus* (Linn.), noddy; *Puffinus auduboni* Finsch, Audubon's shearwater; *Phaëthon flavirostris* Brandt, yellow-billed tropic bird; *Fregata aquila* (Linn.), man-o'-war bird; *Ardea virescens* Linn., green heron; *Nycticorax violaceus* (Linn.), yellow-crowned night heron; *Ægialitis wilsonia* (Ord.), Wilson's plover; *Columbigallina passerina* (Linn.), ground dove; *Speotyto cunicularia floridana* Ridgw., Florida burrowing owl; *Strix flammea pratincola* Cory, Bahama barn owl; *Chordeiles virginianus minor* (Cab.), Cuban night-hawk; *Loxigilla violacea bahamensis* Ridgw., Bahama grosbeak; *Tyrannus dominicensis* (Gmel.), grey king-bird; *Euetheia bicolor* (Linn.), grass quit; *Certhiola bahamensis* Reich., Bahama honey-creeper; and *Mimus gundlachi* Cab., Bahama mocking-bird. It will be noticed that of the nine land-birds enumerated above, only two, the ground dove and burrowing owl, are North American, the remainder being purely West Indian. Perhaps the most conspicuous bird of them all, and certainly the most attractive, is the Bahama mocking-bird.

which has an exceedingly rich and mellow song. It is seldom molested, and individual birds habitually sing at a certain time of day from some favorite perch, pouring out a perfect flood of melody, evidently much to the delight of the performer. So far as I have ascertained, the natives do not cage any of these birds, although the children sometimes capture and play with the young.

A few frogs and lizards are found on the island, the latter being very abundant and known as chameleons. Some of them have a bladder-like contrivance under or at the side of the neck, which they expand into a bright red, globular inflation. This may serve to attract insects, as any bit of color is known to do, and thus be an example of alluring coloration.

Only a few species of fish were secured, most of them being purchased from the native fishermen. Among the food-fishes may be mentioned a *Scomber*, which is locally known as the "jack-fish," but seems different from the jack-fish of the North, and a species of *Balistes* or file-fish. Another species which I have been unable to identify, has two very heavy and broad incisors in each jaw, no lips, the incisors being almost entirely bare and exposed, very large cycloid scales, and a low dorsal which is entire and without spines. Captain Flowers, while fishing from the schooner, caught a large jew-fish. *Stereolepis* sp., which was probably the heaviest true bony fish that we secured during the voyage. It proved excellent eating. We noticed that the scales were carefully saved by the native who cleaned the fish. He said that they were highly prized for working into the beautiful shell-work baskets for which the Spanish Wells people are noted. Another large fish caught in the harbor was the barracuda, *Sphyræna* sp. On this and other occasions, the writer has found it excellent eating, in spite of the belief on the part of the natives, and even some sailors, that it is poisonous. I am strongly of the opinion that this is a baseless slur cast upon the reputation of an excellent food-fish. Several species of a finely marked moray, *Muræna melanotis* Gthr., were secured here. The ground color is black, dotted with linear light yellow markings. The teeth are sharp as needles, one or two particularly long ones being planted in the roof of the mouth. They are said to inflict an ugly wound, and appear quite capable of it. This fish is eel-shaped, and will defend itself savagely when an attempt is made to capture it. A large porcupine-fish, *Diodon hystrix* L., was bought from a fisherman. It is armed all over with very strong spines, and can inflate itself into an almost perfectly spherical ball. We found it no easy matter to skin this animal, but finally succeeded in removing the body through the mouth, thus securing a skin without a cut. A relative of the porcupine-fish was found in the "swell-toad," *Tetrodon spengleri* Bloch, a species that we had already encountered at the Tortugas. Another singular form is the remora, *Echeneis naucrates* L., that has a series of suckers on the top of the head which open and shut like the slats of a window-blind. They serve to attach the fish to the body of a shark or other large animal, and thus the remora gets free transportation, and at the same time is always on hand to pick up the crumbs from the shark's table. It is said that some of the orientals use this animal for fishing purposes, tying a line around it and letting it go forth to fasten itself upon the quarry, after which both captor and captive are hauled in by the line. A very small specimen of the black fish that we secured on the Bahama Banks, which I described as a *Ceratias* (?) (page 49) is included in the collection from Spanish Wells. Since writing the former description, however, the specimen has been examined by Professor Samuel Garman, of Harvard, who pronounces it probably a melanotic specimen of *Antennarius tigris* Poey. It is now in his hands for description. A form which I am unable to even approximately locate with the literature at hand is a small species, with the general facies of a *Zoarces*, but with the ventral fins united so as to form a sucking disk, and the body covered with large cycloid scales.

We found the edible fish abundant and cheap at Spanish Wells, and were glad to have our table supplied with this excellent food by the native fishermen, who seemed to have no trouble in furnishing all that we could dispose of.

"More insects were obtained in the vicinity of Harbor Island and Spanish Wells than at any other point on the voyage, and as many are of interest, either because of their size, bright colors, habits, or distribution, they are accorded a little more space. The ants have been kindly identified by Mr. Pergande, of Washington, and we mention the following as being conspicuous: *Brachymyrmex heeri* Forel (var. *obscurior*), a little species which was extremely common on the bushes and continually fell in the beating net; *Dorymyrmex pyramicus* Rog., a long-legged ant of rather small size, common in like situations on both islands; and *Pseudomyrma flavidula* Smith, a long, yellow ant with a wide head and a black spot on each side of the abdomen. The remainder of the Hymenoptera were examined by Mr. Ashmead, who furnished the names of the entire collection. The succeeding seem worthy of note: In the ANDRENIDÆ a new *Nomia* and a specimen of *Agapostemon femoralis* Guér.; in the BEMBECIDÆ the beautiful *Monedula signata* Linn., with its contrasting black and yellow markings. The LARRIDÆ were represented by *Stizus hogardii* Latr., a large, reddish wasp which was noticed carrying away a cicada at least twice its own size. Of the SPHEGIDÆ we got *Pelopæus fasciatus* Lap.; of the VESPIDÆ *Polistes minor* Beauv. and *P. americanus* Fabr., the latter building its paper nests in the bushes on both islands. *Polybia cubensis* Sauss. was also found here. Several other things in this order were obtained, but space forbids further mention at present.

"Of Lepidoptera the most striking species was a beautiful moth found not uncommonly about the sapodilla trees. The primaries are black with numerous white spots and a large red mark at base, the thorax black with white dots, while the abdomen is of a velvety blue above, banded with black and white beneath. A large *Erebus* was often seen flying in the evening, while during the day it was to be noticed in caves. Probably in this diurnal habit of concealment in such places is to be found an explanation of the way stragglers have of entering houses in the United States.

"Asilid flies are not uncommon on the islands, and Muscids and TABANIDÆ were common enough, though little attention was given their capture. The Coleoptera, as usual, received the lion's share of notice, and in this order some very nice things were obtained. *Cicindela marginata* Fabr. was not rare along the white sandy beaches, but the sun was too fervent to encourage a great deal of chasing after these agile creatures. We took a *Scarites* like a small specimen of *subterraneus* Fabr., also *Plochionus pallens* Fabr., as representatives of the CARABIDÆ. The little red lady-bird, *Coccinella sanguinea* L., was found here, as at almost every other point in the West Indian region at which collecting was done. At night the lights of a species of *Pyrophorus* could be seen flashing in every direction through the groves of cocoa-palms, and after many an awkward tumble, taken by running across unfamiliar ground in the dark, it was considered easier and more productive to depend on the native children for a supply of these fire-flies, they catching them at night and bringing them to the vessel for sale next day. A fine Buprestid (*Gyascutus carolinensis* Horn) was found on bushes close to the sea. The Longhorns were quite a noticeable feature here, the most common, and at the same time beautiful, one being *Elateropsis rugosus* Gahan, the females of which have the head, thorax and elytra ornamented with broad white stripes, while the males are uniform black above. An *Eburia* was found which seems to be *E. duzalii* Chevrolat, described from Cuba, and a nice Elaphidion occurred with it. The weevils, of course, are comparatively numerous in species. *Pachnæus opalus* was common, a fine Otiorhynchid near *Barynotus* was taken rarely at Harbor Island, and on Eleuthera we found a few specimens of a beautiful form of a reddish-chestnut color, the whole upper surface being overlaid with stripes and spots of greenish scales. The small Curculionids were not wanting.

"The Hemiptera were numerous and conspicuous. A large Cicada is not uncommon, and is known by the natives under the name of "singer" or "old witch." *Zelus longipes* Linn. is a pretty Heteropteron banded above with black and red. It frequents bushes where it feeds on insects. *Sphic-tyrtus whitei* Guér. is red and bronze-green above, but when flying the former color alone shows. It is found in the same situations as the preceding species, but no notes were made of its feeding habits.

"None of the few Orthoptera secured are yet identified. One large species belongs to the Acridiidæ and is over two inches in length. Another is a Mantis, which, as it was seen in various stages, evidently breeds here. Of crickets a little *Tridactylus* or allied form was found in a well, and a large brownish species of undetermined genus is found in the caves among the loose rocks on the floors or in crannies far back from the entrance. The antennæ are immensely elongate. Cockroaches were seen in some numbers.

"The papery nests of two colonies of white ants were seen by the party on Eleuthera Island. One of these was built on a horizontally projecting branch of a small tree a short distance from the ground; the other was built directly on the ground and was of such girth as to render its packing for transportation impracticable."

We were confined at this station, as at the Dry Tortugas, to shore and shallow-water collecting of marine forms. One of the most striking facts brought out by a survey of the Crustacea from this region is that the littoral and shallow-water species are in a majority of cases identical with those found on the other side of the Gulf Stream at the Dry Tortugas. Out of about eighteen species collected at Harbor Island and Spanish Wells, twelve are identical with species from the Tortugas, leaving only one-third the number as peculiar to Eleuthera. This is quite different from the result of a comparison between the deeper water forms from Havana on the one hand, and the Pourtalès Plateau on the other. Out of the thirty-odd species from the Pourtalès Plateau, only three, or perhaps four, were found at Havana. Out of the seven found at Havana, only two were found on the Pourtalès Plateau proper, one being a shallow-water form. We thus see that there is a much closer relation between the littoral crustacean faunæ on the two sides of the Gulf Stream than exists between the faunæ at a depth of eighty to two hundred and fifty fathoms. Our series of forms is not sufficiently large to justify dogmatic generalizations, but they are nevertheless significant, being borne out, moreover, by a comparison of series of invertebrates belonging to other groups. The Dry Tortugas are about three hundred and eighty miles from Spanish Wells, while the Pourtalès Plateau is only about eighty miles from Havana. The Gulf Stream interposes the same barrier in both cases. Without discussing the question of a previous land connection, it seems that there must be some method by which Crustacea and other groups of invertebrates are distributed in a manner practically independent of the current or depth of the Gulf Stream. Many crustacean larvæ are pelagic, and are probably transported long distances by the more superficial currents. A larva starting at the Tortugas during the prevalence of northerly winds would perhaps be borne across the Gulf Stream before the Bahamas were passed. Whether the eggs have any considerable power to withstand dessication or not I do not know, but if they have, it seems likely that they would often be transported on the feet of water-birds.

All of the six crustaceans that we found near Eleuthera which have not hitherto been mentioned, are brachyuran crabs. *Epialtus bituberculatus* M. E. is represented by a minute specimen with a very broad rostrum ending in two blunt points. *Acanthonyx petiverii* M. E. has the distal portion of each of the walking legs expanded into a lamella which apposes the hook-like dactylopodite so that a pseudochela is formed for prehension. The carapace suddenly narrows back of the eyes, and a number of hair-like cirrhi are borne above the rostrum and in bristle-like bunches on the inner sides of the chelæ. The rostrum itself is produced forward into a pair of flattened and expanded teeth. *Mithrax spinosissimus* (Lamk.) is a very large, dark red spider-crab, with a spread of legs of twenty-one inches, and is characterized by having a row of smooth round knobs on the upper edge of the hand. The carapace is orbicular, six inches in diameter, and covered with blunt spines, those on the margin being much the largest, and the anterior marginal spines are bifid. The tips of the walking legs are black. *Eriphia gonagra* (Fabr.) has a broad, rounded carapace, with an antero-lateral row of sharp, recurved spines. The hand and carpus are covered with very peculiar, smooth, shining, round nodules arranged in longitudinal series. The chelæ are bright crimson in color, and the right finger bears a large truncated prominence on the basal part of its cutting edge. One of the most beautiful crustaceans in the entire collection is a specimen of *Plagusia depressa* Say. The carapace is orbicular and covered with nodules interspersed with round, bead-like granules. The anterior part is strangely shaped, having a projecting lip or ridge passing under the eyes and antennæ, and showing deep clefts above for the recesses into which the antennæ are folded. The superior surface of the carapace is mottled with crimson and grayish pink, and that of the chelæ and walking legs is marked with broad, longitudinal bands of the same color. The chelæ are especially gorgeous in their ornamentation, which consists of rows of nodules and the crimson stripes mentioned above. The ventral surface is, as usual, without bright markings. *Carpilius corallinus* (Hbst.) is a very large, bright-red crab, with perfectly smooth, rounded carapace and massive chelæ. The fingers are jet black.

The land-crabs are very abundant on the island, and appear to belong to three or four species. There is the small and ever present *Geocarcinus lateralis* (Frem.) ,with its bright red and yellow coloring. It was especially abundant in the cave where the "leaf-nosed" bats were secured. Next we have *Cardiosoma guanhumi* (Latr.), the common large edible species of a grayish color, and with no bright markings. In addition to these are what appear to be two other species which the writer secured during his former visit to Eleuthera. Both are about as large as *C. guanhumi*. One is of a deep rich wine-color, with two round, light yellow spots near the posterior margin of the carapace. The other is green in color, and has the branchial region covered above with well differentiated swollen lobes of the carapace marked longitudinally with furrows and lines resembling the midrib and veins of a lanceolate leaf. The anterior part of the rostrum between the eyes is much narrower than in *C. guanhumi*, and the carpus and meros of the cheliped are ornamented with prominent rows of spines at the angles. These crabs furnish a no insignificant portion of the food of the natives, who hunt them at night with torches. So completely terrestrial are they, that they can easily be drowned in water. Another crustacean that enters into the dietary of the Bahamans is the spiny lobster, *Palinurus longimanus?*, a truly gorgeous creature terrible to look at because of its bristling spines, but like many another with appalling mien, entirely harmless, being devoid even of the claws so common among its fellows.

A large series of Mollusca was secured in the vicinity of Spanish Wells, embracing most of the more familiar West Indian species. Here again we find considerable resemblance to the fauna of the Dry Tortugas. The following list includes not only the forms collected by this expedition, but also those secured in 1888. While there is no claim to exactitude in the determinations, such as would attend the work of a specialist in this group, it is hoped that the list as a whole will serve to show the character of the collection, and the general relationship of the forms, together with some hints of value concerning the geographical distribution of the species mentioned. Cephalopoda: *Spirula peronii* Lam., a small species less than an inch in diameter, with the whorls not in contact with each other. Gastropoda: *Strombus gigas* Linn., *Murex* sp. (near *M. pomum.*) This is the largest *Murex* found. *Triton chlorostomus* Lam., *Fasciolaria gigantea* Kiener, *F. tulipa* Linn., *F. trapezium; Purpura hæmastoma* Linn., *Columbella mercatoria* Linn., a pretty species ornamented with rows of square brown spots; *Cyphoma gibbosa* Linn., *Cassis cameo* Stimp., a species highly prized as specimens for the cabinet and called the "queen conch" by the natives; *Dolium perdix* Linn., *Oliva reticularis* Lam., a very abundant species; *Conus mus* (?) Hwass; *Conus* sp. ?; *Cypræa exanthema* Linn.. *Trivia quadripunctata* Gray; *Natica affinis* Gmel.; *Obeliscus* sp. ? resembling *O. sulcatus*, a Pacific and Red Sea species; *Cerithium* sp., strikingly ornamented with longitudinal rows of round black dots; *Littorina scabra* Linn., *L. ziczac* Chemn., a very abundant form; *Tectarius muricatus* Linn.; *T. nodulosus* Gmel., abundant; *Architectonica granulata* Lam.; *Nerita peloronta* Linn.; *N. tessellata* Say; *Astralium longispina* Lam.; *Trochus jujubinus* Linn.; *Livonia pica* Linn.; *Fissurella nodosa* Born; *F.* sp. ?; *Emarginula* sp. ?; *Crepidula fornicata* Linn.; *Chiton* sp. ?; *Bulla occidens* A. Ad.; *Hemitrochus varians*, a common striped landsnail abundant on bushes near Spanish Wells: *Strophia incana* Binney. Lamellibranchiata: *Pholas* sp. ?; *Thracia plicata* Desh.; *Tellina alternata* Say; *T. rastellum* Hanley; *Lucina jamaicensis* Lam.; *L. divaricata* Linn.; *L. tigerina* Linn.; *Cardium muricatum* Linn.; *Lævicardium serratum* Linn.; *Arca noæ* Linn.; *A. transversa* Say; *A. donaciformis* Reeve; *Mytilus* sp. ?; *Pinna muricata* Linn.; *Meleagrina margaritifera* Linn.; and *Pecten irradians* Lam.

The Bahamans utilize many of these shells in the beautiful shell-work for which they are justly famous. Baskets and breastpins, ear-rings, brooches and pendants are designed and executed with good taste and excellent workmanship. As before indicated, the scales of certain fishes, e. g., the jew-fish, are worked in with good effect as petals of artificial flowers, which are often brightly colored. A very pretty ornament is made by decorating a large star-fish, *Pentaceros*, with a symmetrical design in shell-work.

Coming to the Echinodermata, we again find a number of the species met with at the Tortugas. *Pentaceros reticulatus* Linck is the most abundant and conspicuous star-fish. A species of *Astropecten* is common in the shoal water between the reefs and the island. *Luidia clathrata* Lütken was found a little farther out on the flats. This creature is most disheartening to the collector, from its reprehensible tendency to fly all to pieces when not satisfied with its treat-

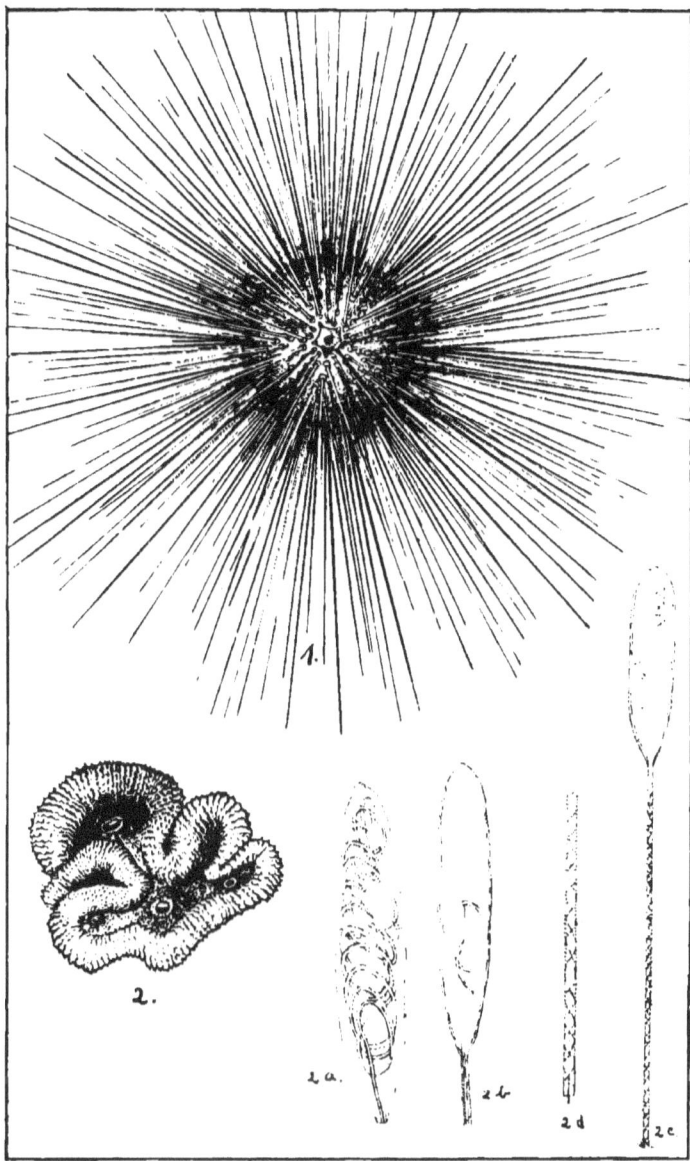

M. F. LINDER, DEL.

Specimens from Spanish Wells.

Fig. 1. DIADEMA SETOSUM (Gray), showing natural disposition of spines.
Fig. 2. ISOPHYLLIA DIPSACEA. Dana.
Fig. 2a. Nematocyst, showing coiled thread.
Fig. 2b. Nematocyst, showing thread partly extruded.
Fig. 2c. Nematocyst, showing thread entirely extruded.
Fig. 2d. End of thread, showing barb.

ment. I have watched them dismember in a large glass vessel, when there appeared to be no rational incentive whatever for such conduct. The OPHIURIDÆ were for some reason almost entirely overlooked in our work at this place, *Ophiura cinerea* Lyman being the only species saved.

The coral rock out on the reef was fairly riddled with holes made by the black sea-urchin, *Diadema setosum* Gray, portions of the old decomposing coral heads presenting a honey-combed appearance after the urchins have been removed. When occupying these retreats, the animals have the spines all directed outward in a great bunch, making a defensive armature that would certainly prove effective against almost any foe. How these animals, with their exceedingly brittle and slender spines and unusually thin, fragile tests, manage to make these excavations is something of a mystery. It may be noted, however, that the teeth of *Diadema setosum* are very strong, and the jaws capable of much more extensive protrusion from the test than in most other species. These teeth can be extended at least an inch beyond the corona, and seem to me to be the means by which the borings are made. *Hipponoe esculenta* A. Ag. is found in countless numbers on the sand-flat east of the island on which Spanish Wells is located. This beautifully white species is an excellent one upon which to observe the "righting movements" and other experiments described by Romanes in his very suggestive work on "Jelly-Fish, Star-Fish and Sea-Urchins." Some of the experiments made during my previous visit are perhaps of sufficient interest to note in this connection. These animals remove their excrement, which is in the shape of hard, rounded bodies and is ejected from the apical region, by means of a combined wriggling of the spines and pedicellariæ. Some of these balls were dipped in acetic acid and then placed on the apex of the test. There ensued a violent motion on the part of the spines and pedicellariæ, and the irritating substance was quickly passed on lines radiating from the apex along the ambulacral areas and dropped from the equatorial region of the test. It appeared, therefore, that these organs worked in coördination to pass the offending objects away from the test. In order to show whether this action was entirely automatic or partook of the element of choice, the following experiment was tried. An animal was placed with the actinal pole against the side of a large glass vessel, to which the ambulacral feet soon adhered. In this position a portion of the equator was uppermost. The balls treated with acid were then placed as exactly as possible upon the equator. They were promptly rolled off in the direction opposite the normal one, that is, toward the apical system. This seemed a clear indication that choice was exercised in deciding the direction of removal. If the action of the spines and pedicellariæ had been purely automatic, they would have removed the objects in the customary direction. This would have brought the irritating substance in contact with the numerous sensitive ambulacral feet, which were adhering to the glass on the actinal side. The conclusion that volition was involved was further strengthened by placing non-irritating balls in the same position, when they were worked off in both directions indifferently.

Another experiment was tried to determine whether there was any rudiment of memory to be discovered in the sea-urchins. Placing a specimen on the table, a lighted match was held near the test. The heat caused the animal to move away from the match. After it had progressed some distance, another lighted match was held on the side opposite the one originally irritated. The animal at first retreated directly away from the second match, but upon approaching the place where it had been burned by the first match, it *turned and took a course at right angles to a line drawn between the two sources of danger.* The first match was no longer burning, of course, and we may reasonably surmise that the animal changed its course upon *remembering* its former experience. The other experiments were substantially the same as those tried by Romanes.[1]

[1] "Jelly-Fish, Star-Fish and Sea-Urchins," page 301 et seq. The student will be well repaid should he find time for the perusal of this entire work, one of the most suggestive of the many contributions to science made by Professor Romanes.

Among the cœlenterates a great quantity of gorgonians were secured, most of which have not yet been identified. Among them were *Briareum asbestinum* Pall., a heavy, fleshy species of a pink or purplish color, and without a horny axis cylinder. This is a good form to study, as the polyps are large and will expand freely in aquaria. *Plexaurella dichotoma* is very common, with thick, fleshy branches covered with slit-like apertures, and having the calicles included, and a well marked axis cylinder. *Eunicea tourneforti* M. Edw. has thick branches and exserted calicles. The spicules of this gorgonian are among the most beautiful of objects under the microscope, being unusually large and brilliantly colored with pink and red and purple. *Eunicea tourneforti* M. Edw. is flabellate in form, very dark in color, and has non-retractile polyps. The spicules are very large and massive, without coloration. The most beautiful of the gorgonians is *Rhipidigorgia flabellum* Linn., the familiar "sea-fan." The red variety sometimes grows to a height of four feet, while the yellow specimens are usually much smaller, seldom, if ever, attaining a height of eighteen inches. *Niphigorgia anceps* M. E. is also common, with long branches resembling grass-like leaves of purple and yellow. The polyps are arranged in linear series.

The reef corals at Spanish Wells were practically the same as those found at the Tortugas, but several species were more abundant, notably *Madrepora prolifera* Lam., of which we secured a splendid series; *Mycedium fragile* Dana was found here and not at the Tortugas. *Isophyllia dipsacea* Ag. is interesting from the fact that it has enormous nematocysts and affords, when alive, an excellent opportunity to study these remarkable organs. The nettling cells are found in the tentacles which surround the mouth of the polyp. It is hard to determine just what kind of stimulus will cause the threads to be projected. The writer has found that the tentacles may be touched with a needle or buffeted by the squirmings of a small worm without effect. On the other hand, he has seen scores of them set off without any known cause. A careful study makes it evident that the threads are thrown out by a partial eversion. The point or barb seems to have a rotary motion when passing across the field of the microscope although this may be an optical delusion. A number of actinians were secured here, and one hydroid, a beautiful new *Pennaria*.

CHAPTER VIII.

LITTLE CAT ISLAND AND HOMEWARD BOUND.

On the morning of July 13th, the boats were sent to collect the gorgonians and madrepores that had been left on the beach to dry, and returned loaded to the gunwales with a magnificent collection of sea-fans, yellow and red, gorgonians of a score of species, and *Madrepora cervicornis* or *prolifera*, enough to supply good specimens for all the party. These branching corals required most careful handling, as they are perhaps as brittle a substance as one could imagine. They were carefully stowed in the long boat, and the sea-fans and other gorgonians were tied in large bales and bundles and stored in the hold. The work of packing the coral was commenced at once, and most of the branching madrepores were safely stowed in barrels, with a packing of coarse grass brought from Eleuthera several days previously and dried on deck.

In the afternoon we tried to get the schooner out of the harbor, but failed on account of adverse winds. The next day the wind was still unfavorable. The pilot had no desire to put us aground again, and would not take avoidable risk. A new species of shark was bought from the natives and skinned, as well as a fine porcupine-fish, although handling this exceedingly spiny species was attended with some danger of rather troublesome wounds. In the afternoon we had a grand swimming party over the side of the schooner, the last event of the kind enjoyed during the cruise. Most of our young men and women could swim by this time, and some of the former were accomplished divers. Philip, the pilot, demonstrated his ability to get bottom at a depth of five fathoms, or thirty feet, and claimed to be able to go a depth of nine fathoms. We did not have an opportunity to test this claim, much as we would have been interested in the trial. Another Bahaman claimed to be able to dive fourteen fathoms, but upon being pressed for an explanation of this unheard-of feat, confessed that he meant seven fathoms down and seven up again! The next morning we tried to get away by taking the inland passage around Egg Island, but again failed, being forced to drop anchor near the condemned brig that is allowed to obstruct the harbor entrance in a most unaccountable manner. Thinking to improve the time while waiting for a favorable breeze, some of us went ashore to see if we could dig a well and fill the empty water casks. One only has to dig three or four feet to strike water here. It is rtue that the water will rise and fall with the tides, but sometimes it will be so little brackish as to be quite endurable although not at all palatable. In one place we found that two "wells" had been dug only a few feet apart. Fresh water could be drawn from one and salt water from the other. We had succeded in sinking an old barrel into the good well, and had nearly filled one of the casks when we saw the signal flying from the schooner, which meant that all hands were wanted on board at once. On reaching the vessel, we found that the pilot considered the wind favorable to get out of the harbor, and the captain decided to try it without delay.

The passage was a somewhat anxious one, as the jagged black rocks on every hand were anything but reassuring, especially as we had to beat our way through the narrow channel between the reefs and Eleuthera. The passage through the reefs was off Ridley's Head. Philip, the pilot, seemed to understand his business this time, and after an hour's anxiety we found blue water once more under the schooner's keel, and breathed a sigh of relief at getting out without accident. The pilot was discharged, and thus we parted with the last, but by no means the least, of our good Spanish Wells friends.

The next two days were spent in beating our way against a head-wind along the east coast of Eleuthera, our object being to see what could be found by dredging across the shallow ridge between the northeast end of Eleuthera and Little Cat Island. The delay was particularly vexatious, as our time was getting short, and the thoughts of the party were turning homeward. After ten weeks of the cramped quarters and necessary discomforts of sea life, it was but natural that the romance of the situation should have been pretty well dispelled, and that there should be a longing for the fresh meat and roomy, clean beds of home. The captain, too, was getting anxious to have his responsibilities come to an end. He had given up the comfortable cabin, to which he was used, to make room for the ladies of the party, and he was obliged, moreover, to put up with many little annoyances and discomforts which must at times have severely tried his patience. It was easy to see that most of the party would have been glad to find the bowsprit pointed north instead of experiencing this continual beating against a head-wind, and the monotonous cry of "Hard-a-lee!" as the vessel came about on another tack. It seemed best, however, to make the most of our opportunities, and use the vessel as near the limit of our charter as possible; and so we stuck it out until the desired spot was finally reached, about 3 o'clock in the afternoon of July 18th, our schooner having sailed along the entire coast of Eleuthera, a distance of about eighty miles. This island is exceedingly narrow, averaging only about three miles, and extends northwest and southeast. About twenty-four miles east of its southern extremity is the northwest end of "Cat Island," as it is known to sailors, although the world at large calls it by the more euphonious name of San Salvador. The two main islands are connected by a string of rocky islets, the westernmost of which is Little San Salvador, or "Little Cat." Between this and Eleuthera, a distance of about ten miles, there is a submarine ridge, rising at one point to within nine fathoms of the surface, and sinking rapidly to a great depth on either side. At one place there is a drop from thirteen to nine hundred fathoms within a mile.

We had come to this locality for the purpose of dredging over this submarine ridge, feeling confident from the general lay of the land and currents that an exploration carried on here would not be fruitless. We also intended to send a party of botanists, ornithologists, and entomologists to work on Little Cat Island. This latter plan was frustrated, however, by a piece of carelessness on the part of the mate, who lost his bearings during the night, and worked the vessel so far to leeward of the island that we could not afford to beat up to it again.

We found the dredging here exceedingly difficult, owing to the rocky nature of the ridge. We did not dare use anything but the tangles, and they were constantly getting fouled, and endangering our gear. We made three hauls in the afternoon of the day upon which we arrived at that locality, and seven the next day. The bottom must have been of the roughest possible description, and was probably covered with massive corals interspersed with the branching forms, *Millepora* and gorgonians. The tangles wore out here more rapidly than anywhere else during the voyage, and the strain on the dredging spar, rope, etc., was such as to render the experience anything but an agreeable one to those who had in remembrance the sudden catastrophe while dredging on the Pourtalès Plateau.

The collection secured here was peculiar from the fact that it did not embrace a single crustacean. Hardly a haul of the dredge or tangles at our other fields of work came up without at least a few crabs. Practically all the specimens secured here were either echinoderms or cœlenterates, and nearly all were serpent-stars or hydroids.

The small but exceedingly interesting series of OPHIURIDÆ contains several species not met with elsewhere. There were two species of *Ophiocoma*, one of which had the arms banded, one tentacle-scale, almost circular mouth-shields, and the disk conspicuously and evenly granulated. The other was a small species related to *O. æthiops* Lütken, which is a Pacific species. Our specimen was black on the dorsal surface, and very light buffy, almost white, on the lower side. Arm-spines small, the upper being the longest. Three remarkably pretty species of *Ophiothrix* were collected. One was bluish violet in color, with a disk covered with forked, stumpy spines, and a few long, slender, needle-like spines. This species is beautifully marked, the disk with sharp, radiating lines of purple and white, and the arms with pairs of pure white lines enclosing bands of deep cobalt blue. Arm-spines six, the uppermost being the longest. Another *Ophiothrix* was blue, the disk without long spines, but thickly beset with trifid stumps. This species was ornamented by transverse series of white blotches between the upper arm-plates, and round, white blotches on the under arm-plates. Arm-spines seven, the lowest furnished with hooklets. The third species of this genus is probably *O. suensonii* Lütken, an exquisitely beautiful object under a lens of moderate power. The disk is beset with exceedingly long, glassy spines, arranged along ten radiating lines, and is of a delicate lavender color, with ten sharp, radiating lines of purple running in pairs from centre to circumference, each pair enclosing a band of light violet. There are four concentric purple lines running around near the upper edge of the disk. The lower surface is marked by similar concentric lines of white and purple alternating. Along the upper side of each arm runs a purple band between two fine white lines. On the under surface a similar band extends from the tip of the arms to the mouth. But the most striking feature of this remarkable form is the arm-spines, which are the longest of any in the collection, being nine times as long as the arm-joints. As usual in this genus, these spines are glassy, with a row of spinelets on each side. A species of *Ophiomyxa*, from which the label is lost, but which is associated with the serpent-stars from this locality, is of a buffy white color, with comparatively long arm-spines. Several specimens of a species, which can probably be referred to the genus *Sigsbeia*, were secured at this time. They were smaller than *S. murrhina* of Lyman, or the *Sigsbeia* mentioned in the account of the Havana collections, page 79.

although the specimens from Little Cat Island may be young individuals. The disk is highly vaulted and covered with large plates. The radial shields are very large and prominent, and alternating with them are ten series of squarish plates. Five large radial plates form a pentagonal figure around the center of the dorsal surface. The mouth-papillæ and teeth are quadrate. There is a single minute tentacle-scale and two arm-spines which are lobate and ctenate on their edges like the mouth-papillæ and teeth of *Ophiomyxa*. There are large accessory plates extending downward from the upper arm-plates. The arms roll naturally in a vertical plane. Color in alcohol buffy; the arms banded with pinkish brown.

Coming to the true basket-fish, or ASTROPHYTIDÆ we find the only representatives of the genus *Astrocnida* in our entire collection. This genus is of special interest, as it shows one of the intergrading steps between a simple-armed species, such as *Astrogomphus*, and the branched basket-fish of the true *Astrophyton* type. The arms in this species, which may be *A. isidis* Lyman, are branched two or three times near their ends. One specimen has six and the other seven arms, a very unusual feature in this group. The mouth-parts are spiniform; the disk closely beset with rounded nodules which form raised concentric rings; arms swollen at base and ornamented with raised transverse ridges of granules which bear microscopic hooks as in *Astrogomphus vallatus*. A small specimen of an *Astrophyton* was found here, of a species represented by several larger specimens taken from the Bahama Banks early in the cruise. The species is allied to *A. costosum* Seba, but is probably not identical. The color is brighter than in any other of that genus that I have seen, being a dark pink, which is relieved on the outer branches and twigs of the arms with bands of very light buffy, almost white, giving a beaded appearance which is highly ornamental. The disk has high radial shields beset, especially on their outer parts, with very large stumpy spines in two series, these spines reaching to the second forking on the arms. There is one madreporic body situated as in *A. costosum*.

But a single sea-urchin was secured here, an *Aspidodiadema*, which does not agree very well with either species described by Agassiz. The spines are very long and banded regularly with purple and white. The characteristic sheathed pedicellariæ are well shown, but differ somewhat from those previously described. So far as I can ascertain, this genus has not hitherto been found at a less depth than ninety-five fathoms.

The comparative meagreness of the collections so far as the higher forms are concerned, was more than atoned for by the marvelous series of hydroids from the ridge connecting the two islands. No less than twenty-six species were brought up in the ten hauls of the tangles, of which eighteen are apparently new. It will thus be seen that this spot is one of perhaps unprecedented richness in its hydroid fauna. In less than a single day's dredging here, we brought up a greater number of species of this interesting group than rewarded our week's work off Havana, where we secured twenty-one species in sixteen hauls, or on the Pourtalès Plateau, where we secured twenty-three species in forty-three hauls. The proportion of new species was also far in excess of anything found elsewhere.

The family HALECIDÆ was represented by *Halecium macrocephalum* Allman, characterized by very large hydranths and small hydrothecæ, and a new species of *Halecium* which is very minute, and was, found on a bit of sea-weed completely buried in a growth of algæ and other matter adherent to the sea-weed. It had the curious habit of growth by which new hydrophores sprouted from the old ones just below their margins. The common *Obelia marginata* Allman was found here, and a species of campanularian, for which a new genus may be necessary unless it can be accommodated in the genus *Calycella* of Hincks. Three species of *Hebella*, all apparently new, complete the list of campanularians.

Among the SERTULARIDÆ are two new species of *Sertularia*, one of which resembles the next genus in the fact that the hydrothecæ are in pairs and contingent, although they are not inserted on the front of the stem. The other *Sertularia* is a beautifully ornamented form, the hydrothecae being long and tubular, with close-set thin, but highly elevated ridges giving a closely annulated appearance to the unusually large hydrothecae. *Thuiaria distans* Allman, in which each internode of the stem supports three shallow and distant hydrothecae, and another, probably new, species of the same genus, in which two pairs of hydrothecae are borne on each internode of the stem, were also included. Two species of the genus *Desmoscyphus* were found, neither of which can be placed in any species described in the somewhat full literature at my disposal. I was greatly interested in finding, while working over this collection a species which was described in 1786 by Ellis, one of the very earliest writers on the hydroids, under the name *Sertularia quadridentata*, from the island of Ascension off the African coast. The species is figured in his "Natural History of many Curious and Uncommon Zoöphytes Collected From Various Parts of the World." In 1821 Lamouroux, in his "Exposition Méthodique," describes the same form under the name *Pasythea quadridentata*. From that time on, this curious genus seems to have been lost sight of up to the time when we found our specimens near Little Cat Island. This interesting species is peculiar in having the calicles in groups of four, the lower pair being larger and somewhat different in shape from the upper.

No less than twelve species of PLUMULARIDAE are included in the collection made here, and two-thirds of them are probably undescribed. The genus *Plumularia* is represented by two closely related species, both apparently new. *Halopteris carinata* Allman is a very pretty species which has the cup-shaped hydrothecae surmounted by a pair of fixed lateral nematophores borne on long processes from the stem. The name "carinata" was suggested by the keel that runs down the anterior face of the hydrotheca. The bulkiest hydroid secured during the whole cruise was a species which is in some respects allied to *Hippurella;* but does not show the peculiar reproductive contrivances of that genus. The speci-

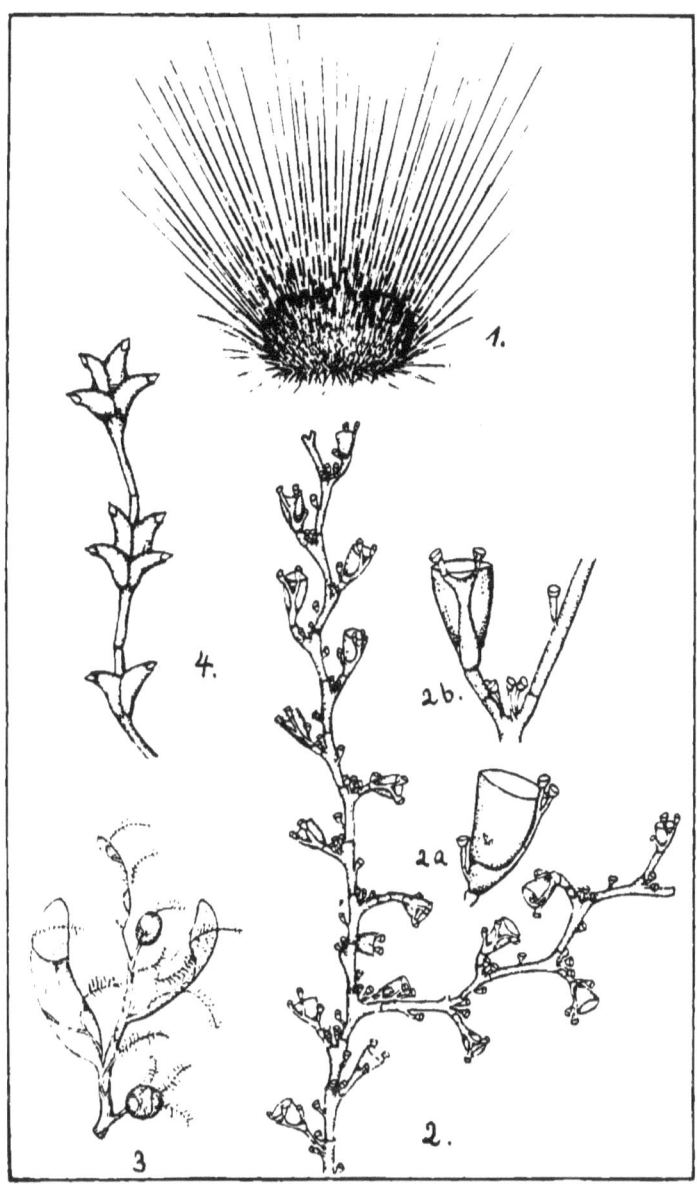

Specimens from near Little Cat Island.

Fig. 1.   ASPIDODIADEMA sp.
Fig. 2.   Plumularian Hydroid.
Fig. 2a, 2b.   Details of same.
Fig. 3.   AGLAOPHENIA PERPUSILLA (Allman) growing on seaweed.
Fig. 4.   PASYTHEA QUADRIDENTATA (Ellis).

men is very massive and bushy, the main stem being over
half an inch in diameter and branching profusely, the whole
colony attaining a height of over two feet. The hydrothecæ
are quite small, and the pinnæ much annulated. One of the
most delicately beautiful of all the Plumularians is a species
allied to *Plumularia obliqua* Sanders, the pinnæ of which are
very short and bear but a single conical hydrotheca. There
are four nematophores in the axil of each pinna. One of the
smallest of the PLUMULARIDÆ is *Aglaophenia perpusilla* Allman, a species resembling a small feather, but only one
quarter of an inch high. The corbula, hitherto unknown,
resembles that of *A. perforata* Allman.

When Dr. S. F. Clarke reported on the hydroids of the
"Blake," he found a remarkable form characterized by peculiar
processes at the bases of the pinnæ, and nematophores of
a new type on the main stem of the colony. This interesting
species was made the type of a new genus and called
Nematophorus grandis Clarke. In our collection from Little
Cat Island are three species of this same genus, one being
the form described by Clarke, and the other two being new.
All three agree in having an unusual amount of very dark
or black pigment distributed throughout the colony. The
peculiar protoplasmic processes described by Clarke, as issuing from the nematophores are shown in our specimens to be
the barbed threads of particularly large nematocysts. There
are many points of unusual interest yet to be studied in connection with this very well-marked genus. *Halicornaria
speciosa* Allman was also secured here, together with two
apparently new species of the same genus which were found
growing on *Nematophorus*. A large quantity of gorgonians
and millepores came up during our work here, but were
mostly of the species secured at Spanish Wells.

At four P. M. July 19th, the tangles were hauled on board
for the last time, and the order given to point the schooner's
jib-boom straight for Baltimore. Notwithstanding all the
pleasure and advantages for study that had been so thoroughly
enjoyed and faithfully embraced, there was no one on board

the "Emily E. Johnson" who was not ready to join heartily in the cheer that went up from her deck as the vessel came about and sail was set for home. The confined quarters and restricted cuisine and cabin-top beds had long since been shorn of their novelty. The work for which we had come had been accomplished, and we felt that it had been well done. It was therefore natural that thoughts of home and friends should once more occupy the imagination, and find vent in an impatience at every lull in the breeze which bore us northward.

The homeward voyage, like the rest of the cruise, had its full quota of work for all. The collections were to be packed for shipment from Baltimore to Iowa City, and it was necessary to thoroughly overhaul all the equipment and put it in as good shape as possible for transportation. Personal effects were furbished up in anticipation of once more entering into the round of civilized life. The collection and equipment were found eventually to necessitate the packing of one hundred and thirty-one barrels, boxes, crates and other parcels, and the proper disposition of all this material was a task involving no little labor. A list was of course kept of the articles packed, and each parcel carefully marked and checked.

During the homeward voyage the provisions became so reduced in variety that there was little left save flour, butter, coffee, tea, and some canned fruits and vegetables. The meat was almost completely gone before the end of the cruise, owing largely to the fact that the corned beef and pickled pork which had been packed in barrels had become tainted during the prolonged sojourn in a hot climate. We found that dried apples and peaches kept remarkably well, and so did rice and beans. The failure of the potatoes caused one of the most serious deprivations. Of course there was no fish to be had while we were under way, and the absence, or at least very scanty supply, of meat was a hardship which would have been felt more severely had we not been homeward bound. There was no danger of actual want, however, so long as the flour and coffee held out, and we had a superabundance of both of these staples. The thing most to be

feared was a long calm, which might possibly have caused our
water supply to run short, a danger never lost sight of by
those accustomed to the peculiar conditions surrounding the
navigation of sail vessels, which are, of course, absolutely
dependent upon winds and currents. On this account skippers are always relieved after they have crossed the belt of
calms known as the "Horse Latitudes," between Lat. 31°
and 33° N. Those who sail in the "fruiters" trading between
the Bahamas and Baltimore have terrible stories to tell of fruit-
laden vessels being caught in these regions by the dreaded
calms, and having to roll week after week on the glassy surface of the ocean, exposed to the pitiless glare of the sun
and, worst of all, the fearful odors of the mass of rotting fruit
in the hold, which must all be thrown overboard if the calm
lasts many days. The stench from this putrid mass must
be unspeakable, if that yielded by only a few rotting "pines"
can be taken as a sample.

We were wonderfully fortunate throughout our cruise in
the matter of weather. Three months are rarely passed at
sea without encountering at least one really severe storm, and
perhaps several trying calms. We escaped them both, as
nothing like a storm or long calm was met with during the
whole cruise. The squalls on the outward voyage were
some of them rather severe, and for one day we were compelled to lay to, but neither of these amounted to what sailors
would call a storm or a gale. So wonderfully were we favored
in this matter that the captain grew uneasy, feeling that such
a stretch of fine weather was abnormal and almost uncanny.
He was evidently most anxious to get his vessel safely into port,
having an ill-concealed fear that there was something porten-
tous in the meteorological conditions. And he was doubtless
right, as will be acknowledged when we reflect that shortly
after our return the West Indies and our South Atlantic coast
were visited by a hurricane of appalling force and fury,
attended by the greatest loss of life and shipping that has ever
been experienced in those regions. It seems to be the belief
of sailors that long-continued periods of fair weather are

"hurricane breeders," as they call them, although the landsman is apt to regard this as one of the ways in which the sailor keeps up his reputation as a chronic "growler."

Another matter in which the party was most fortunate was the continued good health enjoyed throughout the cruise. Of course, seasickness was to be expected, and several persons were always more or less affected when the water was at all rough. Aside from this, however, there was apparently no exception to the excellent physical condition of all on board. Several of the party were materially, and we hope permanently, benefited by the voyage. There was just about enough real work to keep us well, and the sea air and out-of-door life agreed admirably with the young people. As a matter of information for anyone desiring to follow in our footsteps, it may be of interest to state that the records of the commissary committee prove that more food was consumed each week, after the first, than had been disposed of during any preceding week. The appetites thus developed were in most cases good, and in several instances really phenomenal. Fairly hard work and good appetites, in conjunction with provisions which were wholesome and abundant in the main, brought the party home in the best of health.

The homeward voyage was uneventful, the wind being fairly propitious, and no dead calms were experienced. A few rain-squalls varied the monotony, but the weather was pleasant as a rule. After the packing was attended to, considerable leisure was at our disposal, and, if the truth must be told, we were inclined to thoroughly enjoy a season of rest. A sea life offers the best of opportunities for indolence, and possibly this constitutes a material element in the charm which it has for many of us. On July 24th Hatteras Light was sighted, but the wind failed soon after, and little progress was made during the night. On the following day, however, a good breeze sprung up, and the "Emily E. Johnson" seemed imbued with our longing to get home as soon as possible, for she slid through the water at a rate not before attained, rounding Cape Henry early the next morning. The wind lasted to the Baltimore quarantine station, where we spent the greater part of the night of July 26th, and the next morning the schooner was taken to one of the B. & O. railroad wharves, and the voyage was ended.

During the eighty-three days of her absence from Baltimore, the vessel had sailed just about an even three thousand miles, counting straight courses, and not the extra distance actually involved in beating against the wind, and we were gratified to be able to hand her over to her owners in excellent condition. Not a spar nor sail had been materially damaged, and she had suffered no injury beyond the ordinary and inevitable wear and tear incident to a three months' cruise in tropical waters. The vessel had served her purpose admirably, and we often felt grateful for the good fortune that had led to her selection. Should a similar expedition be organized in future, no better vessel could be secured than our old friend, the "Emily E. Johnson." I wish, also, to bear testimony to the courtesy and fair-mindedness of her chief owner, Captain C. C. Paul, of Baltimore. Our business dealings with this gentleman were most pleasant and satisfactory.

We had some trouble in disposing of the ballast, for which we had paid a good price before leaving, and we were finally forced to give away the lumber used in fitting the vessel. The lamps, dishes, kitchen-ware, range, etc., were sold to Captain Paul and left on the schooner.

Considerable annoyance and delay were experienced in getting our collections through the custom house. Not a thing on board was dutiable, but some of the minor officials were determined that each package should be carted over the cobble-stones of the Baltimore streets to the public stores and there opened and examined, a process which would have been fatal to our splendid collection of corals and caused almost irreparable damage to much of the other material. The Chief Appraiser was finally seen and proved to be a gentleman able to appreciate the absurdity of such requirements, and he readily agreed to send an inspector on board to examine our effects at the railroad dock. This was an immense relief to us, as we were almost in despair over the insistence of the minor officials.

This matter having been satisfactorily disposed of, the next thing was to secure a car and attend to loading it with our equipment and collections. This was not left to the railroad men, but every package was handled by members of the expedition, the car being loaded under the direct superintendence of Messrs. Houser, Larrabee and Powell. The care exercised in this matter was both demonstrated and rewarded by the entire absence of breakage or other damage during the transit of the car to Iowa City.

It can scarcely be a matter of surprise to any one who has read the preceding pages, that it was with a real feeling of sadness that we left the "Emily E. Johnson," which had been our home for so many weeks and the scene of such delightful experiences; nor is it to be wondered at that a strange mist gathered in the eyes of more than one of the party when we bade good-bye to Captain Flowers, who had endeared himself to all of us and will remain in our estimation the very type of an honest and manly man and skillful seaman. We felt that his watchful care had averted many a danger, and that his mastery of his calling had been, after all, one of the main reasons for our unvaried success, especially while dredging.

Nor can the leader of the expedition close this narrative without a word of hearty commendation for the young men and women who placed their safety and well-being so largely in his keeping during this novel voyage. That they have become endeared to him is but the natural result of their hearty and ready coöperation at all times, and the zeal with which they carried on the often arduous labors of the cruise. No work was too trying or too disagreeable for them, and the hardest service was always sure of prompt volunteers. It was with the deepest gratitude that the writer learned that all returned in health and safety to their homes.

Perhaps the most remarkable feature of this cruise was its cheapness. The party traveled about five thousand miles, in round numbers, and lived for three months at a total expense of $205.00 for each individual.[1] The original estimate made in 1891 was $200.00 for each person. Just before reaching Baltimore it was deemed desirable to make an assessment of $5.00 all around in order to meet some extra expenses at that place. As a matter of fact, enough remained to give a reunion banquet to the whole party in June, 1894, and still a few dollars remain in the treasury. In addition to the privileges enjoyed during the cruise, each member of the party is entitled to a series of the marine forms collected, after the University has received the first complete series from each locality visited. Several individuals have already sold enough of this material to realize the $200.00 originally expended, so that in these cases the trip cost nothing at all except the time. I am inclined to think that this is a record-breaker in the matter of cheapness.

The amount of zoölogical material collected was perhaps as great as has been secured by any other dredging expedition in the same length of time, and the number of new forms shows that its scientific value will ultimately prove to be equal to that of other much more pretentious cruises. The different groups are to be worked up by the best specialists that can be found, and the readiness with which the masters in marine zoölogy have undertaken to report on the groups in which they are most proficient is in itself the best proof of the scientific value of the collection. These reports will appear from time to time in the "Bulletins from the Laboratories of Natural History of the State University of Iowa." The following specialists have undertaken to work up certain portions of the material as indicated below:

Professor Samuel Garman, of Harvard, the fishes; Mr. William H. Ashmead, of the National Museum, the Hymenoptera (excepting the ants); Mr. Theodore Pergande, Department of Agriculture, Washington, D. C., the ants; Dr. John B. Smith, Rutgers College, the Lepidoptera; Professor Herbert Osborn, Iowa Agricultural College, the Hemiptera;

[1] This sum provided for every necessary expense from Iowa City, the starting point, and return, including a berth in a sleeper and a seat in a palace car from Chicago to Baltimore, for each.

Dr. George Marx, Department of Agriculture, the spiders, except the ATTIDÆ; Professor George W. Peckham, of Milwaukee, the ATTIDE; Mr. H. F. Wickham, State University of Iowa, the Coleoptera; Miss Mary J. Rathbun, of the National Museum, the brachyuran crabs; Mr. James E. Benedict,[1] of the National Museum, the Anomoura; Professor F. H. Herrick, Adelbert College, the Alphei; Dr. W. H. Dall, of the National Museum, the Mollusca; Professor A. E. Verrill, of Yale College, the star-fish, serpent-stars, and Alcyonaria.[2] The report on the Hydroida will be embodied in a forthcoming monograph of the American Hydroids, which is now being prepared by the writer for publication by the United States National Museum. Professor W. G. Farlow, of Cambridge, has in hand the collection of marine Algæ.

The report on the brachyuran crabs is the farthest advanced, and Miss Rathbun announces that there are about one hundred and thirty-one species of that group in the collection, including a number of new forms. Among the hydroids, the writer has found eighty-eight species, more than half of which are new, constituting perhaps the largest single collection of this group that has ever been made in West Indian waters, so far as the results of the various expeditions are at present known.[3]

The educational benefits of this cruise have, it is hoped, been made sufficiently manifest in the preceding pages; but these results must not be regarded as limited by the advantages secured by the members of the party. Far more important considerations are the increased facilities for the investigation of marine forms now offered by the State University to the students of Iowa, and the demonstration of the practicability of accomplishing such results at a cost which is merely nominal.

[1] Mr. Benedict will probably work up the Vermes also.
[2] Professor Verrill may also undertake the Crinoidea.
[3] The collections of the "Albatross" will undoubtedly prove to be more extensive than this, and will be included in the monograph referred to above.

APPENDIX A.

LIST OF COMMISSARY STORES ACTUALLY USED DURING THE EXPEDITION.

BY GILBERT L. HOUSER.

Sugar cured hams,	350 pounds	Canned string beans,	56 pounds
Canvased bacon, boneless	55 "	" succotash,	72 "
Corned beef,	200 "	" peas,	96 "
Pickled pork,	100 "	" tomatoes,	216 "
Mackerel,	15 "	" peaches,	360 "
Boneless codfish,	55 "	" apples,	240 "
Canvased dried beef,	55 "	" cherries,	96 "
Canned corned beef,	168 "	" blackberries,	72 "
" roast beef,	96 "	" raspberries,	48 "
" salmon,	12 "	" apricots,	72 "
" oysters,	72 "	" gooseberries,	144 "
" lobsters,	24 "	" apple butter,	35 "
" turkey,	6 "	Marmalade,	12 "
" tongue,	24 "	Currant jelly,	10
" soups (Huckins')	36 "	Raspberry jelly,	10 "
Wheat flour,	6 barrels	Pickles,	½ barrel
Graham flour,	75 pounds	Vinegar,	15 gallons
White cornmeal,	150 "	Lemons,	2 boxes
Oatmeal,	50 "	Lime juice,	3 gallons
Cracked wheat,	48 "	Raisins,	20 pounds
Rice,	50 "	Condensed milk,	5 cases
Hominy,	50 "	Lard,	225 pounds
Cabbage,	1 crate	Canned creamery butter	200 "
Potatoes,	45 bushels	Cheese,	38 "
Onions,	4 "	Eggs,	80 dozen
Beets,	2 "	Ground mustard,	3 pounds
Navy beans,	100 pounds	" black pepper,	2 "
Dried apples,	35 "	" cinnamon,	1 pound
" peaches,	50 "	" cloves,	1 "
Prunes,	55 "	Table salt,	112 pounds
Canned corn,	144 "	Granulated sugar,	600 "

C sugar,	110 pounds	Coffee (roasted & ground)	45 pounds
Maple sugar,	55 "	Tea,	18 "
Baking powder,	32 "	Cocoa,	7 "
Bi-carb. soda,	1 pound	Coal oil,	52 gallons
Dry yeast,	1 case	Matches,	3 doz. boxes, 500
Corn starch,	15 pounds	Soap, 50 cakes ivory; 25 cakes rosin	
Tapioca,	15 "	Crackers,	75 pounds
Extract lemon,	1 pint	Pilot bread,	63 "
" vanilla,	1 "	Wafers,	21 "
Catsup,	6 pints	Can-openers,	½ dozen
Worcestershire sauce,	5 "	Toothpicks,	½ doz. packages
Saratoga chips,	12 pounds		

DISHES.

Soup plates,	2 dozen	Water pitchers,	⅙ dozen
Dinner "	2 "	Sugar bowls,	¼ "
Dessert "	2½ "	Castors,	¼ "
Cups,	2 "	Knives,	2 "
Saucers,	2 "	Forks,	2 "
Soup tureens,	1½ "	Carving knife and fork	
Cream pitchers,	½ "	Tea spoons,	2
Vegetable dishes,	1 "	Table "	1
Steak platters,	1 "	Teapot	
Bowls,	⅙ "	Coffee pot	
Tumblers,	2 "		

GALLEY OUTFIT.

Range		Coffee boiler	
Teakettle		Skillets,	2
Pots,	2	Dish-pans,	2
Ham-boiler		Ladle	
Saucepan		Potato-masher	
Waffle irons and muffin cups		Coffee-strainer	
Drip pans,	6	Iron spoons,	2
Hash knife and tray		Cake-turner	
Biscuit board and pin			

APPENDIX B.

LIST OF DREDGING AND SHORE STATIONS, S. U. I. BAHAMA EXPEDITION, 1893.

I. DREDGING STATIONS.

1. May 17th. Bahama Banks. 3 fathoms.
2, 3, 4. May 24th. Off Havana, Morro Castle bearing S.W. by W., about 2½ miles. 110 fathoms.
5, 6, 7, 8. May 25th. Off Havana. Morro Castle bearing S.W. by W, about 2½ miles. 140 fathoms.
8½, 9, 10, 11. May 26th. Off Havana. Nearly same ground as No. 5. 200 fathoms.
12, 13, 15. May 27th. Off Havana. 200 fathoms.
14. May 27th. Off Havana. 260 fathoms.
16. May 29th. Off Havana. Nearly same ground as No. 12.
17, 18, 19, 20, 21, 22, 23. June 15th. Off Fort Jefferson, Tortugas. 1½ to 8 fathoms.
24, 25. June 19th. Off Key West. Sand Key Light bearing W.N.W., Key West Light bearing North. 60 fathoms.
26. June 19th. Nearly same ground as No. 24.
27. June 19th. Sand Key Light bearing N.W. by N. Key West Light N. ½ E. 50 to 60 fathoms.
28. June 19th. Sand Key Light bearing N. about 6 miles. 116 fathoms.
29. June 19th. Near last station.
30, 31. June 20th. Off Key West. Sand Key Light bearing N.N.W. About 100 fathoms.
32. June 20th. Sand Key Light bearing N. by W. about 8 miles. 126 fathoms.
33. June 20th. Sand Key Light bearing N. ½ W. about 6 miles. About 105 fathoms.
34. June 20th. Sand Key Light bearing N. about 8 miles. About 120 fathoms.
35. June 21st. Off Key West Sand Key Light bearing N.N.W. about 5 miles. About 90 fathoms.
36. June 21st. Bearings about same as No. 35; distance, 7 miles; depth, about 100 fathoms.
37. June 21st. Bearings as in No. 35; distance, 8 miles; depth, 125 faths.
38. June 21st. Bearings and depth about as in No. 37.
39. June 24th. Off Key West. Sand Key Light bearing W. ½ N., about 6½ miles. 20 fathoms.
40. June 24th. Sand Key Light bearing W. about 8 miles. Depth, 15 fathoms.
41, 42, 43. June 24th. Sand Key Light bearing W. about 8 miles. Depth, 15 fathoms.
44. June 26th. Off Key West, about 1 mile from light. 5¼ fathoms.
45, 46. June 26th. Off Key West, shallow water.

47. June 26th. Key West Light bearing N.W. by N., Sand Key Light W. by N. About 80 fathoms.
48. June 26th. Key West Light bearing N.W. by N., Sand Key Light W. by N. ½ N. About 80 fathoms.
49. June 26th. Sand Key Light bearing W.N.W., American Shoal Light N.E. 85 to 95 fathoms.
50. June 26th. Sand Key Light bearing N.W. by W. ½ W., about 15 miles. About 120 fathoms.
51. June 27th. American Shoal Light bearing N. by W. 10 miles. Depth about 100 fathoms.
52. June 27th. American Shoal Light bearing N. by W. ¼ W., about 10 miles. 105 to 110 fathoms.
53. June 27th. American Shoal Light bearing N.W. by N. ¼ N., about 10 miles. 110 fathoms.
54. June 27th. Bearings as in No. 53, distance 15 miles. About 130 faths.
55. June 27th. About same ground as No. 54.
56. June 27th. Pourtalès Plateau, 24° 16' N. Lat., 81° 22' W. Long. Depth about 200 fathoms.
57. June 27th. 24° 18' N. Lat., 81° 18' W. Long. 200 to 225 fathoms.
58. June 28th. 24° 19' N. Lat., 81° 19' W. Long. About same depth as No. 57.
59. June 28th. 24° 20' N. Lat., 81° 20' W. Long. About 130 fathoms.
60. June 28th. 24° 15' N. Lat., 81° 20' W. Long. About 125 fathoms.
61. June 29th. Key West Light bearing N.W., American Shoal Light N. E. 75 to 80 fathoms.
62. June 29th. American Shoal Light bearing N.E. by N., 8 miles. 70 to 80 fathoms.
63. June 29th. American Shoal Light N. by E. ½ E., about 8 miles. 85 to 95 fathoms.
64. June 29th. American Shoal Light N. by W., about 8 miles. About 110 fathoms.
65. June 29th. American Shoal Light bearing N. by W. ½ W., 10 miles. About 115 fathoms.
66. June 30th. Key West Light bearing N., depth, 6 fathoms.
67. June 30th. Off Key West.
68 to 78. July 18th, 19th. Off Little Cat Island, on the submerged bank connecting it with Eleuthera. 3 to 13 fathoms.

II. SHORE STATIONS.

1. Egg Island, Bahamas, May 13th.
2. Water Cay, Bahamas, May 20th.
3. Havana, Cuba, May 21st to 28th.
4. Bahia Honda, Cuba, June 1st to 3rd.
5. Dry Tortugas, Florida, June 7th to 13th.
6. Key West, Florida, June 17th to July 1st.
7. Harbor Island, Bahamas, July 8th.
8. Eleuthera, Bahamas, July 9th to 15th.

INDEX.

Abaco Island, 46.
Acanthogorgia, 86.
Acanthomyx petiverii, 209.
Accident on Pourtalès Plateau, 141.
Achelous spinimanus, 125.
Acridiidæ, 208.
Actæa palmeri, 51.
    spetigera, 124.
Actinians at Bahia Honda, 99.
    method of killing, 99.
Actinometra near Havana, 76.
Actinopteryx fucicola, 121.
Ægialitis semipalmata, 40.
    wilsonia rufinucha, 40.
Agapostemon femoralis, 206.
Agassiz, Alexander, 2, 169, 173, 180.
    introduction of iron rope in dredging by, 3.
    advises dredging on Pourtalès Plateau, 139.
Agassiz, Louis, 2.
Agave, 43.
    at Bahia Honda, 99.
Agaricia agaricites, 134.
Aglaophenia, 89, 179.
    apocarpa, 179.
    gracilis, 179.
    lophocarpa, 89.
    minuta, 30, 54.
    perforata, 54, 225.
    perpusilla, 225.
    rhynchocarpa, 89.
    rigida, 179.
    sigma, 180.
Aground, 187.
Aid rendered by Alexander Agassiz, 8.
Aid rendered by Capt. J. W. Collins, 8.
    Jas. E. Benedict, 8.
    Hon. Marshall McDonald, 8.
Alcohol, storage of, 21.
Alcoholic specimens, method of preserving, 56.
"Albatross," 3.
Alcyonaria, comparison of forms from deep and shallow water, 87.
    near Havana, 85.
    of Pourtalès Plateau, 175.
Allopora miniacea Pourtalès, 177.
Alpheus, 52, 126, 160.
    heterochelis, 161.
American flag, absence of in Havana harbor, 61.
American Shoal light, 139.
Amphiuma, 45.
Amphiura, 45, 170.
Anamathia crassa, 156, 161.
Anasimus latus, 156.
Anchonus, 96.
Anchorage inside the reefs, 144.
Andrews, Dr. L. W., 186.
Andros Island, 46.
Andrenidæ, 206.
Angel-fish, 120.
Anemones, 177.
Annelids, 127.
Anomalot ie furcillatus, 156.
Anomouran crabs, 158.
Anous stolidus, 40, 203.
Antenella gracilis, 88.
Antennarius, 28, 29, 121, 149.
Anthenoides, 166.
    piercei, 169.

Antipatharian corals, 176.
Antipathes, 87.
Anthonomus jülichii, 153.
Ants, 121.
Aphrocallistes bocagei, 180.
Apocynum, 44.
Arachnida, 161.
Arachnopsis filipes, 156.
Arbacea, 83.
  punctulata, 98.
Arbaceidæ, 83.
Arca, donaciformis, 212.
  noæ, 98.
  transversa, 212.
  velata, 129.
Architecture of Havana, 63.
Archaster, 53.
Architectonica granulata, 212.
Ardea virescens, 203.
Arey, Prof. M. F., 19, 188.
Argemone mexicana, 44.
Argonauta (argo?), 164.
Artipus, 41, 58.
  floridanus, 122, 153.
Asaphis, 98.
Ascorhynchus, 161.
Ashmead, Mr. William H., 206, 231.
Asilid fly, 153, 207.
Aspidodiadema, 83, 223.
Assignment of work, 20.
  to duty while dredging, 47, 48.
Asterias, 168.
  volsellata, 168.
Asteriidæ, 167.
Asterinidæ, 78.
Asteroidea, 165.
Asthenosoma hystrix, 173.
Astralium, 52, 126.
  cælatum, 158.
Astrocnida, 222.
  isidis, 81, 222.
Astrogomphus, 80, 81, 222.
  costosum, 222.
  vallatus, 81, 172, 222.
Astropecten, 130, 135, 166, 212.
Astropectenidæ, 130.
Astrophytidæ, 79, 81, 222.
Astrophyton, 170, 222.

Astrophyton agassizii, 132.
  costosum, 132.
  mucronatum, 172.
Attidæ, 97.
Attractive coloration, 124.
Aulostoma, 148.
Avicula, 52.
  margaritifera, 129.
Awnings, 17.
Axohelia mirabilis, 84.

Bahama Banks, 37, 186.
Bahama expedition, assignment of
    work in, 18.
  equipment of, 7.
  help rendered by the University, 5.
  incipiency of, 5.
  laboratory of, 7.
  ladies admitted to, 5.
  management of, 6.
  origin of, 4.
  personnel of, 19.
  requisition for admission to, 17.
Bahama fly catcher, 41.
Bahama Islands, zoölogical reconnoisance of, 5.
Bahia Honda, actinians of, 99.
  birds of, 95.
  botany of, 99.
  channel at, 104.
  corals of, 98.
  difficulties at, 93-95.
  insects, 96.
  mollusks of, 98.
  plants of, 99.
  restrictions imposed by officials, 94.
  scenery near, 93.
Balistes, 28, 189, 204.
Ballast, 17.
Ballord, Webb, 19, 40.
Baltimore to Egg Island, 20.
Banana, 101.
Barnacles, 161.
Baris chalybea, 96.
  quadrimaculata, 96.
Barrett, A. M., 19.

Barynotus, 207.
Basket fish, 78, 132.
Bat fish, 50, 151.
Bathynectes longispina, 158.
Bearing of crinoid ground, 165.
Becalmed in Florida Straits, 138.
Bembidium contractum, 152.
Benacus, 69.
Benedict, James E., 8, 56, 72, 232.
Bermuda Islands, land birds, 118.
Berry Islands, 46.
Bibb, 2.
Bill of fare committee, 22.
Bird Key, 109, 113.
Birds along Gulf Stream, 29.
  at Dry Tortugas, 118.
  of Bahia Honda, 95.
  of Egg Island, 40.
  of Eleuthera, 203.
Black chelæ of crabs, 124.
Black-whiskered vireo, 41.
"Blake," 3, 92, 165.
Blapstinus opacus, 122, 153.
Boats at Spanish Wells, 200.
Booby gannet, 119.
Botany of Bahia Honda, 99.
  of Egg Island, 42.
Brachymyrmex heeri, 206.
Brachyurans, 77, 122, 155.
  report on, 232.
Brain of turtles, 105.
Briareum asbestinum, 215.
Bridled tern, 40, 119.
Brooks, Prof. W. K., on Alphei, 160.
Brown pelican, 119.
Bungo, 62.
Bunks, 16.
Buprestid, 153, 207.
Butterflies at Havana, 70.

Cactus, 44.
Cafius, 41.
  bistriatus, 121.
Calappa angusta, 158.
  marmorata, 125.
Caligorgia gracilis, 175.
Callichorma columbina, 70.
Calms, 185, 227.

Calvin, Prof. S., 6.
Calycella, 223.
Campanularian hydroids, 30, 53, 178, 223.
Camponotus tortuganus, 121.
Cancroidea, 124, 158.
Canned goods, 138.
Canning factory, 137.
Canthon lævis, 152.
Canvas covering for dredges, 10.
Cape Henry, 228.
Captain, selection of, 15.
  of port, 94.
Carcharhinus glaucus, 145.
Cardiosoma guanhumi, 210.
Cardium isocardium, 129.
  muricatum, 212.
"Carey chickens," 33.
Car, loading of, 230.
Carpillius corallinus, 210.
Caryophyllia, 84.
Cassis cameo, 211.
Cat Island, 219.
Catorama punctulata, 122.
Cenobita diogenes, 126, 158.
Cephalopod, 164, 211.
Ceratias uranoscopus, 49, 205.
Cerithium, 42, 52, 98, 128, 212.
Certhiola bahamensis, 41, 203.
"Challenger," 2.
  reports of, 4, 165.
Channel at Bahia Honda, 104.
  off Eleuthera, 218.
Chelæ, modification of in hermit crabs, 42.
Chelymorpha (argus?), 153.
Chesapeake Bay, sail down, 22.
Chief appraiser, 229.
Children at Spanish Wells, 197.
Chilocorus cacti, 152.
Chione cingenda, 129, 162.
Chiton, 41, 212.
Chordeiles virginianus minor, 203.
Chrysogorgia, 85.
Chrysogorgidæ, 85.
Chrysomelidæ, 96, 153.
Cicada, 207.
Cicindela marginata, 52, 207.

Cicindela olivacea, 97.
  tortuosa, 97, 152.
Cidaridæ, 173.
Cidaris tribuloides, 132, 173.
Cirrhipathes, 176.
Citizens of Spanish Wells, 197.
Cladocarpus, 89, 180.
  dolicotheca, 89.
Clarke, S. F., 179.
Clorocoris loxops, 122.
Cocoanuts, 99.
  palms, 42, 193.
Coccinella sanguinea, 207.
Coccinellidæ, 152.
Codling, 148.
Cœlenterates, near Havana, 83.
  of Pourtalès Plateau, 175.
  of Egg Island, 45.
Cœlopleurus floridanus, 83, 173.
Coleoptera of Egg Island, 41.
  of Eleuthera, 207.
  of Key West, 152.
  of Tortugas, 121.
  of Water Cay, 58.
Collecting in Gulf Stream, 27.
Colors of dolphin, 146.
  of water and clouds, 186.
  of crustacea, 124, 158.
Columbella, 128, 162.
  mercatoria, 211.
Columbigallina passerina, 40, 203.
C matulæ, 76, 165.
Commissary committee, 18.
Compositæ, 100.
Conus mus, 212.
Cook suffers from heat, 143.
Corallines, 115.
Coral reef, description of, 201.
  rock, 44.
Corals at Bahia Honda, 98.
  near Havana, 83.
  northern limit of reef-building species, 25.
Cornulariidæ, 86.
Corticaria, 122.
Cost of cruise, 231.
Cotton plant, 101.
"Crawfish," 196.

Crepidula fornicata, 212.
Crinoids, 164.
  actions of, 74.
  great abundance of, 165.
  near Havana, 71.
  near Tortugas, 131.
  preserved in sealed pans, 56.
Crustacea, at Bahia Honda, 97.
  Tortugas, 122
  Pourtalès Plateau, 155.
  Egg Island, 45.
  lack of, at Little Cat Island, 220.
  protective form and coloration in, 51.
Cryptocephalus marginicollis, 70.
Cryptophagidæ, 152.
Cryptopodia concava, 52, 158.
Cryptozonia, 167.
Ctenophore, 99.
Cuba, coast of, 59, 92.
  Consul general of, 62, 90.
  officials, 60, 91.
  size, 59.
"Current," the (Eleuthera), 202.
Currents off the Florida reefs, 106.
Curculionids, 207.
Custard apples, 102.
Custom house, 229.
Customs regulations at Havana, 60.
Cyathophylloid corals, 176.
Cybister lherminieri, 69.
Cymopolus asper, 158.
Cyphoma, 128.
  gibbosa, 211.
Cypræa, 128.

Dall, Dr. W. H., mollusca, 232.
  deep sea mollusks, 163.
  symmetrical hermit crabs, 163.
Dascyllidæ, 152.
Dasygorgia, 85.
Decker, E. G., 19.
  ornithologist of expedition, 40.
Deep sea, coloration in, 83.
Degeneracy from intermarriage, 196.
Deltocyathus, 84.
Dendronotus, 20.
Dentalium, 163.

INDEX. 241

Department of State, letter from, 6.
Dermestes vulpinas, 153.
Desmoscyphus, 54, 88, 224.
Diadema setosum, 45, 132, 202, 213.
Diodon, 28, 49.
   hystrix, 205.
Diplomatic service, working of, 190.
Diploria cerebriformis, 134.
Diplopteron, 89.
Diptera, 153.
Distichopora, 177.
   contorta, 84.
   sulcata, 85.
Ditzen, Henry, 19.
   in charge of vermes, 126.
Diving of Bahamans, 218.
"Dog watch," 184.
Dolium perdix, 211.
Dolphin fishing, 145.
Dorocidaris bartletti, 82, 173.
   blakei, 173.
   papillata, 161, 173, 174.
Dorymyrmex pyramicus, 206.
Double Headed Shot Cays, 57.
Dredge, anchors the schooner, 142.
Dredge, 10, 11.
   effectiveness of, 48.
Dredging machine, first trial of, 47.
   management of, 73.
Dredging off Little Cat Island, 220.
   on Pourtalès Plateau, 139.
Dredging rope, 9.
   care of, 13.
   reeling of, 13.
   rigging of, 13.
Drew, Prof. Gilman, 19.
   Mrs., 19.
Dry Tortugas, 103, 108, 117.
   fumigation of vessel at, 107.

Eburia, 207.
   duvalii, 207.
Echinanthus, 48, 53.
   rosaceus, 133.
Echeneis naucrates, 205.
Echinodermata of Bahia Honda, 98.
   of Spanish Wells, 212.
Echinoderms of Egg Island, 45.

Echinoderms of the Great Bahama
   Bank, 52.
   of Havana region, 77, 78.
Echinoidea of Pourtalès Plateau, 172.
Echinometra subangularis, 133, 174.
Echinus gracilis, 174.
Educational value of expedition, 140.
   benefit of expedition, 231.
"Eel Pout," 148.
Egg Island, anchorage at, 15.
   birds of, 40.
   botany of, 42.
   coleoptera of, 41.
   cœlenterata of, 45.
   crustacea of, 45.
   description of, 37.
   echinoderms of, 45.
   entomology of, 41.
   harbor of, 36.
   insects of, 41.
   mollusca of, 41, 45.
   plants of, 42.
   products of, 39.
   view from, 39.
Elateridæ, 96.
Elateropsis rugosus, 207.
Eleuthera, first seen, 36.
   coast of, 192, 219.
Ellis, 224.
El Morro, 60.
Emarginula, 212.
"Emily E. Johnson," description of,
   16.
   condition of at end of cruise,
   229.
Entomology of Bahia Honda, 96.
   of Egg Island, 41.
Epialtus bituberculatus, 209.
Erebus, 206.
Eriphia gonagra, 210.
Eristalis vinctorum, 154.
Errantia, 127.
Etropus, 50.
Enetheia bicolor, 41, 203.
Eunicea, 46.
   tourneforti, 215.
Eunicidæ, 127.
Eupactus viticola, 152.

Enpagurus discoidalis, 159.
  granulatus, 126.
Euphoria sepulcralis, 58.
Euthuorus filum, 70.
Euschistus crenatus, 153.
Evania appendigaster, 154.
Evenings on shipboard, 184.
Examination of schooner by health officers at Havana, 91.
Excavations made by sea-urchins, 213.
Executive committee, 19.
Expedition, cheapness of, 230.
Eyes of Alpheus, 52.

Fan palms, 100.
Factory for pineapples, 189.
Farlow, Prof. W. G. (algæ), 232.
Farming on Eleuthera, 199.
Farrea facunda, 180.
Fasciolaria, 128.
  gigantea, 128, 211.
  trapezium, 211.
  tulipa, 211.
Fauna, richness of at Pourtalès Plateau, 140.
Fewkes, Dr. J. Walter, 179.
Fiddler crabs, 125.
File-fish, 50.
Fish at Tortugas, 119.
  brought up on tangles, 48.
  flying, 33.
  vivid hues of, 119.
Fishes at Spanish Wells, 204.
  of Gulf weed, 28.
  of Pourtalès Plateau, 147.
Fissurella, 41, 98, 128.
  nodosa, 212.
Flocks of sea-birds, optical delusion concerning, 114.
Flounder, 50, 121.
Flowers, Capt. Chas., 11, 15, 89, 105, 109, 142, 143, 230.
Flute-mouth, 148.
Flying-fish, 33.
Fort Jefferson, description of, 111.
Fort Taylor, 137.
Fourth of July, 185.

Fregata aquila, 203.
Frogs, 204.
Fruits of Egg Island, 44.
Fumigation of vessel at Tortugas, 116.
  benefit of, 117.
Fusus (F. eucosmius ?), 162.

Gale, 34, 135.
Games at Spanish Wells, 197.
Garden Key, 113.
  reefs at, 114.
Garman, Prof. Samuel, fishes, 205, 231.
Garzetta candidissima, 95.
Gastropods of Gulf weed, 29.
  at Egg Island, 41.
  at Tortugas, 128.
  toleration of immersion in alcohol, 129.
Geiger tree, 101.
Gelochel don nilotica, 203.
Geocarcinus, 97.
  lateralis, 210.
Geographical distribution of marine life, 140.
Ginglymostoma cirratum, 110.
Goat fish, 120.
Goodman, Dr., 111.
Gonangia (of F ia), 180.
Gonian itus marginipunctatus, 122.
Gonodactylus, 161.
  chiragra, 126.
Gorgonellidæ, 86.
Gorgonia, 85.
Gorgonians of Spanish Wells, 215.
Gorgonidæ, 82, 86.
  of Egg Island, 45.
Grammaria, 179.
Grapsus maculatus, 45.
Grass finch, 41.
Graves at Tortugas, 114.
Great Bahama Bank, 46.
  animals of, 49.
  color of water on, 47.
  crustacea of, 50.
  dredging on, 47.
  echinoderms of, 52.

Great Bahama Bank, fish of, 49.
    geography of, 46
    hydroids of, 53.
    mollusca of, 52.
Griburius larvatus, 153.
Grosbeak, 41.
Ground dove, 40.
Gulf Stream, 24.
    beneficent work of, 26.
    collecting in, 27.
    course of, 26.
    list of animals of, 31.
    off Cuba, 92.
    temperature of, 24, 25.
Guns, care of at sea, 38.
    for tropical shooting, 40.
Gymnasteriidæ, 166.
Gyascutus carolinensis, 207.

Halecidæ, 223.
Halecium, 53.
    filicula, 178.
    macrocephalum, 223.
Halicornaria speciosa, 225.
Halieutichthys, 151.
Halobates, 154.
Halopteris carinata, 224.
Hammerhead shark, 144.
Haplophyllia paradoxa, 176.
Harbor Island, 182, 188, 189.
    churches in, 190.
    harbor at, 187.
    houses in, 189.
    jail at, 190.
    magistrate at, 189.
Hatteras light, 228.
Havana, 59.
    astrophytidæ near, 79.
    alcyonaria near, 85.
    basket fish near, 79.
    business at, 68.
    cathedrals of, 67.
    climate of, 69.
    cœlenterates near, 83.
    corals near, 84.
    crustaceans near, 76.
    danger at, 71.
    drives of, 66.

Havana, echini near, 82.
    echinoderms near, 77.
    English sparrows in, 65.
    harbor of, 60, 61.
        night scene in, 61, 62.
    heat at, 68.
    history of, 63
    hydrocorallinæ near, 84, 85.
    hydroids near, 87.
    insects of, 69.
    leaving, 91.
    museum in, 66.
    natives of, 64.
    ophiuridæ of, 78.
    parks of, 64, 65.
    photographs of, 70.
    poorer quarters of, 67.
    reception of party at, 62.
    return to harbor of, 89.
    serpent-stars near, 78.
    sights of, 63.
    soldiers in, 67.
Health throughout the cruise, 228.
Heat at Egg Island, 41.
    off Cuban coast, 91.
    on Pourtalès Plateau, 143.
Hebella, 179, 223.
Heidemann, Mr. O., 122, 154.
Hemiptera, 207.
    at Key West, 153, 154.
    at Tortugas, 122.
    of Egg Island, 41.
Hemiptychus similis, 152.
Hemitrochus varians, 212.
Hermit crabs, 42.
Herrick, Prof. F. H., 160, 232.
Heteropteron, 207.
Hexactinellidæ, 180.
Hippocampus, 148.
Hipponöe esculenta, 133, 202, 213.
Hippurella, 224.
Hoist, 8.
Hold, arrangement of, 17.
"Hole in the wall," 46.
Holopus rangei, 105.
Holymenia, 153.
Homeward voyage, 226.
"Horse latitudes," 227.

House at Egg Island, 40.
Houser, G. L., 7, 18, 19, 70.
Howe, Miss M., 19.
Hurricane, 227.
Hydra viridis, 30.
Hydrocorallinæ near Havana, 84, 85.
Hydroida, 232.
Hydroids, from Little Cat Island, 223.
  from near Havana, 87.
  of Bahama Banks, 53.
  of Gulf weed, 30.
  of Pourtalès Plateau, 178.
Hydrophilus triangularis, 69.
Hymenoptera, 154.
Hymenorus convexus, 122, 153.

Ice, absence of on board, 146.
Icteris hypomelas, 95.
Idia, 180.
Insects at Bahia Honda, 96.
  at Egg Island, 41.
  at Havana, 69.
  at Key West, 152.
  at Spanish Wells, 206.
  at Tortugas, 121.
  at Water Cay, 57.
Iridescent colors of vermes, 127.
Iron plates brought up in dredging, 142.
Iron rope, equipment of, 49.
  strength of, 142.
  successful use of in dredging, 49.
Isis, 175.
Islands, composition of, 114.
  coral in incipiency, 118.
Isolated life, effect of, 195.
Isophyllia dipsacea, 134, 215.

Jelly fish, 31.
Johnson, Dr. Leora, 19.
  work of at Spanish Wells, 196.
  observations on people, Spanish Wells, 196.

Key West, buildings at, 137.
  canning factory at, 137.
  description of, 136.

Key West, harbor of, 107.
Kodak, use of at Havana, 70.
Korethraster, 167.

Laboratory, fitting of, 16.
Lachnopus, 96.
  floridanus, 153.
Ladies, accommodations for at Tortugas, 111.
  admitted to party, 6.
Lævicardium serratum, 212.
Lafoëa convallaria, 88.
Lambrus, 157.
  agonus, 157.
  fraterculus, 157.
  pourtalesia, 157.
Lamellibranchiata, 212.
  at Tortugas, 129.
Lamouroux, 224.
Land crab, 125, 159.
  anatomy of, 97.
  of Eleuthera, 210.
Lantana, 43, 103.
Larrabee, Wm. Jr., 19, 141, 229.
Larridæ, 206.
Larus atricilla, 203.
Latreutes ensiferus, 29.
Least sandpiper, 40.
Leguminosæ, 44, 103.
Lepas, 29, 161.
Lepidoptera at Bahia Honda, 97.
  at Spanish Wells, 206.
  at Tortugas, 121.
Leptodius floridanus, 124.
Leptogonaster, 169.
Leptopodia sagittaria, 122.
Library, fitting of, 16.
Lictorella, 88.
"Lightning," the, 1.
Linerges mercurius, 31, 55, 134.
Liomera longimana, 124.
Lippia, 43.
Lispognathus thomsoni, 156.
Littorina, 98.
  scabra, 212.
  ziczac, 212.
Little Cat Island, 217, 219.
Little Egg Island, 38, 44.

Little Egg Island, gastropods of, 41.
Livonia, 128.
    pica, 45, 212.
Loberus impressus, 152.
Locusts of Havana, 70.
Logger ead Key, 113.
Loggerhead turtles, he'plessness of, 119.
Longhorns, 207.
Lophaster, 167.
Lophiidæ, 150.
Loxigilla violacea, 41.
    bahamensis, 203.
Lucina divaricata, 212.
    jamaicensis, 212.
    tigerina, 129.
Luidia, 166.
    alternata, 166.
    clathrata, 212.
Luperus malachioides, 96.
Lycænid, 121.
Lygæus, 153.

Mackerel, 121.
Macroceloma, 51, 156.
    trispinosa, 123.
    septemspinosa, 156.
Macroura near Havana, 76.
Macrotus waterhousii, 203.
Mad dog on deck, 71.
Madrepora cervicornis, 134
    palmata, 183.
    prolifera, 215.
Maioid crabs, 155.
Malthe, 50, 151.
Mameys, 102.
"Man-eating" sharks, 145.
Mangos, 101.
Mangroves, 43.
Mangrove swamps, 99.
Manicina areolata, 134.
Manilla plants, 39.
"Man-o'-war" bird, 57.
    at Tortugas, 111, 119.
Mantis, 208.
Mariel, 103.
Marine Hospital, U. S., 137.
Marine mollusca of U. S., 162.

Martin Wagner & Co., 137.
Marx, Dr. George, 232.
Meandrina clivosa, 99.
    sinuosa, 99.
Melagrina meleagris, 98.
    margaritifera, 212.
Memory in sea-urchins, 214.
Metachroma, 96.
    pellucida, 153.
Metalia, 134.
Microphrys bicornutus, 123.
Midgets at Spanish Wells, 197.
Millepora, 54.
    expanded zoöids of, 54.
    alcicornis, 134.
Mimus gundlachii, 41, 203.
Mithrax, 123, 157.
    forceps, 123.
    hispidus, 123.
    spinosissimus, 209.
Moat at Fort Jefferson, 113.
Mocking bird, 41.
Modern crinoid fauna, 164.
Modifications of chelæ, 42.
Mollusca of Bahia Honda, 98.
    of Egg Island, 41.
    of Great Bahama Bank, 52.
    of Gulf weed, 29.
    of Pourtalès Plateau, 162.
    of Spanish Wells, 211.
    of Tortugas, 128.
Mollusks, colors of, 128.
Monedula signata, 206.
Monocanthus, 28, 50.
Monocrepidius, 96.
    lividus, 152.
Monroe, Mr., U. S. Agent, 190.
Moon flower, 100.
Morals of negroes, 190.
Morro Castle, 54, 60.
Mother Carey's chickens, 29, 33.
Mudd, Dr., 112.
Munida, 76, 159.
Murgantia histrionica, 122.
Murex, 98, 128, 162.
    cabritii, 162.
    fulvescens, 163.
    nodatus, 163.

Murex pomum, 163, 211.
Murices, 163.
Muræna melanotis, 204.
Murray, Dr. David R., 111, 117, 135.
Murrill, George, mate, 19.
Muscids, 207.
Musquitoes at Bahia Honda, 93, 95.
Myiarchus lucaysiensis, 40.
Mycedium fragile, 215.
Myriopods, 96.

Nacerdes melanura, 70.
Nassau, N. P., 186.
Natica, 98.
    affinis, 212.
Nautilograpsus minutus, 29.
Negroes, 188.
    morals of, 190.
Nematocarcinus, 159.
    ensiferus, 159.
Nematophorus, 89.
    grandis, 225.
Neptunus, 51.
    sayi, 29.
Nerita, 98.
    peloronta, 212.
    tessellata, 41, 212.
Nets, 10.
Nettling cells, observations on, 215.
Noctiluca, 55.
Noddy terns, 110, 119.
Nomia, 206.
Nurse sharks, 110.
Nycticorax violaceus, 203.

Obelia hyalina, 30.
    marginata, 87, 223.
Obeliscus, 212.
    sulcatus, 212.
Oculina arbuscula, 176.
    from great depth, 176.
    varicosa, 99.
Octopus, 128.
Ocypoda arenaria, 125.
Ocypodoidea, 125.
Officials, customs, at Havana, 60.
"Ollas," 147.
Oliva reticularis, 211.

Ophidiaster, 167.
    tubifer, 167.
Ophiocamax, 78, 82, 170.
Ophiocantha, 53, 78, 81.
Ophiocoma, 131, 170, 220.
    æthiops, 220.
    echinata, 131.
    riisei, 131.
Ophiocreas, 80.
    lumbricus, 171.
Ophioglypha, 78, 169.
Ophiolepis, 78.
Ophiomitra, 78.
Ophiomusium, 78, 79.
Ophiomyxa, 80, 221.
    flaccida, 132, 170.
Ophionereis reticulata, 131.
Ophiopæpale, 78.
    goësiana, 81.
Ophiothyreus, 78, 81.
Ophiothrix, 45, 53, 221.
    orstedii, 132.
    suensonii, 221.
Ophiozona, 78.
Ophiura, 78, 130.
    appressa, 131.
    cinerea, 130, 131.
    lævis, 131.
    rubicunda, 131.
Ophiuridæ, 78, 82, 169, 213.
    near Havana, 78, 81.
    of Pourtalès Plateau, 169.
    of Spanish Wells, 213.
Orbicella annularis, 134.
Oriole, 95.
Origin of deep-sea fauna, 164.
Ornithology of Bahia Honda, 95.
Ornamentation of deep-sea shells, 163.
Orthoptera, 208.
Osachila tuberosa, 77, 158.
Osborn, Prof. Herbert, 231.
Otiorhynchid, 207.
Othonia, 123.
Oxacis, 122, 153.
Oxybelus emarginatus, 121.
Oyster dredge, 11.

Pachnæus opalus, 41, 70, 207.
Palæmon natator, 29.
Palæotropus, josephenæ, 174.
Palinurus longimanus, 211.
Pangæus bilineatus, 122.
Panopeus, 124.
Pans, as receptacles, 56.
Paracyathus, 84.
Paramuricea, 86.
" Parka Centrale," of Havana, 65.
Parthinopidæ, 157.
" Passage, inside," 191.
    narrow to Spanish Wells, 192.
Passion vines, 100.
Pasythea quadridentata, 224.
Paul, Capt. C. C., 229.
Pawpaws, 102.
Peckham, Prof. Geo. W., 232.
Pecten ornatus, 129.
    irradians, 212.
Pediculati, 149.
Pelagic forms, difficulty of collecting, 32.
Pelagic hemiptera, 154.
Pelia mutica, 156.
Pelopæus fasciatus, 206.
Pennaria, 216.
Pentaceros reticulatus, 52, 187, 202, 212.
Pentacrinidæ, 165.
Pentacrinus, asteria, 73.
    decorus, 73, 74.
    mülleri, 73, 74.
Pentacrinus ground, 71, 165.
    first haul of, 73.
    first specimen of, 75.
    transportation of, 74.
Pentagonasteridæ, 160.
Pepper coral, 54.
Pergande, Mr. Theo., 121, 206, 231.
Pericera cornuta cœlata, 123, 156.
Petalium bistriatum, 122.
Petalosticha, 83.
Petrel, stormy, 33.
    Wilson's, 29.
Petrolisthes, sex-spinosus, 126.
Phaëthon flavirostris, 203.
Phakellia tenax, 181.

Phaleria, 41, 58, 152.
Pheidole megacephala, 121.
Philip, the pilot, 218.
Pholas, 212.
Phosphorence of sea, 31, 54, 55.
Photography, arrangements for, 16.
Photographs taken by Mr. Houser, 113.
Phrymodius maculatus, 124.
Phrynus, 58.
Phycis regius, 148.
Physalia, 121.
    in Bay of Fundy, 26.
    arethusa, 134.
" Pier Rock," 200.
Pilot at Bahia Honda, 92, 104.
    at Harbor Island, 187.
Pilotage at Key West, 106.
Pilots' Association at Key West, 106.
Pilumnus caribæus, 51.
Pindar, Mr., 39.
Pineapple, culture of at Spanish Wells, 198.
Pines, 101.
Pinna, 98, 202.
    muricata, 212.
Pipe fish, 119.
Pita plant, 43, 99.
Plagusia depressa, 210.
Plans and equipments, 1.
Plants of Bahia Honda, 99.
    of Egg Island, 42.
Platycaulus, 175.
Platylambrus serratus, 123, 157.
Plexaura dichotoma, 46.
Plexaurella dichotoma, 215.
Pliobothrus symmetricus, 84, 177.
Plochionus pallens, 207.
Plover rufous-naped, 40.
    semipalmate, 40.
Plumularia, 224.
    attenuata, 179.
    geminata, 179.
    megalocephala, 88.
    obliqua, 225.
Plumularians of Gulf weed, 30.
Plumularidæ, 88, 179, 224.
Podochela, 77, 155.

Podochela gracilipes, 155.
  lamelligera, 156.
Porocidaris sharreri, 82.
Polistes americanus, 206.
  minor, 206.
Polybia cubensis, 206.
Polyclonia frondosa, 134.
Polycesta, 153.
Polyps, method of killing, expanded, 46.
Pomacanthus, 120.
  arcuatus, 120.
  ciliatus, 120.
Pompilus, 154.
Ponciana regia, 101.
"Porcupine," the, 2.
Porcupine fish, 217.
Porichthys, 121, 150.
Porites, 127.
  astraeoides, 134.
  clavaria, 99, 134.
  furcata, 134.
Poronia, 166.
Potamides, 98.
Potatoes, rotting in hold, 138.
Pourtalès, Count, 2, 157.
Pourtalès Plateau, 139, 161.
  alcyonaria of, 175.
  anemones of, 177.
  corals of, 176.
  crinoids of, 164.
  crustacea of, 155.
  fishes of, 146.
  hydroids of, 178.
  location of, 139.
  mollusks of, 162.
  pelagic hemiptera from, 154.
  sea-urchins of, 173.
  serpent-stars of, 169.
  sharks of, 144.
  simple armed basket fish of, 170.
  siphonophores of, 177.
  sponges of, 180.
  star-fish of, 165.
  vermes, 161.
Powell, W. P., 7, 19.
Prionotus arcuatus, 120.
  evolans, 120.

Protective coloration in crustacea, 29.
  in fishes, 28.
Prouty, Miss Edith, 19.
Provisions grow scarce, 226.
Pseudebaeus oblitus, 122.
Pseudomyrma flavidula, 206.
Psyllobora nana, 122, 152.
Pterogorgia, 46.
Pterophysa grandis, 177.
Pteropods, 164.
Puffinus auduboni, 203.
Purpura haemastoma, 41, 211.
Purslane, 44.
Pycnogonida, 161.
Pyromaia cuspidata, 156.
Pyrophorus, 207.
Pyrosoma, 55.

Quarantine officer, 107.

Rain squall, 32, 69.
Rathbun, Miss Mary J., 152, 232.
Reef corals at Spanish Wells, 215.
Reefing boards, 16.
Reefs at Tortugas, 115.
  description of, 201.
Richness of fauna, 118.
"Ridley's Head," 192, 218.
Rhipidigorgia flabellum, 45, 215.
Rhizocrinus, 164, 165.
Rhizotrochus, 84.
  fragilis, 176.
Rhynchophora, 153.
"Robert E. Patterson," the, 111.
Rock crabs, 45.
Rock purples, 163.
Rogers, A. M., 19.
Romanes, 213.
Rope, length needed in dredging, 12.
Rose apples, 102.

Sabin, Edwin, 19.
Sage brush, 100.
Sand burr, 44.
Sand Key light, 139.
San Salvador, 193, 219.
Sapodillas, 102.

Saprinus ferrugineus, 122.
Sargasso Sea, 28.
Sargasso weed, 27.
  inhabitants of, 28.
Sars' collection, 1.
Scaphopoda, 163.
Scarites, 207.
Scatophilus sarpedon, 70.
Schaeffer, Pres. Chas. A., 6.
Schizotricha, 179.
Scirpetrella, 86.
Scomber, 204.
Scorpion, 58, 96.
Sculpin, 120.
Seymnus, 122, 152.
Sea birds at Tortugas, 118.
Sea-fan, 45.
"Sea gardens," 192.
Sea grape, 43, 139.
Sea-horse, 148.
Sea-oats, 122.
Sea-robin, 120.
Seasickness, 22.
  freedom from, 139.
Sea-spiders, 155.
Sea-urchins, experiments with, 213.
Serpent-stars at Bahia Honda, 98.
  of Great Bahama Banks, 53.
  of Havana, 78.
  of Little Cat Island, 220.
  of Pourtalès Plateau, 169.
  of Tortugas, 136.
Serpulidæ, 127.
Serranus, 120.
Sertularella gayi, var. robusta, 179.
  distans, 179.
Sertularia, 88, 223.
  integritheca, 88.
  quadridentata, 224.
  tubitheca, 88.
Sertularidæ, 179-223.
Shark, 217.
  flesh of, palatable, 145.
  dissection of, 145.
Sharks at Tortugas, 109.
  during calm, 144.
Shell-work, 212.
Shore collecting, appliances, 14.

Siderastræa galaxea, 99, 134.
Sidewalks of Havana, 63.
Sigsbee, Lieut. Commander, on colors of pentacrini, 74.
Sigsbeia, 79, 221.
Simple-armed basket-fish, 170.
Simple corals, 176.
Singing at Spanish Wells, 197.
  of children at, 198.
Siphonogorgia, 86.
Siphonophores, 177.
Siphostoma, 119.
Skylights, 16.
Sladen, W. Percy, F. L. S., 165.
Smith, Dr. John B., 231.
Solomon, Mr., 190.
Sombrero light, 139.
Sounding line, 13.
  methods, 13.
Soundings on Bahama Banks, 47.
  off Havana, 72.
Southern Cross, 47.
Spanish consul at Baltimore, 19.
Spanish cruisers, 61, 69.
Spanish Wells, 192, 193.
  birds of, 203.
  cemetery at, 194.
  children at, 197.
  citizens of, 197.
  corals of, 215.
  crustacea of, 208.
  experiments with echinoderms at, 212.
  fishes of, 204.
  food of inhabitants at, 195.
  gorgonians of, 215.
  insects of, 206.
  men of, 195.
  mollusks of, 211.
  reefs at, 200.
  unique community at, 194.
Specimens, alcoholic, management of, 184.
Speotyto cunicularia floridana, 203.
Sphærophthalma ferrugata, 154.
Sphegidæ, 206.
Sphictyrtus whitei, 208.
Sphyræna, 204.

Spiders at Bahia Honda, 97.
 at Egg Island, 41.
 at Tortugas, 122.
Spider worts, 44.
Spindalis pretrei, 95.
Spines of Diadema setosum, 132, 133.
 of Ophiuridæ, colors of, 82.
Spirorbis, 30.
Spirula peronii, 211.
Sponges, deep-water, of Pourtalès Plateau, 180.
Spongodes, 87.
Squall, 32, 185.
Squid, 34.
Star-fish, at Tortugas, 130.
 of Pourtalès Plateau, 165.
Start home, 225.
Stench from rotting pineapples, 227.
Stereolepis, 204.
Sterna anæsthetus, 40, 203.
 dougalli, 40.
 maxima, 203.
Stinging power of worms, 127.
Stirrup Key, 46, 186.
Stizus hogardii, 154, 206.
Stolasterias, 168.
Stookey, Prof. Stephen, 19.
Stores removed from vessel, 116.
 restowed, 117.
 shifting in hold, 33.
 storage of, 17.
Stormy petrel, 33.
Strix flammea pratincola, 203.
Strombus gigas, 126, 128, 196, 211.
Strophia, 128.
 glans, 41, 42.
 incana, 212.
Students, difficulty of access to deep-sea forms, 4.
Study at night, impracticability of, 32.
Stylaster filogranus, 84.
Submarine ridge, 219.
Sugar cane, 101.
Sulphur fumes, application in fumigation of vessel, 117.
Surface collecting appliances, 14.
Swell-toad, 120.

Swimming, 144.

Tabanidæ, 207.
Tachys, 152.
Tangles, 12.
 effectiveness of, 48.
 making of, 35.
 suggested by Mr. Jas. E. Benedict, 16.
 used on pentacrinus ground, 72.
Tanks for alcohol, 21.
Tectarius, 128.
 muricatus, 212.
 nodulosus, 41, 212.
Telesto, 86.
Tellina alternata, 212.
 rastellum, 212.
Temnechinus, 83.
 maculatus, 174.
Tenebrionid, 153.
Terebra, 162.
Terebratula, 161.
 cubensis, 161.
Tern, bridled, 40, 44, 57.
 least, 119.
 noddy, 40 44, 57.
 roseate, 40.
Tetramorium cæspitum, 121.
 guineense, 121.
Tetrodon spengleri, 120, 205.
Thalassography, birth of, 1.
"The Core," 190.
Thecopsammia, 84, 176.
Thomson, Sir Wyville, 1, 2.
Thracia plicata, 212.
"Three Cruises of the 'Blake,'" 176.
Thryolambrus, 77.
Thuiaria, 54.
Thyanta custator, 153.
Thyroscyphus ramosus, 87.
Tin pans as receptacles, 50.
Tisiphonia fenestrata, 180.
Torell, 1.
Tortugas, 116.
 birds of, 118.
 coleoptera of, 121.
 corals of, 134.
 crustacea of, 122.

Tortugas, description of, 113.
  description of Fort Jefferson at, 111.
  fauna of, 118.
  fishes of, 119.
  fumigation of vessel at, 117.
  insects of, 121.
  mollusca of, 128.
  sea-urchins of, 132.
  serpent-stars of, 130.
  star-fish of, 130.
Tow-net, failure of, 34.
Toxopneustes variegatus, 98.
Transportation, 18.
  of crustacean larvæ, 209.
Trawls, 9.
Trichius delta, 152.
Trichopteryx, 152.
Tridactylus, 208.
Tringa minutilla, 40.
Triton chlorostomus, 211.
Trivia, 52, 128.
  quadripunctata, 212.
Trochus jujubinus, 212.
Tryon, Marine Mollusca of U. S., 162.
Tubicolæ, 127.
Tubularidæ, 86.
Tug, absence of at Dry Tortugas, 109.
Turtles at Bahia Honda, 104.
Typical coral reef, 200.
Tyrannus dominicensis, 203.

United States Agent, 190.
University class, members organized for expedition, 17.
Upeneus maculatus, 120.

Vermes at the Tortugas, 126.
Verrill, Prof. A. E., 232.
  on colors of deep-sea animals, 158.
Vervain, 44.
Vessel, description of, 16.
View from light house, 39.
Vireo altiloquus barbatulus, 41.

Voluta junonia, 162.

Waldheimia floridana, 161.
Washing clothes by beating, 189.
Water Cay, description of, 57.
  birds of, 57.
  insects of, 57.
Water, clearness of at Egg Island, 38.
"Water glass," 201.
Water supply, 18.
Weather during cruise, 227.
Weevils, abundance of in West Indies, 96.
  of Bahia Honda, 96.
Weights for dredges, 11.
Weld, Prof. L. G., 6, 7.
White ants, 208.
Wickham, H. F., 19, 95, 122, 129, 154, 161, 163, 232.
  Mrs. H. F., 19.
Williams, Hon. Ramon, 62.
  aid rendered by, 62.
  strange mistake of, 90, 91.
Williams, Miss Margaret, 19.
Wilson, E. B., on Pycnogonida, 161.
Wilson, Miss Bertha, 19, 42, 99.
Wilson's petrel, 29.
Worm-like fish, 151.
Worms on Gulf weed, 30.

Xiphigorgia anceps, 215.

Yachting license, 182.
Yams, 196.
Yellow fever, Dr. Murray's opinion of, 135.

Zelus longipes, 207.
Zinnia, 100.
Zoarces, 205.
Zoarcidæ, 148.
Zoölogical material collected during cruise, 231.
Zophobas, morio, 153.
Zoroaster ackleyi, 167.

ERRATA.

Page 19, fifth line from bottom, for A. G. Barrett read A. M. Barrett.
Page 45, foot-note, for Mary E. Rathbun read Mary J. Rathbun
Page 50, fourteenth line from bottom, for *Malthus* read *Malthe*.
Page 51, twentieth line from top, for *C. camptocera* read *M. camptocera*.
Page 77, seventh line from top, for *Libinia* read *Temnonotus*.
Page 84, seventh line from bottom, *Pliobathus* read *Pliobothrus*.
Page 88, first and thirteenth lines from top, for *Lafica* read *Lafoëa*.
Page 125, fifteenth line from top, for *Achelous* read *Achelous*.
Page 179, fifth line from top, for *gaya* read *gayi*.
Page 215, ninth line from top, for *E. tourneforti* read *E. muricata*.

www.ingramcontent.com/pod-product-compliance
Lightning Source LLC
Chambersburg PA
CBHW031327230426
43670CB00006B/261